WOMEN *with a* MISSION

PERSONAL PERSPECTIVES

edited by
Moreen Dee and Felicity Volk

The contributions provided by former and serving female heads of mission in this publication are the personal opinions of the individuals concerned, who are commenting in their private capacity. They should not be attributed to the Department of Foreign Affairs and Trade.

DEPARTMENT OF FOREIGN AFFAIRS AND TRADE

National Library of Australia Cataloguing-in-Publication entry
Women with a Mission : personal perspectives.
Bibliography.
Includes index.
ISBN 978 1 921244 27 8 (hbk.).
ISBN 978 1 921244 26 1 (pbk.).

1. Australia. Dept. of Foreign Affairs and Trade. 2. Women diplomats - Australia - Biography. 3. Diplomatic and consular service, Australian - History. I. Dee, Moreen. II. Volk, Felicity.

327.94

Production management, editing and artwork by WHH Publishing
Design by OCTAVO
Printed by Brown Prior Anderson

Foreword

Australian women of the Department of Foreign Affairs and Trade have made a major contribution to advancing and protecting Australia's national interests overseas. *Women with a Mission: Personal perspectives* applauds this contribution and provides an insight into the life and work of inspiring individuals.

Women today comprise more than half of the department's total staff. In the past decade, the government has appointed forty-six women to serve as Heads of mission or post. In almost every year over the same period, the department has recruited more women than men through the graduate trainee program. The composition of the Senior Executive Service is changing to reflect this new reality: women have accounted for nearly 40 per cent of new SES appointments in the past five years.

It has not always been this way, however. Today's department would be unrecognisable to its first female diplomatic recruits in 1943. As this publication records, women have had to overcome numerous systemic and cultural barriers. This challenge was met by a small number of courageous and determined women who have paved the way for today's female diplomats. These are some of their stories.

I hope this publication inspires more women to join the foreign service and to represent Australia at the highest levels overseas. Australia's national interests will be best served by the equal contribution of women to this important task.

It is with pleasure that I commend *Women with a Mission: Personal perspectives* to you.

Alexander Downer
Minister for Foreign Affairs

Contents

Preface

W*omen with a Mission: Personal perspectives* is an initiative of the Department of Foreign Affairs and Trade to mark International Women's Day 2007 by commemorating the role of female heads of mission and post in the history of Australia's foreign service.

The volume derives from the *Women with a Mission* seminar held in the department on International Women's Day 1999, at which a small number of senior diplomats spoke about the progress made by women officers in the diplomatic service. It has been prepared by the department's Historical Publications and Information Section and its publication has been undertaken with the generous support of the Minister for Foreign Affairs, Alexander Downer, and the secretaries of the department during its preparation, Dr Ashton Calvert AC and Michael L'Estrange AO.

The nine former and current heads of mission and post who have contributed to this book represent a timeline from the first career appointment of a female head of mission in 1974 to the present day. Their appointments provide a view of the wide range of geographical locations and the differing political, cultural and social conditions of the countries with which Australia has established diplomatic relations. Each officer followed a unique path, as the personal perspectives here show, navigating not only changing geo-political landscapes but also evolving social mores in both Australia and the countries to which they were posted. We thank them all for the contributions and assistance throughout the project.

While this volume has been published under the auspices of the Department of Foreign Affairs and Trade, the analyses, arguments, opinions and conclusions presented throughout are those of the authors and should not be attributed to the department or to its ministers.

In bringing this project to fruition, particular debts of gratitude are owed to many. The editors are grateful, for their comments and guidance, to Deputy Secretary Gillian Bird and Rod Smith, First Assistant Secretary, Consular, Public Diplomacy and Parliamentary Affairs Division; Janette Ryan and Janet Tomi, Assistant Secretaries, Information Resources Branch; and Dr David Lee, Director, Historical Publications and Information Section. Special thanks are extended to Di Johnstone for her extensive research assistance in preparing the introduction and to Melissa Hitchman, Mack Williams, Rosaleen McGovern and Jeremy Hearder for their comments on this chapter. We also acknowledge the research assistance provided by Deborah Bowman and Leanne Ferguson; assistance with photographs from Alan Walsh and Diana Psaila and from Steve McLeish, Currawong Childcare Centre; and by Maria Young, Domestic Legal Branch. Dr Michael Hussey, US National Archives and Records Administration, in College Park, Maryland, was especially helpful in locating records pertaining to anecdotal history recounted in the introduction. WHH Publishing gave close support through the following people: Virginia Wilton (publishing consultant); Janet Mackenzie (initial copy editing); Robyn Leason and Kornelia Kaczmarek (artwork) and Penny Chamberlain (proofing). The indexer was Barry Howarth and the cover and internal design was by Octavo.

For their kind permission to publish photographs from their collections, the editors thank and acknowledge the National Library of Australia, the National Archives of Australia, the Photographic Archive of the United Nations, and *AR—La revista de Ana Rosa* magazine, Madrid, Hachette Filipacchi S.A. publishers. Unless otherwise acknowledged, photographs are from the personal collections of contributors.

Dr Moreen Dee
Historical Publications and
Information Section

Felicity Volk
Consular, Public Diplomacy and
Parliamentary Affairs Division

Department of Foreign Affairs and Trade
Canberra

Abbreviations

APEC	Asia–Pacific Economic Cooperation
ASEAN	Association of Southeast Asian Nations
BIGA	Business Interest Group of Australia (Sri Lanka)
BTIC	Bilateral Trade and Investment Commission (Chile)
CANZUS	Canada, Australia, New Zealand and the United States grouping
CEDAW	Convention on the Elimination of all Forms of Discrimination Against Women
CMD	Corporate Management Division (DFAT)
DFAT	Department of Foreign Affairs and Trade
DRC	Democratic Republic of the Congo
EADS CASA	European Aeronautic Defence and Space Company, Spanish arm of
EEO	equal employment opportunity
EU	European Union
FCO	Foreign and Commonwealth Office (United Kingdom)
FLP	Fiji Labor Party
FPDA	Five Power Defence Arrangement
GATT	General Agreement on Tariffs and Trade
IAEA	International Atomic Energy Agency
JVP	*Janatha Vimukthi Peramuna*, People's Liberation Front (Sri Lanka)
LTTE	Liberation Tigers of Tamil Eelam (Sri Lanka)
MFO	Multinational Force and Observers (Sinai)
NATO	North Atlantic Treaty Organization
NPT	Nuclear Non-Proliferation Treaty
NSG	Nuclear Suppliers Group
OECD	Organization for Economic Co-operation and Development
PNG	Papua New Guinea
SES	Senior Executive Service
SVT	*Soqosoqo ni Vakavulewa ni Taukei*, Fijian Political Party
UNIDO	United Nations Industrial Development Organization
UNP	United National Party (Sri Lanka)
WEOG	Western and Others Group

1 Women diplomats and Australia's foreign service

Moreen Dee

The first woman diplomat recorded in the history of diplomacy since the sixteenth century was Catherine of Aragon, daughter of King Ferdinand II of Aragon. In 1507, Catherine carried formal credentials as her father's envoy when she travelled to England to negotiate with Henry VII about the delay in her proposed marriage to his son, Prince Henry. Spain thus pioneered the appointment of women as diplomats, but it was France that led the way well into the second half of the seventeenth century. In 1529, Louise of Savoy (mother of King Francis I of France) and Margaret of Austria (aunt of the Hapsburg Emperor Charles V) negotiated the Treaty of Cambrai, ending one phase of the wars over France's claims in Italy;[1] later that century, Madame Delahaye-Vautelaye was appointed French Ambassador to Venice; in 1645, the Maréchale de Guebriant became French Ambassador to Poland; and in 1670, the daughter of Charles I, Henrietta Anne, Duchess of Orleans, acted as Louis XIV's representative when negotiating the Anglo-French Treaty of Dover.[2]

France's efforts in appointing women diplomats, albeit political appointees, were to prove a brief flutter. By the eighteenth century the practice had been discontinued, and it was not considered again, by any country, for more than two hundred and fifty years. But women still undertook the duties of representing their countries. The UK Foreign and Commonwealth Office has recorded that on her husband's death in 1763, the widow of the British consul in Tripoli took over the management of consular affairs until his successor arrived in 1765. Secretary of State Lord Halifax reportedly dismissed her efforts as 'strange and ridiculous'. Another enterprising wife successfully carried on the British spy network in Rotterdam for fourteen years after the death of her husband in 1771. The Foreign and Commonwealth Office also accepts that there were probably many cases throughout the nineteenth century where the wives of British representatives conducted their husbands' official correspondence while they were away on tour.[3] In 1870, when the US consul in Canton died,

---

Note: This chapter is based on a background paper prepared by Diane Johnstone, Ambassador to Nepal 1986–1989.

the city merchants asked his widow to continue the regular trade reports required by the State Department. She carried out this task competently, but when she later applied for further appointments the US Secretary of State acknowledged that she had 'mastered the duties of the office' but rejected her application because 'questions are likely to arise which would be improper for a woman to discuss'.[4] Although 'necessary women'—that is, housekeepers and housemaids—were employed by the British Foreign Service from 1782 and 'lady typewriters' from 1889,[5] career diplomacy remained a male preserve. Active discrimination against the recruitment of women to any foreign service continued into the twentieth century until after World War I.

The early twentieth century—barriers, discrimination and prejudice

During the period from the late 1920s to the 1930s, Chile, Spain, the United States, the Soviet Union, Norway, Bulgaria, Uruguay and the Dominican Republic all appointed women to senior diplomatic and consular positions. But most foreign services still retained their strong bias against the recruitment of women. This stance reflected deep-seated community attitudes to the role of women in society, as well as discrimination against the employment of women in the white-collar workforce. At the time, many jobs were not legally open to women; in those that were available, formidable barriers effectively denied women equality with male colleagues in terms of general conditions of service and advancement into senior positions. Women's wages were significantly lower than those of their male counterparts—on the widespread presumption that women were not breadwinners and thus could be paid less.

This situation continued even where legislation was enacted to open positions to women. In the United Kingdom, for example, the passing of the Sex Disqualification (Removal) Act in 1919 technically opened the way for women to pursue a career in diplomacy, but it was 1946 before the first women career diplomats were recruited.[6] Women had worked as clerks and assistants in the Foreign Office during World War I, but with the cessation of hostilities they lost these positions to ex-servicemen. From 1921 the Foreign Office did engage women as permanent clerical and executive officers, but by the outbreak of World War II very few had obtained promotion.[7]

This prejudicial attitude towards female white-collar workers was not, of course, confined to the foreign service, but there was particular prejudice against employing women as diplomats. Arguments not to employ women included a vivid mixture: women's inability to exercise influence in high-level affairs; their likely lack of acceptance by male counterparts in other countries and cultures; the possibility of danger including mixing with 'low types'; the possibility they might not have the constitutional ability to handle the rigours of the profession; and the risk of sexual misadventure. Opponents of women diplomats also argued that the hierarchic structures and arcane traditions that were seen as essential to the proper practice of the diplomatic art would be eroded, even destroyed, should women be admitted.[8] Ambassador Joyce E. Leader from the United States, in a speech in 2001, described the service until the last quarter of the twentieth century as 'a male bastion par excellence'.[9]

As part of a wider investigation into the admission of women into the British Civil Service by a special committee in 1933–1934, the Foreign and Commonwealth Office sought the views of Britain's representatives abroad. There were a few favourable replies but the overall response was 'unenthusiastic', with comments found to be 'merely flippant, some superficial and some clearly biased'.[10] Of the favourable responses, the most open-minded came from the ambassador in Brussels, who wrote to London that 'a good girl is going to be a more valuable member of staff than a bad boy. In fact the more I think about it, the plainer it becomes that the truth of the matter lies in this'. But the others ranged from the view that 'the clever women would not be liked and the attractive women would not be taken seriously' to concerns that women would require 'an handsome dress allowance'. One 'clearly biased' representative exclaimed: 'I am against female suffrage, female MPs and female magistrates. I think that all this has done, and will continue to do, my country immense harm.'[11]

The situation was little better in the US Foreign Service where the first female career officer joined in 1922 and went on to serve in Switzerland and Panama before resigning on marriage in 1927. As in the United Kingdom, initially numbers were small: despite the promising start, between 1926 and 1929 only four women were recruited into the service, and then none between 1930 and 1941. Furthermore, American male ambassadors were similar to their British counterparts in their attitude towards female officers, with one objecting to a woman's posting on the grounds that he did not know where to seat her at dinner parties.[12]

In the first four decades of the twentieth century, the debate surrounding the admission of women as career diplomats was not an issue in Australia. Although Australia established an overseas office in London in 1910, until late 1935 it did not have an independent foreign service. Australia's foreign relations abroad were handled through British legations. The first Australian overseas representation in its own right was established in 1937 with the appointment of an Australian counsellor in Washington, albeit attached to the British embassy. An Australian legation was opened in February 1940, followed in succession that year by representation in Ottawa and Tokyo. The deteriorating situation in the Pacific also saw a post established in New Caledonia in 1940 and others in Portuguese Timor, Singapore and China the following year. By the end of the war, Australia had representation to the Netherlands government in London (1942), the Union of Soviet Socialist Republics (1943), New Zealand (1943) and India (1944).

World War II and the winds of change

The shortage of men on the home front during World War II opened new opportunities for women to serve successfully in war bureaucracies in many countries. The fledgling Australian foreign service began to recruit female diplomats in their own right in 1943; others, like the British Foreign Service, appointed women to 'temporary administrative posts' that included diplomatic postings abroad.[13] The Canadian service, where shortages saw officers' wives working in the Department of External Affairs on a voluntary basis, hired a small number of women in 1942–1943 but these women were ineligible to become foreign service officers.[14] It was not surprising, therefore, that when the war was over there was increased pressure for women to enter the non-traditional workforces, such as foreign services, particularly from influential women's groups. Additionally, the long experience of the war impressed on governments the importance of taking full advantage of the total range of abilities and skills available in a country's potential workforce.

Nonetheless, in the twenty-year period after the war, the numbers of women recruited into Western foreign services remained small. Early efforts to engage female diplomats were followed by periods of limited or no recruitment.[15] The various forms of discrimination with which women were confronted also took many years to be removed. These barriers included formal and informal quotas on the number of women who could be appointed; restricted employment opportunity; the requirement for women to resign on marriage, or their ineligibility for posting if married; unequal pay; and discrimination in the promotions process and in access to senior appointments.

During this period, women also found themselves relegated to administrative or consular work, or 'soft policy' areas such as human rights or cultural relations. They were denied postings to a wide range of countries considered unsuitable for women. Female officers who tried to improve their circumstances by highlighting discrimination were tagged as troublemakers, with additional problems for their careers. Most were thus reluctant to lobby for equal conditions of service for fear of the possible impact on their career, and simply hoped that doing much better than their male colleagues would bring recognition. Class action sex discrimination suits filed in the 1970s by female officers in the US District Court over policies, practices and customs in the State Department that had blocked their promotion were not finally decided in the officers' favour until some twenty years later, in 1996.[16]

But the most significant barrier for the female career diplomat was the marriage bar—the requirement to resign on marriage or, if married, being regarded as unsuitable for posting. These restrictions limited women's opportunities and compelled some women to take tough decisions about their personal lives. The marriage bar reflected the views that a married woman should be supported by her husband, and that married women took men's jobs. It was also argued that recruiting women was an inefficient use of resources: why employ women when they would marry sooner or later, more often sooner, and have to resign? The resistance to appointing married women rested on claims that there would be no place for a male spouse at an overseas mission and that it would be socially inappropriate—if not scandalous—to post a married woman without her husband.

With Australia taking the lead in 1966, becoming the first Western foreign service to lift the bar,[17] slowly the barriers have come down. At the start of the twenty-first century, formal discrimination—in particular against the recruitment of women—has been eliminated in most foreign services. However, informal practices and cultural issues still affect the advancement of women in some countries. These can include attitudes of male managers, low expectations of women's abilities, concern about placing women in positions involving danger, and views—often not tested—about the attitudes of other countries to women diplomats. Where these work-related issues no longer have an impact on the careers of female officers, there remain the domestic difficulties surrounding child care and employment of spouses, and the larger issue of balancing work and family, particularly where there is a culture of long work hours. Of course, many of these issues apply equally for male colleagues, and the gains made by women in resolving some of them are producing the same positive outcomes for their male counterparts.

Australia's record—a good start, then ...

The many changes for the world's foreign services caused by World War II also affected Australia's newly independent Department of External Affairs. Australian policies and attitudes towards women in the fledgling diplomatic service broadly reflected those evident in the foreign services of the Western countries with which Australia most identified, but the department was unhindered by entrenched diplomatic practices. So it was that when External Affairs established a Diplomatic Cadet Scheme in 1943, to support the growing need for Australian representation overseas during wartime, preference was to be given to ex-servicemen but three of the twelve available places were allocated to women.

The 1943 recruits to Australia's Diplomatic Cadet Scheme: (L–R) Mick Richardson, Professor Bland (Director of the External Affairs Cadet Training Course), Ric Throssell, Neil Truscott, Colonel Hodgson (Secretary, Department of External Affairs), Alexander Borthwick (obscured), Alf Body, Lloyd Tilbury, Barry Hall, Alan Treloar (obscured), Bronnie Taylor, Julia Drake-Brockman, Diana Hodgkinson. (Missing from photo: Alan Renouf) [Department of Foreign Affairs and Trade]

Dr H.V. Evatt, as Minister for External Affairs, personally announced the names of the three selected women—Julia Drake-Brockman, Diana Hodgkinson and Bronnie Taylor—and was given credit for their inclusion among the first intake. Hodgkinson later recalled that the inclusion of women had been largely due to the urging of the noted women's rights lobbyist, Jessie Street, who would later be the sole woman representative in the Australian delegation to the founding Conference of the United Nations in 1945 and instrumental in the establishment of the UN Commission on the Status of Women.[18] The appointment of the three female cadets was heralded by Australian women's groups and created interest overseas, particularly from the National Council of Women of Great Britain, which was interested in promoting the admission of women into the British foreign service.[19] Interestingly, though, in later arguing the need to expand Australia's overseas diplomatic service, the influential scientist Professor Ian Clunies Ross, in what may have only

Jessie Street at the Status of Women Commission, New York, 1947. [National Library of Australia]

been the generalised manner of the time, still spoke of recruiting the 'very best men available'.[20]

The Australian scheme was both innovative and popular, attracting 1,500 applicants for the first twelve places.[21] At a time when women were excluded from other professions, it provided opportunities for bright young female graduates not available elsewhere, albeit potentially short-lived. All three of the women selected in 1943 had married by 1947 and been obliged to resign under the marriage bar even though, by then, the Diplomatic Cadet Scheme was considered by one observer to be attracting a better calibre of women than men. A letter from Dr Grenfell Price, Opposition representative on the selection committee, to Dr John Burton, Secretary of the Department of External Affairs, noted that for the 1948 intake, three women in particular 'were in ability and personality streets ahead of most of the men on the list'.[22] Nevertheless, the Public Service Board felt that as women would ultimately marry and leave the service, funds spent on training women were expended needlessly.[23] Citing this potential 'wastage', the board would only agree to three of the five women selected by the committee being accepted for recruitment in 1948, despite vigorous efforts by Burton to persuade them to recruit all five.[24] In the years from 1943 to 1950, 17 per cent of the cadets were women—fifteen of the eighty-four recruits.

As women's prospects for recruitment through the cadet scheme were so restricted, several joined the department through other channels: as research

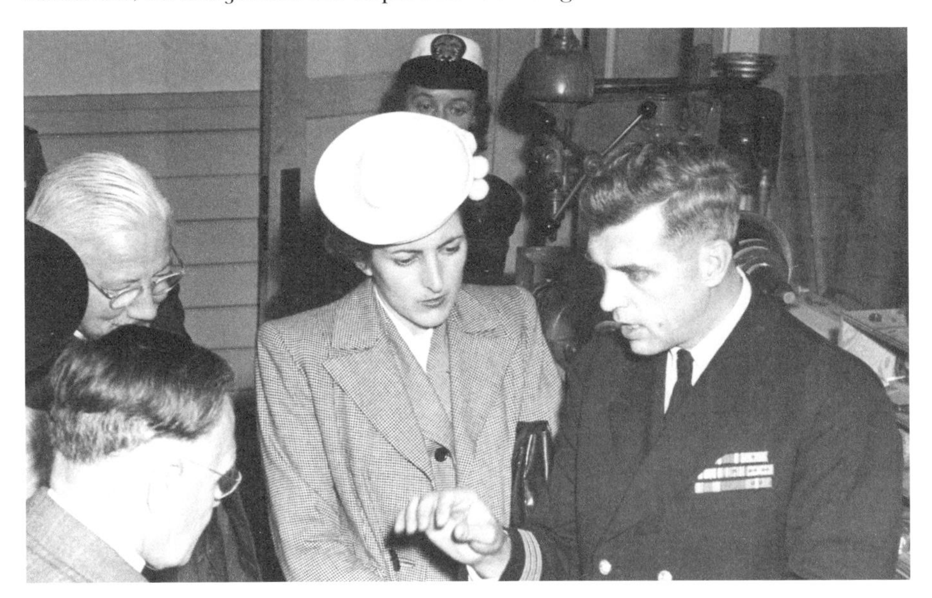

Diana Hodgkinson (second from right), Vice Consul in San Francisco, during the visit of Norman Makin, Minister of External Affairs, to Mare Island Naval Base in San Francisco Bay, c. 1946.
[Department of Foreign Affairs and Trade]

officers or administrative assistants. These women later moved to diplomatic work, with some awarded senior appointments. Included in this group were two who would become career heads of mission or post:[25] Ruth Dobson, who was not selected in the 1943 cadet scheme but was invited to join as a research officer, and Maris King, who joined the department as a typist in 1942 and became a senior research officer in 1956.[26]

As in the other Western foreign services, after this promising start in Canberra, the number of women recruits fell dramatically in the 1950s. Only three women were recruited in the period 1951–1959. A significant reason for this decline was that many young women were reluctant to pursue a career where it appeared entrenched bias negated ability in relation to their male colleagues. By the end of the 1950s, on university campuses around Australia, departmental recruiters were confronted by women who expressed concerns about discrimination against women within the department.[27] These concerns were legitimate. For example, in 1949, the Australian Mission to the United Nations in New York had made an explicit appeal that the new third secretary not be a woman.[28] In response to press accusations of bias against employing women in 1953, the department set out the general policy of employing female diplomatic cadets (termed a policy of 'complete equality') for the then Minister for External Affairs, Richard Casey. The assertions were that more male applicants had been chosen because they were usually more widely experienced and that 'the usefulness of women in the Service [was] limited' because of the high incidence of women marrying; many posts were in tropical or disturbed areas; the pressure and frequent movement requirements of posts in conference areas imposed a 'severe physical strain' on staff; and some posts '[bore] heavy responsibility for

Cynthia Nelson (second from right), Australia's first female chargé d'affaires, during the presentation of credentials by Australia's first ambassador to the Republic of Vietnam, William D. Forsyth, 21 August 1959. (L–R: Ngo Dinh Diem, President of the Republic of Vietnam, W.D. Forsyth, C. Nelson, D. Anderson, Third Secretary, Australian Embassy.) [Department of Foreign Affairs and Trade]

dealing with deserting seamen which is thought, is not fair for women to deal with'.[29]

Ten years later, the situation had improved little. In 1963, a trade official writing to the Director of the Trade Commissioner Service to oppose women's recruitment as trade commissioners summed up the prejudices of the time. He suggested that women 'could not mix nearly as freely with businessmen as men do'; they could not withstand the 'fairly severe strains and stresses, mental and physical' of the trade commissioner's life; and that 'a spinster lady can, and often does, turn into something of a battleaxe with the passing years—whereas a man usually mellows'. The writer was most concerned that women recruits 'would take the place of a man and preclude us from giving experience to a male officer'.[30]

The marriage bar goes—but other hurdles remain

Throughout this period, women employed in many other foreign services, as well as the wider Australian Public Service, had to resign on marriage. By 1961, this marriage bar meant that only five of the nineteen women officers recruited to External Affairs since 1943 remained[31]—a state of affairs that affected the numbers of senior women in Australia's diplomatic service for decades to come. With the lifting of the marriage bar in 1966, the numbers of women recruits increased and some who had previously left on marriage but still wanted a diplomatic career chose to return. One of these officers was Tonia Shand, who went on to become Australia's high commissioner to Sri Lanka.[32]

The introduction of equal pay in 1972, and flex-time and paid maternity leave in 1973, removed further barriers to women's employment. Throughout the 1970s more women were included in the larger numbers of young graduates being recruited to a rapidly expanding foreign service. From about one in six in the early years of the 1970s, the proportion of women rose until, in 1985, for the first time more women than men were recruited. From then the numbers were roughly 50 per cent each, with men overall in a slight majority. However, in the 1999 intake, the balance shifted towards women, an outcome that, with the exception of the 2001 intake, has been maintained.[33]

Even as the number of female recruits was steadily rising, significant prejudice continued against female officers within the department. In 1973, the ambassador in South Africa asked that a female officer not be sent to the post as it was unsuitable for a woman. Senior officers in Canberra also appeared to consider that some posts in the Middle East and Africa were unsuitable for women diplomats (the same caveat was not applied to secretarial or communications staff). For the Middle East region with seven possible posts at the time,[34] Mary McPherson had been posted as third secretary to Tel Aviv 1951–1953, but it was another twenty years before Helen Churchward

Ruth Pearce addressing the National Press Club on International Women's Day, March 1995. [National Library of Australia]

went to Beirut as the third secretary in 1972, followed two years later by Christine White as third secretary in Tehran.[35] Ruth Pearce, who served as ambassador to the Philippines and to Moscow and as high commissioner in Solomon Islands, told the National Press Club in 1995 that at the time she applied in 1978 for a posting to Baghdad, she was told that the department would never send a woman to Iraq.[36] Although a small number of women continued to be posted to the diplomatic staff of Australian missions in the Middle East, the first female head of mission was not appointed until 1990, when Victoria Owen became Australia's ambassador to Lebanon and Syria.

Africa, with five possible posts,[37] fared similarly, with only Jennifer Turnbull posted to Pretoria in 1972, followed by Diane Johnstone in 1974, and Pera Wells going to Accra that same year. Regrettably, there is no contemporary record of the number of women who, like Ruth Pearce, expressed a particular wish to be posted to the Middle Eastern or African regions. This is not to say that women were not being posted to Australia's other missions around the world. A 1970s departmental Statement of Service shows that of the fifty-one women listed, thirty-eight had had at least one overseas posting.[38] Nonetheless, in Canberra, as in other Western foreign services during that period, female officers were assigned in the main to the 'soft policy' areas—a fact not lost on female officers in these early years and a practice that remained an issue for many of them into the 1980s.

Throughout this period, there were important positive influences at work for women who had decided to make Australia's foreign service their career. One of these was the formation of informal networks among female colleagues, who otherwise felt isolated in policy areas where they were, more often than not, the only woman officer. These networks allowed women officers to compare experiences, offer support, and plan ways of addressing issues for women. A second important and positive influence was the support and encouragement given to a number of women by several supportive male supervisors. These colleagues not only acted as mentors but were also prepared to argue for women to be given positions of greater responsibility and the more challenging work or assignments not usually available to women. In late 1979, a senior male officer in Canberra successfully argued for Diane Johnstone to set up the liaison office in the then war-torn Southern Rhodesia over the objection of senior defence and foreign affairs personnel.

Women responded with alacrity to this support, determined to prove that they could rise to the challenge and conscious that a failure on their part would have consequences for the careers of other women officers. Two significant milestones for women in the department that served to inspire women officers to aspire to senior positions in the Australian foreign service also came in the mid-1970s. The first was Ruth Dobson's appointment in 1974 as ambassador to Denmark—the first ambassadorial posting for a female career diplomat. The second, three years later, was Rosaleen McGovern's appointment as the department's first woman officer to the Second Division of the Australian Public Service, later the Senior Executive Service (SES).[39]

Australia's first female career ambassador, Ruth Dobson, arriving to present her credentials in Copenhagen, Denmark, 1974. [Department of Foreign Affairs and Trade]

Equal employment opportunity and institutional change

Although by 1984 most forms of overt discrimination had been removed, informal barriers remained, including negative attitudes about the professionalism of women officers. A survey of women officers in that year also found that women felt inhibited by a predominantly male culture and the domination of male executives. Over half felt that being a woman had affected their career. In areas where they were the only woman, most felt isolated at some time and under special scrutiny. Married women believed that institutional barriers to their promotion and postings continued, as well as negative assumptions about their ability to manage work and family commitments.[40] Some men remained adamantly opposed to women working on these grounds. Penny Wensley's account in this book recalling a comment by a senior officer—when she was required to collect her children from day care—that she needed to decide whether she was a mother or an officer, reflected a then prevalent view that it was not possible for women to be both.[41]

The catalyst for real institutional change came in 1984 with the passage in the Australian Parliament of the *Sex Discrimination Act* and the *Public Service*

Reform Act. Under this legislation, the government committed the federal bureaucracy to implement equal employment opportunity (EEO) programs and to identify and remove barriers to equal employment opportunity. A strategy to develop gender-sensitive analyses of the government's budgets was introduced through the Women's Budget Program,[42] requiring all departments and agencies to review thoroughly every aspect of their activities that could be regarded as having implications for women. The 1984 survey was the first phase of the Department of Foreign Affairs' response.

In order to respond to the views reflected in the survey in a systematic and forward-looking way, in 1985 the department introduced an EEO program that required the achievement of indicative outcomes in significant areas for all women officers—diplomatic and administrative. Taking a zero-based approach to all aspects of women's service, within three years the department's EEO outcomes included reducing the number of posts deemed unsuitable for women officers;[43] reviewing the status of women in delegations to international conferences to increase their inclusion and broaden their involvement from the usual social or 'soft' areas into mainstream issues; strengthening EEO within the department by appointing an officer as an ombudsman for women officers; supporting the department's family-sensitive operations with family liaison officers; reviewing recruitment procedures to remove perceived gender imbalance; and encouraging mentoring for junior officers in all streams. These EEO programs served to change—or at least moderate—attitudes among male officers to their female colleagues and to raise awareness about practices that were disadvantageous for women officers. From December 1992 there was also a Women's Policy Officer, but this position was merged with that of the EEO Officer in 1997.

A continuing issue for women into the 1990s was the promotion process. In late November 1988, Dr Stuart Harris, then recently retired as secretary of the department, told the National Organisation Change Conference in Canberra that the Department of Foreign Affairs and Trade had still to implement a merit promotion process effectively. He contended that aspects of the process, such as an emphasis on seniority, or numbers of overseas postings undertaken, were unrelated to merit and produced biases against women. Harris was concerned that these biases existed 'despite a forward-looking EEO program'.[44] A particularly striking fact was that, at the end of 1990, nearly 80 per cent of the women in the department were within the junior bands of the workplace structure, namely, the first four levels of public service officers.[45] By 1994, this figure had fallen to 69 per cent, following a significant improvement in the proportion of women in the feeder-groups for the SES and a gradual increase in the number of women entering the SES. Women then filled 9 per cent of senior positions within the department, up from 2.1 per cent in 1989. But this proportion still fell well below the target level of 15 per cent by 1995 set under the government's EEO policy agenda for the Public Service.[46] (At the time, the Public Service average exceeded this target, standing at 17 per cent.) A contributing factor here was that women (along with some of their male colleagues) were holding back from applying for promotion because of negative perceptions about their prospects for success as women. A survey of selected women officers that year, however, also found that women felt constrained by the legacy of a predominantly male culture, which continued to produce misleading assumptions, particularly in regard to management of domestic responsibilities and professional duties.[47] A consequence of the limited number of women at senior management levels was that it restricted the numbers of women eligible for most head of mission and post positions and, of more concern, had a dampening effect on the career aspirations of capable women at lower levels.

A number of other issues emerged from this 1994 survey that indeed applied to the promotion prospects for both men and women officers. These included the continued culture of long hours—the perceived career advantage of being seen to work late, regardless of efficiency; and the need for greater departmental support for officers to fulfil family responsibilities. Michael Costello, then secretary of the department, acknowledged the findings of the survey and introduced focus group meetings with women at all levels to

Senior Executive Meeting, April 1996: (R–L) Joanna Hewitt, Deputy Secretary (the first woman appointed as a deputy secretary in the Department of Foreign Affairs and Trade), Bob Cotton, First Assistant Secretary CMD, Les Rowe, Assistant Secretary EXB; Kim Jones, Deputy Secretary; Geoff Forrester, Deputy Secretary; Philip Flood AO, Secretary; Peter Grey, Deputy Secretary; Trevor Kanaley, Director-General, AusAID.
[Department of Foreign Affairs and Trade]

advise him on issues of concern.[48] These meetings were important in providing a high-level imprimatur for initiatives that addressed the issues women had identified and encouragement for these to be widely accepted. One important procedural change was the requirement for a female representative on any promotion committee.

In 1995, the public profile of female officers and their role in the policy process received a boost from a highly successful International Women's Day address to the National Press Club in Canberra by three SES officers.[49] The following year, Joanna Hewitt, on her appointment as the department's first deputy secretary, used the same occasion for her first public engagement, taking as her theme the contribution of women to Australia's foreign service. This latter event led to a well-attended monthly lecture series at the Press Club that served to counter negative publicity at the time about the department's record on promoting women and appointing women heads of mission.

A significant development that helped women officers to achieve a successful diplomatic career commensurate with their abilities was the establishment in October 1996 of the Currawong Childcare Centre within the department in Canberra. It was one of the first work-based childcare centres in the federal bureaucracy and became a model for other such facilities. In 1998, the department also received a private ruling from the Australian Tax Office that allowed it to offer salary packaging of child care fees for staff using the centre. In other family-friendly initiatives, the department established a 'family room' for parents to care for non-contagious sick children, and a 'babycare room' for women officers to breastfeed in private; introduced approved employer-

Secretary of the department, Michael L'Estrange AO, with departmental officers Margaret Bowen and her daughter Eri (left) and Mardi Wu with her daughter Sienna, after he officially opened an extension to the Currawong Childcare Centre on 25 February 2005.
[Department of Foreign Affairs and Trade]

funded child care for officers travelling on short-term overseas missions; and encouraged managers to accommodate permanent part-time work and job-sharing arrangements for officers with family responsibilities. The initiatives taken in addressing these so-called 'women's issues' applied equally to, and similarly assisted, male officers within the department with families. The on-site child care made it easier for officers, both male and female, to balance work and family responsibilities; as did the subsequent vigorous 'working smarter' campaign that addressed the issue of long hours; the reciprocal work agreements with many foreign governments that made it easier for spouses to work overseas; and additional flexibilities in working hours, and forms of carers leave. In 1996 the department's progress in these areas was recognised when it was placed first in the Public Service Commission's regional category of the annual Australian Public Service Equality Award for innovative practice.

There is no doubt that from the mid-1990s women in the department had a higher profile. Visible examples of this were the annual activities that the department sponsored at home and overseas to mark International Women's Day, celebrating a growing list of achievements by women in Australia's foreign service, including service on dangerous assignments. More significantly, by the end of the decade, an increased number of women were filling the ranks of senior career officers, including Joanna Hewitt's deputy secretary appointment, and larger numbers of women headed Australia's overseas missions and posts.

Dame Annabelle Rankin, Australia's High Commissioner to New Zealand with Mr Gough Whitlam, Prime Minister of Australia (centre), and Mr Norman Kirk, Prime Minister of New Zealand, during Mr Whitlam's visit to New Zealand, January, 1974. [National Archives of Australia: A6180, 11/2/74/61]

Australian women heads of mission and post

Australia's first female head of mission was Dame Annabelle Rankin; like the early recorded Spanish and French women diplomats, she was a political appointee and not a member of Australia's career diplomatic service. A former senior Liberal cabinet minister, Dame Annabelle was appointed in 1971 as Australian High Commissioner to New Zealand. The appointment was extensively covered in both the Australian and New Zealand press and widely lauded as recognition of her considerable achievements. The former cabinet minister, however, approached the position in much the same way that a career diplomat would today. She deflected questions about being a pathfinder for women by pointing out that 'it is important for a woman to remember that when taking up an executive position or any job with a big responsibility, she should do so as a citizen not only as a woman'.[50] On her position as a head of mission, she was quick to dispel the widespread view that 'a High Commissioner's job ... is just a matter of rounds of social engagements, and entertaining'; she stressed—in an explanation that applies equally today—that 'the job properly demands a lot of hard work and homework'.[51]

The first career head of mission was Ruth Dobson, who became Australia's Ambassador to Denmark in 1974. Dobson was the longest-serving female officer in the department, having joined the Department of External Affairs as a research officer in 1943. Previously she had had postings to London, Geneva (where she served on the Third Committee of the UN General Assembly, which drafted the Convention on the Status of Women), Wellington, Manila and Athens. In Canberra, she had headed the department's Western Europe

Diane Johnstone, Australia's Ambassador to Nepal, greets the King of Nepal, Birendra Bir Vikram Shah Dev (right) on the occasion of the King's Birthday, 29 December 1988. [Department of Foreign Affairs and Trade]

Section and was seconded to the Governor-General's staff as private secretary to Lady Casey. From Denmark, Dobson subsequently became Ambassador to Ireland in 1978. Shortly before the end of her term in Dublin and approaching retirement, she spoke in a newspaper interview of the calibre of Australia's women diplomatic officers: 'we have some outstanding women coming on quickly now. We want to be thought of as dedicated professionals and we should be because, though many things have changed, a woman still has to be that bit better than a man to get each promotion.' Wryly, she also reflected that being a female in the predominantly male diplomatic corps in a country at least gave her the advantage of always being remembered when she needed to deal with 'some tricky issue'; and as for the social responsibilities of the position, 'the trick is to be able to play an ambassador's role and that of the ambassador's wife at the same time'.[52]

Neither of Dobson's appointments nor those that followed, however, signalled a significant change in the approach towards appointment of women heads of mission or post. From 1974 to the end of 1992, only thirteen female officers were appointed to head Australian missions and posts overseas:[53]

1977	Maris King	Nauru
1982	Mary McPherson	Cyprus
1983	Rosaleen McGovern	Sweden
	Joan Norwood	Vanuatu
1986	Susan Boyd	Bangladesh
	Diane Johnstone	Nepal
	Penny Wensley	Hong Kong (Post)
1988	Beris Gwynne	Nauru
	Rosaleen McGovern	Singapore
	Dr Helen Ware	Zambia
	Tonia Shand	Sri Lanka
1990	Victoria Owen	Lebanon and Syria
1992	Ruth Pearce	Solomon Islands
	Stephanie Daly	Bali (Post)

In September 1992, there were two female heads of Australia's seventy-nine missions abroad and women numbered around 6 per cent of SES officers from whom these appointments were made. Diane Johnstone, who had been Australia's ambassador to Nepal (1986–1989), took the lead in an initiative to redress this poor representation. Having set out her concerns about the situation in detail for the secretary of the department, Dr Peter Wilenski, in

April,[54] she wrote to the ministers for Foreign Affairs and Trade, Senator Gareth Evans and John Kerin, and provided a personal brief for the Joint Parliamentary Committee on Foreign Affairs Defence and Trade.[55] In arguing the need to promote more women into SES-level positions, Johnstone proposed that the department open all but the most senior overseas posts to merit selection from among officers in the levels immediately below SES, in which women were well represented. With women then comprising 13 per cent of the SES across the Public Service and 12.5 per cent of federal Parliament at that time, she also suggested that it would not be 'unreasonable' to agree to a minimum target for women to head 15 per cent of Australia's missions within the next two to three years.[56] The Foreign Affairs and Trade Association subsequently wrote to both ministers and the secretary endorsing Johnstone's views and supporting increased opportunities for women to be appointed heads of missions and posts.[57] But by this time, Gareth Evans and John Kerin had already noted their understanding of the problem and stressed the importance of female officers as well as their male counterparts in the immediate pre-SES levels considering themselves 'as qualified, serious candidates' for senior appointments. Evans also said that, rather than a commitment by the Australian Government, the setting of a target within a specific timeframe would be more properly addressed in the context of the department's EEO program. The program was at that time being reviewed to establish achievable targets for numbers of female heads of mission and heads of post to the year 2000.[58]

But the selection and appointment process was not the only factor in the low numbers of female Australian representatives. Another reason was identified by Wilenski in speaking to female officers of suitable rank in late 1992, and confirmed in the survey of women officers in 1994: many women—especially those with spouses or families—were ambivalent (as were some men) regarding the personal or career advantage of becoming a head of mission or post. The turning point came with a 1996 seminar on this topic, at which four female heads of mission and post spoke frankly to a large number of senior and middle-level women officers about the specific problems of taking up a representative posting. Some of these were difficulties of employment for their spouses, and the assumptions made in some societies that male spouses should work; the requirement for a woman head of mission to run a residence as well as a busy mission; the intense scrutiny, particularly if they were the sole female among all the diplomatic representatives in a country. In addition, some societies found single women culturally puzzling; some Australian expatriates were isolated from contemporary Australian social attitudes; and there was pressure from local and Australian women's groups to take the women's view on any 'women's issues'. Although a number of posts included household support, women with children had the challenge of managing child care without the traditional support systems available to them in Australia.[59]

The women also outlined a number of the advantages they believed they brought to their positions. As women they were seen to be more ethical and, because they were often more consultative, better managers of staff. They had access to a broader range of contacts because they could talk to women, who in many societies might not be politically or economically visible, but who were influential. In developing countries their access to women gave them an advantage in dealing with projects for women, which were often those at the forefront of development programs. Where they were the only, or one of a few, female heads of mission in a particular country, they were role models raising Australia's profile in the local community.

The outcome of the 1996 seminar and the department's renewed focus on appointing women to head its diplomatic missions was that many more

Penny Wensley, Australia's Ambassador to the United Nations in New York, addressing the 53rd Session of the United Nations General Assembly in 1998. [United Nations Photographic Archive]

women applied for these positions in the following months. From seven such appointments in 1995, by February 1998 the Minister for Foreign Affairs, Alexander Downer, was able to announce that eleven women now headed Australia's overseas missions and posts. This number included two in the Middle East—Merry Wickes in Amman and Victoria Owen in Cairo—and Penny Wensley in the prestigious post of ambassador and permanent representative to the United Nations in New York. In March 1999, this number rose to fourteen, a point at which the momentum stalled until 2005.

The Department of Foreign Affairs and Trade 2006 graduate intake with Secretary Michael L'Estrange AO (front, centre), July 2006. [Department of Foreign Affairs and Trade]

These figures reflect the fact that the women then in, or entering, the SES ranks had joined the department some time before the 1985 milestone of approximately equal male–female graduate intake. That is, the group from which diplomatic and consular post appointments were being made was relatively small. The significance of the ratio of intake numbers to appointments is evident in the numbers of female heads of mission and post by the end of 2006. As officers from early to mid-1980s' intakes reach SES level, women fill 25 per cent of such positions within the department, including twenty as heads of the eighty-eight overseas posts currently available.

In 2006, the status of women in Australia's diplomatic service is in line with leading Western foreign services such as those of the United Kingdom, the United States and Canada. This position has been achieved through many changes that have taken place within the Department of Foreign Affairs and Trade and its predecessor departments over the years since the first women diplomatic cadets joined Australia's fledgling diplomatic service. Three factors influenced these changes: forces within, as women maintained their belief in their capacity to manage successfully a full and rewarding career in diplomacy; external pressures, as the government legislated against the inequity of employment opportunities for women; and progressive departmental practice that came with recognition of the various difficulties and implementation of measures aimed at better management practices.

The role of women as Australian heads of mission is secure. Young women now entering Australia's foreign service as graduate trainees do so with every expectation that they might well represent their country at the highest level of international diplomacy.

Notes

1 The treaty is referred to as the 'Ladies Peace'. For further information on this and other phases of the Italian Wars, see <http://columbia.thefreedictionary.com/Italian+Wars> (accessed December 2006).

2 Pact between Charles II of England and Louis XIV in which Charles promised to support French policy in Europe in return for a French subsidy that would free him from financial dependence on Parliament. For further information, see <http://concise.britannica.com/ebc/article-9363049/Treaty-of-Dover> (accessed December 2006).

3 Foreign and Commonwealth Office (FCO), *History Notes, Women in Diplomacy: The FCO, 1782–1991*, Foreign and Commonwealth Office, London, 1999, p. 2.

4 Letter, C.V.D. Chenoweth to President Grant, 9 November 1872, US National Archives and Records Administration: Box 10, RG 59 General Records of the Department of State, Applications and Recommendations for Public Office, 1797–1901, Administration of Grant 1869–1877.

5 FCO, *Women in Diplomacy*, p. 3.

6 The Sex Disqualification (Removal) Act 1919 stated that 'a person shall not be disqualified by sex or marriage from the exercise of any public function, or from being appointed to or holding any civil or judicial office or post', but this was qualified by provisions 'giving power to reserve to men any branch of or posts in the Civil Service in any of His Majesty's possessions overseas, or in any foreign country'. Subsequent regulations made in 1921 specifically restricted to men all posts in the Diplomatic and Consular Services. Ibid., p. 7.

7 By 1939, only two of the women appointed in the early 1920s had been promoted. Ibid., p. 6.

8 FCO, ibid., pp. 7–8, 27–30.

9 Joyce E. Leader, 'Women in the International Affairs Professions', speech delivered at Penn State University, Harrisburg, USA, 5 April 2001. Available at <http://www.fundforpeace.org/media/speeches/leader02.php> (accessed December 2006).

10 FCO, *Women in Diplomacy*, p. 7; and letter, J.W. Nicholls, Foreign Office, to Sir Claud Schuster, Chairman, Committee to consider the admission of women to the Diplomatic and Consular Services, 23 January 1934, quoted in ibid., p. 31. The FCO records that the lack of enthusiasm was 'chiefly on the grounds that local conditions would not allow such an innovation'.

11 See ibid., pp. 7–8, 27–30.

12 Leader, 'Women in the International Affairs Professions'.

13 See FCO, *Women in Diplomacy*, p. 11, which notes that 'by 1945, at least 108 women graduates were known to have been appointed to temporary administrative posts in the [British] Foreign Service. Of these, 31 were [then] serving as temporary Assistant Principals … [in] the Foreign Office, while 16 had served abroad as First, Second and Third Secretaries, as Vice Consuls and as Press Attachés'.

14 Canadian Department of Foreign Affairs and International Trade, *Our Past: The History of the Department of Foreign Affairs and International Trade*, available <http://www.dfait-maeci.gc.ca/department/history/history-en.asp> (accessed December 2006).

15 In the United Kingdom, by the end of 1959, women formed only 2% of the Administrative Grade (Foreign Service Officers). In the United States, although in 1957 women comprised 8.9% of this group, in 1975 the figure had only risen to 9%. FCO, *Women in Diplomacy*, p. 13; and Leader, 'Women in the International Affairs Professions'.

16 The ruling required the State Department to mandate diversity training for all foreign service officers and managers, eliminate sex discrimination in personnel practices, and automatically promote a number of women who had claimed discrimination in promotions. Leader, 'Women in the International Affairs Professions'.

17 The marriage bar was lifted in the United States in 1971, the United Kingdom in 1972 and South Africa in 1986.

18 Diana Hall and Rachel Miller, c. 1993, unpublished manuscript on women in the Department of Foreign Affairs, in possession of authors, Canberra and Sydney. Jessie Street's *Australian Dictionary of Biography* entry is available at <http://www.adb.online.anu.edu.au/biogs/A160396b.htm> (accessed December 2006).

19 Hall and Miller, unpublished manuscript.
20 Quoted in 'Strong Support for Reforms in Australian Diplomacy', *Daily Telegraph*, 9 October 1943. Professor Clunies Ross was also president of the Australian Institute of International Affairs at that time.
21 This number of applications was not maintained, falling to 450 in 1944 and then declining to between 100 and 200 in subsequent years.
22 Letter, Grenfell Price to Burton, 27 December 1947, National Archives of Australia (NAA): A1838, 1260/6/1.
23 A newspaper editorial at the time, titled 'Do Women Make Successful Diplomats?', reflected a similar attitude, questioning 'whether it [was] worth spending a lot of money on having women for a diplomatic career when many may change it for housekeeping in a year or two'.
24 Letter, Burton to Public Service Board, 10 February 1948, NAA: A1838, 1260/6/1.
25 A diplomatic mission is either an embassy or (in a Commonwealth country) a high commission, the heads of which are respectively an ambassador or a high commissioner, appointed as their country's official representative in the country of posting. While any diplomatic representation abroad is often referred to as a 'post', more specifically a post is a consulate-general or a consulate, depending on its size. Heads of post are either a consul-general or a consul and are appointed to promote their country, foster trade and investment, and look after expatriates.
26 An experienced clerk by 1953, in 1954, Maris King was awarded a Public Service Board University Free Place at Canberra University College, where she completed a BA before returning to External Affairs after a period as a Grade 1 Research Officer with the Prime Minister's Department. See Appendix I.
27 Report on visits to universities, R. Harry, former Permanent Delegate, UN Mission and Consul-General, Geneva, and Commissioner, Singapore, 18 May 1959, NAA: A1838, 1260/1/4/1.
28 Letter, John Hood, Minister, UN New York, to Burton, 23 May 1949, NAA: A1838, 1270/2/1.
29 Ministerial note, G. Hartley, Administration Staff, 16 February 1953, NAA: A4311, 87/2.
30 Minute, A. Taysom to Director, Trade Commissioner Service, 13 March 1963, NAA: A3120, 106/1/6.
31 Cynthia Nelson (1946); Mary McPherson (1947); June Barnett (1948); Elizabeth Warren (1948); Patricia Williams (1952). Of these five, Nelson, Warren and Williams would also be obliged to resign on marriage over the next two years. Ruth Dobson (1943) also remained but, as she joined as a research officer she was not included in the numbers recruited as cadets/trainees.
32 See Chapter 5.
33 Women represent 55% of the total number of graduate trainees for the period 1994–2006. There were 13 men and 12 women in the 2001 intake.
34 Israel (opened 1949), Egypt (1950), Lebanon (1967), Iran (1968), Saudi Arabia (1974, Iraq (1976), and Syria (1977).
35 There were also two short-term postings to the Middle East: Tonia Moffat (later Shand), Third Secretary, Tel Aviv, January–April 1963; and Victoria Hamilton (later Owen), Third Secretary, Tehran, January–February 1974.
36 Pearce, a graduate trainee in 1974, had by 1978 served as Third Secretary in Dhaka. See Chapter 7.
37 South Africa (opened 1946), Ghana (1958), Nigeria (1961), Tanzania (1962) and Kenya (1965).
38 The figure of 51 does not include the eight women trainees for 1975. Department of Foreign Affairs Statement of Service 1974–1975.
39 Under Section 35 of the *Public Service Act 1999*, the Australian Public Service (APS) Commission defines the Senior Executive Service (SES) as 'the leadership cadre of the APS. SES members not only provide high level support to their own Agency, but are required to cooperate with other Agencies and to promote APS Values and compliance with the Code of Conduct'. See <http://www.apsc.gov.au/ses/index.html> (accessed December 2006).

The SES replaced the Second Division of the APS under a 1984 amendment to the Public Service Act. For Rosaleen McGovern's story, see Chapter 2.

40 Major Recommendations: 1984 EEO Survey, Attachment A, Discussion Paper: 'Women in Management: The DFAT Experience', 14 July 1994, Department of Foreign Affairs and Trade (DFAT), A9737, 93/02004.

41 See Chapter 4.

42 For further discussion on gender budgets, see Rhonda Sharp and Ray Broomhill, 'Budgeting for Equality: The Australian Experience', in *Feminist Economics*, vol. 8, no. 1, 2002, pp. 25–47.

43 Tehran and Riyadh remained the only posts not available to women.

44 Stuart Harris, 'Change in the Department of Foreign Affairs and Trade: experience and observations', paper delivered to the National Organisation Change Conference, Royal Institute of Public Administration and the Public Service Commission, Canberra, 28–29 November 1988.

45 Minutes of meeting, Equal Employment Opportunity Committee, 17 December 1990, *Interface*, vol. 1, no. 2, p. 10, DFAT.

46 Under the federal government's EEO policy agenda for the APS, a target of 15% of women in the SES was set for 1995, to increase to 20% by 2000.

47 The 1994 survey was conducted in early May, via a 'vertical slice' meeting of selected officers with the Secretary, Michael Costello, and subsequent interviews. The findings were included in DFAT, Discussion Paper: 'Women in Management'.

48 The Secretary convened the initial focus group discussion with 21 female officers on 12 May 1994.

49 Ruth Pearce, High Commissioner to Solomon Islands 1992–1994; Stephanie Daly, Consul in Bali 1992–1994; and Lyndall McLean, Assistant Secretary, Corporate Evaluation Branch.

50 Waveney Browne, *A Woman of Distinction: The Honourable Dame Annabelle Rankin DBE*, Boolarong Publications, Brisbane, 1981, p. 77.

51 Ibid., p. 81.

52 'How to Succeed Diplomatically', interview with Peter Smark, *The Age*, 9 May 1981. Ruth Dobson's posting as Ambassador to Ireland formally ended on 28 August 1981. She retired in Canberra on 24 October 1981.

53 Two additional female appointments in 1992 were from outside the Department of Foreign Affairs and Trade. Maurine Chong headed the Guangzhou post as Austrade Consul-General/Senior Trade Commissioner (Guangzhou did not become a DFAT post until 1996) and Dr Jocelyn Chey, appointed to head the Hong Kong post, was a former Department of Overseas Trade officer who, immediately prior to this appointment, had been Director China/Southeast Asian Branch of the International Wool Secretariat.

54 Letter, Di Johnstone to Dr Wilenski, 21 April 1992, DFAT: A9737, 89/010974 part 5.

55 Johnstone met with Senator Chris Schacht, Chair, Joint Parliamentary Committee on Foreign Affairs and Trade, and several of his colleagues on 18 December 1992.

56 Letters, Johnstone to the Hon. John Kerin and Sen. the Hon. Gareth Evans, 8 September 1992, DFAT: A9737, 89/010974 part 5. In 1992, the percentage representation of female HOMs/HOPs was a little under 4 per cent.

57 Letters, Foreign Affairs and Trade Association to Evans, Senator Peter Cook (Minister for Trade), the Hon. Gordon Bilney (Minister for Development Co-operation and Pacific Island Affairs), and Wilenski, 29 April 1993, DFAT: A9737, 89/010974 part 5.

58 Letters, Kerin and Evans to Johnstone, 19 October 1992 and 7 December 1992, DFAT: A9737, 89/010974 part 5.

59 Summary record, Seminar on Women HOMS/HOPS, 5 September 1996, held DFAT.

References

Unpublished government sources

National Archives of Australia—Canberra

Department of External Affairs/Foreign Affairs

A1838 Correspondence files, 1948–

A4311 'Cumpston Collection' of documents relating to the history of Australian foreign policy

A9737 Correspondence files, annual single number series, 1989– (1947–)

Department of Trade, Trade Commissioner Service Directorate

A3120 Correspondence files, multiple number series [post and policy files], 1963– (1942–)

Newspapers and magazines

Age

Daily Telegraph

Interface (Department of Foreign Affairs and Trade)

Websites

http://www.adb.online.anu.edu.au

http://www.apsc.gov.au

http://columbia.thefreedictionary.com

http://concise.britannica.com

Secondary sources

Browne, Waveney, *A Woman of Distinction: The Honourable Dame Annabelle Rankin DBE*, Boolarong Publications, Brisbane, 1981.

Department of Foreign Affairs and International Trade, Canada, *Our Past: the History of the Department of Foreign Affairs and International Trade*, available http://www.dfait-maeci.gc.ca/department/history/history-en.asp (accessed December 2006).

Foreign & Commonwealth Office (FCO), *History Notes, Women in Diplomacy: The FCO, 1782–1991*, Foreign & Commonwealth Office, London, 1999.

Hall, Diana and Miller, Rachel, c. 1993, unpublished manuscript on women in the Department of Foreign Affairs, in possession of authors, Canberra and Sydney.

Newly appointed heads of mission, certainly in my time and undoubtedly still, were offered counsel by older and more experienced colleagues—most of it was wise, although some verged on trivial. Of the former, I recall some gems passed to me immediately prior to my departure. The first, and most basic, came from a deputy secretary. His message was that outstanding contacts and brilliant reporting would count for nothing if I allowed anything to go wrong with the post's financial management. A colleague who had previously served in the Nordic region warned me that one of the biggest tasks facing the head of mission in Stockholm was keeping the Australia-based staff in good spirits: a challenge that probably applies to any post, but this location had its own peculiarities. My colleague observed that winters in Sweden proved depressing and the brief summers did not fully charge the batteries of solar-powered Australians.

Another senior colleague advised that I should feel free to consult more experienced colleagues in Europe—or anywhere for that matter—in the event that I encountered issues outside my previous experience. But the counsel that I valued particularly, and tried to keep in sight throughout my postings, came from my former ambassador in Jakarta. I had expressed concern to him about the apparent contagion of 'head of mission-itis', a condition suffered when one's exalted position goes to the head. His sage advice was that provided one did not confuse the office with oneself, it should never become a problem.

The Nordic region proved an exceptionally good part of the world in which to cut my ambassadorial teeth. Access to ministers was relatively easy; senior officials were invariably helpful; the leaders of industry were cordial. It was a conducive environment for us to pursue Australia's multilateral and bilateral interests and especially beneficial when organising programs for the seemingly

Accompanying members of a visiting Australian parliamentary delegation during their call on the President of Finland, Mauno Koivisto, in Helsinki, October 1987. President Koivisto is on my right and Senator Peter Baume on my left.

endless procession of visiting ministers and senior officials. During my outgoing call on Australia's Minister for Foreign Affairs in 1983, I was told in plain terms that the Australian government's main interest in Sweden in particular and in the Nordic region generally was 'political'. I was a bit discomfited by this. With Labor in government federally and in several states in Australia at that time, there were clearly close fraternal socialist links. If the number and variety of ministerial visits, both state and federal, were indicators of 'political' interest, the minister's observation could not have been more accurate. Sweden, and to a lesser extent the other countries covered by the post, exercised a magnetic attraction for ministers covering a wide range of portfolios.

It was in multilateral forums that Australian and Nordic interests coincided substantially. Much of the post's work in Stockholm focused on a range of disarmament and other multilateral issues of great mutual interest to both the Australian and Swedish governments and, to a lesser extent, the governments of Finland and Norway. However, our close cooperation in UN human rights forums faltered in 1987—the last year of my posting—over New Caledonia. Australia was lobbying to have New Caledonia reinscribed on the UN list of non-self-governing territories. In representations in all the capitals covered by the post, it was clear that Nordic ministers and officials were struggling over the issue. Against their longstanding advocacy of the economic and political rights of developing countries in the United Nations and elsewhere was the risk of a severe reaction by France (with whom the Nordics had close economic ties), which was strenuously opposing Australia's efforts. Their decision not to support the reinscription was disappointing, to say the least, but hardly surprising. For all governments the balance between national interest and principle is fluid.

Nordic investments in a range of manufacturing industries in Australia were considerable. Their main exports to Australia were components for these industries as well as motor vehicles and electronic equipment. Otherwise trade in goods and services was limited, with Nordic markets extremely difficult to penetrate. Australia's significant success during my time in the region was achieved in wine exports. The volume imported by the countries covered by the post expanded tenfold over the four-year period. The monopolies distributing alcohol vigorously promoted Australia's wines, which were largely imported in bulk and bottled locally. So successful were they that at one stage the importers faced major problems in securing sufficient suitable containers for shipment from Australia. The embassy was asked, tongue in cheek, what it could do to increase Australian imports of bulk whisky. The whisky containers, which were recycled for Sweden's wine imports, were in short supply in Australia.

Inspecting submarine construction facilities in Sweden in 1986, prior to Swedish company, Kockum's, successful bid to sell submarines to the Royal Australian Navy.

Occasionally Australian exporters faced great difficulties in protecting what little market share they had developed, especially in primary products. Seasonal restrictions were placed on some imports, such as fruit and feed grains, to protect local rural industries which, for reasons of geography and climate, were small-scale, generally inefficient and highly subsidised. The markets for Australian suppliers were often minuscule, but principle demanded that we register, in the strongest terms, our displeasure at these restrictions on trade. The merit of our arguments was always acknowledged, but the policies remained in place.

The Australian government's decision to short-list Sweden as one of the two possible suppliers of a new submarine for the Royal Australian Navy brought a completely new dimension to the work of the post. Officers became increasingly involved in negotiations with a wide range of government and private-sector bodies with substantive interests in the project. While technical aspects were the preserve of the navy, on many occasions we were tasked with pursuing highly complex technical issues. The embassy assumed the primary carriage of negotiations on an agreement for assurance of supply, an integral part of the process. The Swedish government dragged its feet; its ministers and senior officials seemed to hope we would grow tired of the process, but eventually it registered with them that the Swedish bid would not be considered by the Australian government without their accession to the agreement.

Adding to the pressures under which we were working throughout these long and sensitive negotiations, an Australian politician, under the cover of parliamentary privilege, accused me of misleading the Australian government on the project and being in the pay of the Swedish government. Absurd and untrue though the allegations were, they were hurtful, given the extraordinary effort the post was making to ensure Australia's interests would be fully protected. My mortgage would have been paid off quite early had litigation been an option.

Amidst the gravitas and protocols which are inevitably part of the head of mission experience, there are moments of levity that help one maintain perspective and avoid the pitfalls of 'head of mission-itis'. On one occasion, the Swedish foreign ministry informed us that the Australian embassy was to be the target of a demonstration by a gay group. The ministry, however, was unable to tell us exactly what the demonstration was about. They assured us that the police, who had given it approval, would protect the integrity of the chancery, which was on the tenth and eleventh floors of a building in the centre of the city. On the appointed day, a small and relatively quiet group assembled on the pavement adjacent to the building. In the absence of signs other than one proclaiming 'Shame, Australia', we spent some time in the dark about the nature of the protest. Finally, a flyer obtained by the head of mission's driver revealed that the demonstration had been prompted by the firing of an allegedly gay teacher from a church school somewhere in Australia. Much later in the day, as the driver and I were leaving the chancery, two young men from the demonstration hopped into the lift on the tenth floor. With elation, one told his companion how pleased he was 'that the ambassador had accepted the protest documents'. Standing at the back of the lift, I kept my composure and counsel until the demonstrators left the lift. It transpired that the senior migration officer, an imposing figure, had accepted the document, thinking that on this occasion pretending to be the ambassador would do everyone a service.

Quite inadvertently, I acquired some notoriety among the Swedish police. After a dinner given for the Australian attorney-general by his Swedish counterpart, I put on what I thought was my navy Burberry only to discover when I got back to my residence that the butler had given me someone else's coat. After considerable detective work, I established that I had the Swedish police chief's coat. When a coat exchange took place the following day, the attorney-general, with tongue in cheek, worried that the ambassador was not only light-fingered but lacking in judgment, having chosen the chief of police as a target for her larceny.

If nothing else, the moments of light relief kept my staff amused. It is a given that success as a head of mission depends to a high degree on having a post where all the officers—Australian and local—are happy and working well together, a status quo often not easy to maintain. By the time I was appointed as ambassador to Sweden, Finland and Norway, I had had extensive management experience, especially in Canberra, involving both large numbers of staff and financial responsibilities. I had also led a small team in Jakarta and been responsible for more than a hundred Australian aid experts and their families in Indonesia. For a variety of reasons, management of a post presented a new set of challenges. The work units were smaller than those I had been accustomed to in Canberra, and professional environments were much more complex. In theory, we all worked for the same firm—the Australian government. With attached staff, however, it was at times difficult to prevent the emergence of the interdepartmental rivalries that tend to afflict the bureaucracy in Canberra, which had the potential to distract the post from its primary purpose. Additionally, as my colleague had forewarned me, environmental factors in Sweden presented challenges to achieving and maintaining harmony among the staff in Stockholm.

Stockholm is relatively remote from the rest of Europe at 60°N of the Equator. Travel to the Continent or to the United Kingdom for much-needed breaks involved either a lot of time or substantial amounts of money for airfares. The barrier of language and the apparent shyness of many suburban Swedes made it difficult to establish contact with the locals. The climate, however, presented the greatest challenge to the Australia-based staff. The long, dark and very cold winters in Sweden proved as depressing for officers on posting as they were for the populace at large. Everyone seemed to get gloomier as winter deepened, which was not surprising: on those rare winter days when the sun actually appeared, it set soon after two o'clock, having risen at about half past ten. Few Australians had encountered such long spells of bitter weather, when the temperatures ranged from minus 26°C to minus 16°C. Moods were not improved when snow and ice caused disruptions to the public transport used by most of the staff. Winters for Australian staff, accustomed to readily accessible outdoor activities regardless of the season, also had the potential to be incredibly boring and, for those with small children, very trying. Families found entertaining their children, most of whom during my appointment were less than five years old, called for a great deal of imagination and ingenuity. The local television stations rarely broadcast programs of interest to Australian children or for that matter to their parents. Videos in English were a novelty, unless family sent them from Australia. Without cable TV and computer games, getting through winter was a great challenge.

Periodic lunches at the residence provided some distraction from winter's dreariness. They also helped to strengthen the esprit de corps within the tiny Australian community. Soccer games on the snowbound front lawn burned up some of the children's surplus energy and distracted them from more mischievous pursuits. I recall one occasion when one of the boys lined up pairs of tiny hands on the piano's keyboard with a view to slamming the lid on them. His nefarious plan was frustrated.

In 1987, I was advised that I was to be cross-posted to Singapore as Australia's high commissioner. By the time I left Stockholm at the beginning of my fifth winter in that part of the world, I knew I had been there long enough—the head of mission driver, who had a seemingly inexhaustible supply of jokes which he shared with me, was beginning to repeat himself.

After Stockholm, Singapore seemed almost like familiar territory. And indeed it should have been, given my work in the Department of Defence covering Southeast Asia, my reasonably regular visits there during my time on posting in Indonesia, and several business trips I had taken before being appointed to Sweden. And although very Asian, Singapore was not as alien as Sweden. Officers and their families in Singapore faced fewer lifestyle challenges than their colleagues in Stockholm and consequently experienced lower levels of stress and frustration. I spent less time managing problems arising from the gulf between staff expectations and the realities of the local

Inspecting the Guard of Honour before presenting credentials to the President of the Republic of Singapore, Wee Kim Wee, in Singapore, March 1988.

environment. English was widely used; the institutions were broadly similar to those in Australia; familiar Australian products were readily available in the local supermarkets, albeit at a substantial additional cost. Good sporting facilities were available, both at the high commission and in Singapore generally. There were also many clubs open to expatriates. The large Australian community in Singapore interacted professionally and socially with officers posted to the high commission. Access to beaches in Malaysia was both easy and not too expensive.

There were many areas of contrast between my two experiences as head of mission, most importantly in the realm of bilateral relations with Australia. Although a small nation state, Singapore had—and still has—an important place in Australia's foreign policy priorities. Connections between Australia and Singapore were longstanding. The memory of the gallantry of Australian military personnel in their efforts to defend Singapore during World War II featured prominently in Singaporean perceptions of Australia and its people. Many major political figures as well as senior bureaucrats and business people in Singapore had been educated in Australia, and Australia was still a preferred destination for large numbers of students. Trade and investment links were substantial. Singapore played a pivotal role for Australia in transport and communications into and through the Southeast Asia region. Defence links were strong through Australia's involvement with Singapore in the Five Power Defence Arrangement. Tourism was also a significant element in links between the two countries.

Welcoming President Wee Kim Wee to an Australian trade exhibition in Singapore, 1989.

Relations between Australia and Singapore, however, hit the occasional rough patch. I had my first experience of this soon after I presented my letters of accreditation to President Wee Kim Wee in March 1988.

In the months before my arrival, the Singapore authorities had targeted the activities of some church workers. They were alleged to have communist connections and were perceived as a threat to national security. Some of those involved were incarcerated under what many countries, including Australia, considered draconian laws. Those not in custody were under close surveillance. Protests by several governments about the fate of these people were made regularly to the Singaporean authorities, who regarded such representations as interference in Singapore's internal affairs. Nonetheless, despite this irritation, relations between Australia and Singapore were cordial enough until Australia's foreign minister decided to have Singapore's high commissioner to Australia called in to register, yet again, Australia's views on the matter. Singaporean authorities took a dim view of their representative being carpeted on what they regarded as purely a domestic matter. They were particularly angry when their high commissioner was door-stopped for comment by Australian media as he left the meeting. Using the *Straits Times*, then a major vehicle for transmitting government policy, the Singapore government on the following day blasted the Australian government and its representatives in Singapore for interference in its internal affairs. The paper announced to its readers, even before I had been summoned to the foreign ministry, that the high commissioner had been called in to receive Singapore's protest.

I had never before been on the receiving end of such a formal protest and did not look forward to my call on the foreign ministry. But the main concern I carried into the meeting related to one of my younger colleagues who had been liaising with the church groups being targeted by the Singaporean authorities. Several weeks beforehand one of his opposite numbers at the US embassy, who had similar connections, had been declared persona non grata by the authorities. The senior foreign ministry official responsible for Australia read me the text of Singapore's protest. A lively exchange followed and I was greatly relieved when it concluded, without my having to take away the message that one of my colleagues had been declared persona non grata. My relief, however, was nothing compared with the officer's.

The challenges in Singapore were not always generated by the host government; some were homespun. The sun had barely risen one Monday morning when an unprecedentedly angry chief of protocol called me at the residence, demanding that I attend a meeting on a very sensitive issue at the foreign ministry at 0830 hours. When I sought some background, I was advised it concerned Australia's deportation of fishermen, at least one of whom was a Chinese national, to Taiwan through Singapore. They had been involved in the murder of some crew members of a fishing boat in Australian waters. The ministry official went on to give me some indication of the upset that it had caused Singapore, berating the Australian government for not having provided prior notice of the deportation, either in Canberra or through the high commission in Singapore. My plea that I was unaware of the issue until his phone call was not well received, but it was believed.

In the short time before the meeting I was unable to obtain much more information beyond what the Singaporean authorities had provided. I did establish that the high commission's duty officer had been advised by Canberra of the deportation late on Sunday afternoon after the aircraft had left Darwin, a mere three hours' flying time from Singapore (and, as it was later revealed, several months after the decision to deport via Singapore was taken). As instructed, the duty officer organised overnight detention for the party before their onward journey to Taiwan.

At the foreign ministry, the reason for the depth of the Singaporeans' upset became apparent. Singapore was in the process of regularising its relations with China, something that was a closely held secret. The negotiations had reached an awkward stage at the time of the deportation. Singapore had been acutely embarrassed when the Chinese Trade Office in Singapore had alerted them to the deportation and the overnight detention of at least one of their nationals. The Chinese ire derived from their belief that Singapore had connived with Australia to facilitate the transfer of a Chinese national to Taiwan, a situation which the Chinese regarded as anathema.

Bilateral relationships recover from these hiccoughs by dint of a strong foundation of past cooperation and recognition of continuing interdependence.

People-to-people links, such as are fostered in the field of education, also provide significant ballast; many Singaporean families have sent their children to Australia for tertiary education. Against the backdrop of cooperation between Australia and Singapore on broader regional issues, intermittent hitches such as the deportation case faded relatively quickly. In the late 1980s, Australia was pursuing a number of regional initiatives that required Singapore's support. The high commission managed a high-profile, active program of visits from federal ministers who were promoting these proposals. More often than not the then Prime Minister, Lee Kuan Yew, made time for Australia's ministers regardless of their portfolio interests. While he usually dominated the discussion, the Prime Minister provided invaluable insights into regional and global issues.

The most frequent visitors were the foreign minister and the defence minister. At that time Australia was at the forefront of efforts to secure political and economic stability and self-determination for Cambodia, a goal whose success depended on support from regional governments. Among the Association of Southeast Asian Nations (ASEAN), Singapore was a most important interlocutor, aiding Australia's proposals by bringing its perspectives to the attention of the other member countries and being highly supportive of Australia's approach.

Another significant Australian initiative around that time was the proposal for an Asia–Pacific Economic Cooperation (APEC) group designed to bring together Pacific Rim countries to consult on economic issues. Securing interest and support from ASEAN was critical to its establishment. Initially the concept met with a degree of suspicion about Australia's motivation in developing a proposal with such wide-ranging benefits. Malaysia was openly hostile, preferring instead a grouping which would exclude Western developed countries. Singapore, on the other hand, espoused the concept with enthusiasm, recognising the benefits that would derive from closer cooperation with major economies, especially those of the United States and Japan.

Eager to see APEC launched, Singapore embarked on a concerted campaign at both ministerial and official level to convince its ASEAN partners that, individually and collectively, participation in APEC would be to their advantage. To capitalise on Singapore's commitment to the concept, the post arranged a series of meetings between Australian ministers and their Singaporean counterparts. It also facilitated a visit by Australia's special envoy, Richard Woolcott, whose program included a call on Prime Minister Lee Kuan Yew. These high-profile interventions complemented the post's regular and detailed briefings on the proposal as it evolved in Canberra.

A significant element in Australia's relationship with Singapore is Australia's membership of the Five Power Defence Arrangement (FPDA)—together with Singapore, Malaysia, the United Kingdom and New Zealand. Occasionally I observed the periodic joint exercises involving the armed forces of all member countries and regularly participated in the meetings between the high commissioners and the senior officials overseeing the operations of the then Integrated Air Defence System, which was the FPDA's only permanent establishment.

Defence staff in the high commission were heavily engaged in supporting Australia's participation in FPDA operational activities. As a general rule, securing the necessary clearances for Australia's military assets involved in these exercises was a routine business, competently handled by these staff. On one memorable occasion, however, the air attaché ran into a brick wall when he sought clearance for a squadron of Australia's new FA-18s to pass through Singapore before participating in an FPDA exercise. I became involved in trying to resolve the impasse through representations at the highest level. The problem proved to be the presence of officers of the US Air Force in the squadron. This was an operational requirement at the time as Royal Australian Air Force aircrews became familiar with this new and very expensive aircraft. I made it clear to the Singapore defence minister that without the US personnel the FA-18s could not and would not be deployed. For its part, Singapore stressed that its then policy of minimising military connections with the United States was being compromised by Australia's requirements and reluctantly granted the necessary clearances.

With Captain Paul Hamon (far right), Defence Adviser, Australian High Commission, and officers of the Royal Australian Navy and Republic of Singapore Navy on an RAN destroyer participating in an FPDA exercise off Singapore, 1989.

In another episode involving our defence forces, during the regional tour of duty of a Royal Australian Navy vessel I was invited to board HMAS *Moresby* as it approached Singapore. I had accepted the captain's offer to be flown to the ship by helicopter, despite a deep-seated fear following an incident on an Indonesian air force helicopter during my time in Indonesia. On that occasion, immediately after take-off, the helicopter had dropped to the ground like a stone, terrifying all those on board. I duly arrived at Singapore's Seletar air base for the flight and was greeted by a perturbingly youthful pilot in one of the most modest aircraft I have ever seen. This young man then ran through what he unceremoniously described as 'ditching procedures' before we took off. With the weather deteriorating, it was hardly a confidence-inspiring start to the trip.

The ship was positioned in the strait adjacent to Changi Airport, and by the time we reached it the wind was so strong that the pilot was refused permission to land. Both the ship and the helicopter were right in line with the main runway of the airport. Not surprisingly, the air traffic controllers, who were handling one of the several peaks in Changi's traffic, demanded that both get out of the runway path as quickly as possible. The pilot opted to ignore the red lights on the ship's landing deck and put his tiny craft down safely, earning himself a stern rebuke from the vessel's captain. The captain's displeasure was as sharp as my relief. I have immense affection for solid ground.

My return to Canberra in mid-1990 was, in its own way, a coming back to earth. I had been overseas for almost seven years when I was asked to undertake the job of principal adviser in the department's Corporate Services Division. Acquiescence in that request proved difficult. I was enjoying the assignment and had made good connections with the Singapore government and especially with the then Prime Minister and with senior officials responsible for areas important to Australia's interests. On the other hand it seemed prudent to agree to the department's proposal.

The role of head of mission, regardless of the size or significance of the post, was a great honour. It brought with it significant responsibilities and, at times, daunting challenges. I was—and remain—grateful to have been an early member of what is now an ever-increasing group of women who serve Australia with great distinction as heads of mission.

3 Diplomacy and crisis management

Sue Boyd

High Commissioner to Bangladesh, 1986–1989

Ambassador to Vietnam, 1994–1998

Consul-General in Hong Kong, 1998–1999

High Commissioner to Fiji, accredited to Tuvalu and Nauru, 1999–2003

In 1999, I had only been a year in Hong Kong as Australia's Consul-General when a telephone call came from Canberra informing me that there was trouble brewing in Fiji. The department wanted me, as an experienced head of mission, to go there urgently. I jumped at the chance.

Friends in super-sophisticated Hong Kong saw things differently and thought I was mad. For much of the world, the Pacific islands are of little interest politically, conjuring instead visions of sand, coral reefs and palm trees. But for Australia, the Pacific is our neighbourhood, important for strategy, trade and investment.

Australia has had a presence in Fiji for almost as long as Australia has existed as a European settlement. From the late eighteenth century and throughout the nineteenth, many of the early traders and settlers came either via or from Australia and were followed closely by the establishment of Australian business houses. The architecture of Suva, in fact, is reminiscent of that of a large Australian country town. The ambience, the rhythm and preoccupations of life there are also rather like that of small-town Australia, albeit with the overlay of the institutions of a capital city. Sport is paramount and everyone is involved. The shops close at lunchtime on Saturdays, so Saturday morning sees the town full and the coffee shops doing good business. The annual flower show is a big event, as is the Hibiscus Festival, with a Miss Hibiscus, a parade of decorated floats and a fun fair and food stalls. Nonetheless, there is a modern touch: a Miss Seniloli—the parallel beauty contest for the gay community, which is a great crowd pleaser and always a sell-out.

In Suva, as in any small Australian country town, everybody knows everybody else—or *about* everyone else. Certainly, there was no such thing as a private life for someone like the Australian high commissioner. This was brought home to me vividly on one occasion when I was talking to a class of primary schoolchildren, and I was asked if there was any downside to my position as the official representative of my country. Mindful of my audience, I said that there was—I always had to be on my best behaviour, and could never be naughty. The response was immediate: 'What would you do if you could be naughty?'

The population of Fiji is mixed and community relations are, on the whole, good. Of the 850,000 Fiji Islanders, 57 per cent are indigenous Fijians or Rotumans, from the island of Rotuma, part of Fiji. The remainder include Indo-Fijians, Chinese, Europeans, part-Europeans, Melanesians and Micronesians. Most of the non-indigenous inhabitants have lived in the islands for a number of generations. Many Indo-Fijians, in particular, are third- and fourth-generation descendants of indentured labourers brought to Fiji by the British, when they were establishing the cotton and sugar cane industries in the nineteenth century.

With Rotuman leaders during a visit to the island of Rotuma in 2002.

Cultural practices and values are many and varied but the communities, on the whole, live together harmoniously and with mutual respect. This was exemplified in the Australian high commission in Suva, where the fifty locally engaged staff come from all communities and work exceedingly well together.

However, as I had been advised, tensions were certainly fermenting when I arrived in Fiji in July 1999. Less than a year later, in May 2000, George Speight invaded parliament and by force of arms took over government. He put aside the constitution and held hostage the Indo-Fijian Prime Minister, Mahendra Chaudhry, and his multi-ethnic government ministers for fifty-six days. But during my time as head of mission, not only did I see the hostages freed and the constitution restored, but I also witnessed fresh elections the following year, in August 2001, and the return to democracy. In time, George Speight and his co-conspirators were convicted of treason and imprisoned on the island of Nukulau, and Fiji's economy recovered.

I considered it to be my good fortune to be Australia's representative in Fiji at this time. Australia played an important role throughout the crisis and in the restitution of normality through our political influence and by focusing on business as usual, even undertaking the new challenge of building practical links to fight transnational crime, an ever-present threat to Australia's security. Against the backdrop of considerable local instability, I needed to call on all the skills developed during a thirty-year career as a professional diplomat in order to influence and help shape events, to garner appropriate resources to apply to the task, and to lead a focused and professional team pursuing Australian interests in Fiji. The high commission advised the Australian government on a day-to-day basis on the sometimes fast-moving events, providing explanations and putting forward the policies and actions that would best advance Australian interests in the circumstances. There were times, however, when decisions had to be made and action taken quickly—and Canberra told about it later. A well-developed sense of humour and a capacity to build relations of liking, trust and mutual respect with all sorts of people were essential components of my skills arsenal.

I had the experiences of a lifetime of diplomacy in this one four-year posting. They included dealing with the aftermath of a dreadful plane crash on my fourth day in Fiji, in which all passengers, including many Australians, were killed; a coup and an army mutiny; managing the evacuation of the Australian community; threats against my life and the security of our diplomatic mission, necessitating Australian Federal Police bodyguards for several months; witnessing the restoration of democracy and the rebuilding of the economy; and, perhaps inevitably, a cyclone. At the same time, there were other particularly sensitive issues to be dealt with that more closely concerned Australian, rather than Fijian, affairs. In the lead-up to the November 2001 election, one such matter was the 'Pacific Solution', which saw the Australian government seek locations in the Pacific to process the asylum seekers who were then arriving by boat and seeking refugee status in Australia, including those picked up by the Norwegian ship, the *Tampa*. And, in my last weeks at the post, I was much occupied by the high commission's role in the implementation of the Australian government's decision to mount a regional force to intervene in Solomon

At the inauguration of an Australian government-funded coastal management scheme on Beqa Island, Fiji, November 2000.

Islands, to assist in the restoration of law and order there.

Of course, through all the crises, the ongoing day-to-day activities of the mission—some routine, others more exacting—still needed attention: immigration; visas; redesigning and applying the aid program to meet the changing needs of Fiji; building cooperation to prevent people smuggling, dealing with international drug trafficking and money laundering; working to develop appropriate roles for, and increase the competency of, Fiji's police and armed forces; assisting in the development of the courts and the public prosecution capacity of Fiji's judicial system; and, last but not least, looking after the welfare of ordinary Australian citizens—the 4,000 living and working in Fiji and the tens of thousands who travel there as tourists each year.

An important function of the high commission is overseeing, supporting and implementing Australian trade, investment and aid. Australia is Fiji's principal trading partner, taking the majority of its imports and supplying much of its imports. Not only is Australia Fiji's largest export destination, but Australian interests also play a major role in most sectors of Fiji's economy: tourism, aviation, garment manufacture, retail and business services. Fiji's major banks are the ANZ, Westpac and Colonial, all of which have been in Fiji for more than a hundred years. The insurance and accounting firms are Australian.

Australia's aid program to Fiji (some $21 million annually during my tenure) assists development in such areas as education, health, community development, reform of government and law and justice. In implementing this program, the high commission works with both the Fijian government and with civil society: supporting small community-based schemes, helping grassroots communities develop, and working in partnership with non-governmental organisations.

Because of Australia's extensive involvement and interests in Fiji the Australian high commissioner is in a position of some influence, with a high public profile and frequently thrust into the spotlight. This situation is not unique to Fiji but perhaps it is more unusual than in many of Australia's diplomatic postings, where the Australian presence is more diluted. I learnt just how much this was the case soon after my arrival in the island nation.

The factor behind my appointment as Australia's head of mission in Suva was the precarious political situation prevailing in the first half of 1999. When I arrived in Fiji in July, the Fiji Labour Party (FLP), led by the veteran Indo-Fijian politician Mahendra Chaudhry, was in power. It had won an overwhelming majority of seats in Fiji's parliament in the first legislative elections held earlier in May under Fiji's new constitution. The FLP had formed a coalition with two of the Fijian parties and had a multi-ethnic cabinet, dominated numerically by indigenous Fijians.

But the Fijian ultra-nationalists were uncomfortable with the symbolism of an Indo-Fijian as prime minister, notwithstanding the multi-racial government and the protections and guarantees of supremacy given to the indigenous community under the constitution. Some of the defeated politicians of the Soqosoqo ni Vakavulewa ni Taukei (SVT) joined in the plotting and scheming, fomenting public sentiment against the new government. Added to this was rivalry for power and influence between provincial-based tribes of Fijians, and resentment among the people in the poorer and less-endowed areas of Fiji that the benefits of development and international cooperation were passing them by.

This flammable mix was ignited, in the end, by a fast-talking, charismatic, mixed-race, failed businessman, George Speight. Prime Minister Chaudhry had exposed Speight's corrupt business dealings soon after the elections and sacked him from a lucrative government business position. He was thus ripe for recruitment by the handful of arch-nationalists who were supported by a small group of elite soldiers within the Fiji Military Forces. This group was motivated, on the one hand, by indigenous nationalism and, on the other hand, by personal and professional rivalry within the senior ranks of the military leadership. Chaudhry's style of government and his impatience to effect change exacerbated these underlying tensions.

On 19 May 2000, George Speight and a small group of soldiers and supporters stormed Parliament House, took the Prime Minister and his ministers hostage and held them under armed guard in the House. Over the next few days, they declared the constitution abrogated, deposed President Ratu Sir Kamisese Mara, and appointed their own president as well as a new 'government' of indigenous Fijian nationalists. In addition to keeping Canberra as informed as possible on the situation, my first response to the events of that day was to go and see Ratu Mara to urge him to deal with the situation in a constitutional manner and offer him Australia's full support.

Such were the imperatives of the situation that we set up a satellite phone link in his office with the Australian Minister for Foreign Affairs, Alexander Downer, who was on an official visit to Cambodia and spoke from a car park in Phnom Penh.

Immediately after the coup, several thousand indigenous Fijians streamed down from the villages, joining ranks with unemployed youth from the city and people with nothing better to do and nothing to lose. They set up camp in the Parliament House grounds, effectively forming a human shield for Speight and his supporters. With the commander of the Fiji Military Forces, Commodore Ratu Voreqe (Frank) Bainimarama, out of the country, the interim military leadership was indecisive and divided in its loyalties and the advantage of an immediate military response to retrieve the situation was lost. As valuable time was frittered away in attempts to negotiate a speedy end to the situation and to bring the rebellious soldiers back into the barracks, it became clear that an armed assault was no longer an option; negotiation was the only way forward. Fiji then entered a tortuous 56-day stalemate as the groups and individuals vying for power competed to find a way to resolve the situation while, at the same time, advancing their own interests.

The high commission kept close to Ratu Mara and his advisers, providing Australia's view that Fiji needed to find a constitutional solution that would enable the international community to provide full support. We also sought to understand the processes and motivations of the other players, and to steer them towards avenues that preserved existing governance structures and practices. We personally dissuaded some who were tempted to join Speight in his illegal government. At no time did anyone decline to talk to us and, as the uncertainty continued, our counsel and advice was sought by players on both sides. Managing the traffic flow at the high commission to keep apart people who would be embarrassed to see each other there was a challenge. It was clear that, for many, Australia's reaction to this crisis in their country was an important factor for consideration.

With Commodore Ratu Voreqe (Frank) Bainimarama, commander of the Royal Fiji Military Forces, June 2002.

Towards the end of May, as the crisis worsened and threats were made to the Ratu Mara's life and to his family, the Fiji Navy spirited him away to one of the Pacific patrol boats originally donated by Australia, which cruised overnight off the coast of the main Fiji island, Viti Levu. There, on 29 May, he was met by the armed forces commander, Frank Bainimarama, now returned to Fiji; the police commissioner; the Great Council of Chiefs Chairman and former Prime Minister, Sitiveni Rabuka; and Ratu Mara's own son-in-law (a former Fiji Army commander). After making the traditional Fijian presentation of a whale's tooth, they pressed him to stand down and hand over power temporarily to a military government. In a later television interview, Ratu Mara said that, in the circumstances, he had no option but to comply. The patrol boat then took the deposed President to his home island in the Lau group. He never returned to power.

As soon as possible after these events, I met with Commodore Bainimarama, now styled Head of the Fiji Interim Military Government. I informed him that Australia could not condone the setting aside of the Fiji constitution and the legal president, Ratu Mara. However, in the interests of practicality, we were prepared to support him in returning Fiji as quickly as possible to democratic rule. The international community expected him to work diligently towards this end, and to be open with us in his plans. We kept in close contact as he worked to meet the challenge of the hostage negotiations and management of government. On 4 July, an interim civilian government was named under Laisenia Qarase, a respected indigenous Fijian businessman, as interim Prime Minister.

In our efforts to resolve the political situation, we were driven by concerns for the welfare of the hostages. Prime Minister John Howard felt personally for his Commonwealth prime ministerial colleague, deposed through force of arms. We left Speight in no doubt about the reaction of the international community should the hostages be harmed.

Australia quietly funded the Red Cross, which provided a daily service to the hostages, bringing clothes, food, medicine and letters from relatives. The Fiji Red Cross Director John Scott was under enormous pressure, absorbing the emotions of the hostages on one side, their families on the other, and running the daily gauntlet of the volatile armed group surrounding Speight. He was already a personal friend, and high commission staff spent considerable time supporting and encouraging him psychologically, while being extremely careful not to compromise the neutrality of the Red Cross.

A potentially serious incident occurred at one early point when a group of visiting New Zealand military cadets innocently (and naively) approached Parliament House to see what was going on. Speight, suspecting this was an Australian military assault, had his men round up the hostages and hold guns to their heads. One of the local staff members of the high commission spoke by mobile phone to Speight, assuring him that no military assault was imminent, and finally persuaded him to turn the guns away from the hostages.

As the critical state of the situation ebbed and flowed, different institutions and leaders became involved: the Great Council of Chiefs; dissident and ambitious chiefs; the military; the police; the churches; and the business community. At the high commission we had to position and reposition ourselves to understand and influence. It was not long before my first thought on waking each morning was: 'What will be the key events today, and who do we need to talk to?'

I had hitherto worked in every other geographical region of the world, but this was my first experience in the Pacific. On arrival, I quickly had to learn the intricacies of Fiji's complex society and build relationships with its decision makers and other key figures of influence. These included government and opposition members, ministers and public servants, judges and lawyers, chiefs, traditional leaders and villagers, business leaders, senior military and police officers, academic and religious leaders, and members of civil society. I was assisted immeasurably in achieving this by the experienced and knowledgeable team I inherited at the high commission in Suva. Another helpful factor was the penetration of society afforded by our extensive aid and military cooperation programs.

Also important were my colleagues in the diplomatic corps. These counterparts, with a shared professional background, values and objectives, provided solid personal as well as professional support when the going got tough. The New Zealand, American and French heads of mission and I shared bodyguard stories as well as political intelligence and information on how we were advising our governments and how they were responding. I was further indebted to my wise and experienced Tuvalu colleague, Enele Sopoaga, and the Papua New Guinea high commissioner, Babani Maraga, who both patiently explained the motivation and values of Pacific island leaders and their peoples. Another source of useful insights was Indian High Commissioner Professor Ishwar Chauhan Singh, a former academic and an expert in Fijian affairs and the Indo-Fijian community.

Key to the success of Australian efforts during this turbulent period were the professional skills and stamina of the high commission staff, both Australian-based and locally engaged. With curfews in place, and long hours of work, my role as leader of the team included making sure that they each got enough rest, took exercise, and were properly fed. This was a particular challenge with my deputy, a brilliant and highly intelligent woman who had no interest in food, exercise or nutrition and whose cook abandoned her in the early days of the coup. It fell to the cook of the high commission residence to keep this able deputy's body going while her mind worked overtime.

For our locally engaged staff, life was particularly difficult. Opinions in the local community were divided, for and against the coup and its objectives. Some staff were closely related to chiefs deeply involved in the political scene.

Staff had to deal with curfews, power cuts, school closures. Some saw the order and normality of life in the mission, as well as the hard work, as a haven from the chaos of life outside. And despite all the difficulties and potential conflicts of interests, they turned up to work every day and gave of their best.

It is in times of crisis such as this that you have to draw heavily on all your leadership skills. For this special group of people, it was important that they understood that I recognised their commitment to the high commission and that I and my senior staff provided encouragement and sensitively took into account the challenges they faced.

In heading a mission at such a time, you must also maintain confidence in the leadership skills you have acquired. At the height of the tension we decided to send away all Australia-based dependants and non-essential staff and to bring the remaining key staff to live in the five houses on the high commission compound. The decision was regrettable but understandable under the circumstances, except perhaps for the high commission's rather 'enthusiastic' defence adviser who was convinced that it was an over-reaction. (This was while rounds of ammunition fired by the rebels in Parliament House were falling in the grounds of Australian staff houses nearby. In fact, one whistled past the ear of the trade commissioner as he went home to collect some clean clothes for the relocation onto the compound.) Further internal wrangling was avoided, however, when the Department of Defence quashed the adviser's request to have my decision rescinded and confirmed that I was the commanding officer and that my decision would be respected.

My leadership style is consultative; the support of senior members of the team and their availability as a sounding board helped me make the difficult decisions. In this I was aided by frequent telephone conversations with colleagues in the Department of Foreign Affairs and Trade in Canberra, particularly Greg Urwin, Australia's most experienced Pacific hand, who had been my predecessor in Suva. In the end, however, many of the decisions were mine, and I was responsible for any consequences.

Indeed, when the crisis reached its climax, we found ourselves to be the only diplomatic mission that had not fled Suva. Until that moment we had thought that some of our New Zealand colleagues still remained, but a telephone call from halfway down the Coral Coast let us know that they too had departed. When Canberra learned of this, they anxiously challenged my judgment that it was safe to remain. Our compound was located a few kilometres from the centre of the city and the action at Parliament House. We were in frequent mobile phone contact with many people in Suva and were surrounded by a high wall and had security guards at the gates. I had calculated that we would have enough warning of any potential trouble to escape in fully fuelled vehicles positioned at the back gate, and make it to safety before any mob reached us. But that night, carrying the full weight of our vulnerability, I hoped fervently that my judgment was right.

After fifty-six days, on 13 July 2000, the hostages were released from Parliament House through a negotiated deal—the Muanikau Accord. Following negotiations including factions of the Great Council of Chiefs, the widely respected former Vice-President, Ratu Josefa Iloilo, became President. Laisenia Qarase's interim government now became a caretaker government to take Fiji to elections. The focus of our negotiations turned to encouraging this government to hold elections earlier than the three years proposed and to agree on how Australia and the international community might best assist.

An issue of immediate importance was the matter of the coup leader George Speight and his co-conspirators. The military had arrested them soon after the hostages' release and it was crucial that their trials be efficient and fair. For them to escape the law would have encouraged further coups by any disaffected group in the future. There were strong local pressures to forgive and forget, the so-called Pacific Way, coming from those who decried the method but supported the nationalist cause. The Australian Federal Police assisted the Fiji Police to collect and prepare evidence in such a way that a trial could successfully be held. Australia provided support to the public prosecutor's office in recruiting an experienced Australian prosecutor, Peter Ridgway, capable of mounting the case against Speight and his co-conspirators.

In the meantime, Australia could not formally support the non-constitutional arrangements in place after Speight's arrest, and so developed a strategy to encourage Fiji back to the rule of law as quickly as possible. With New Zealand and the United Kingdom, we had moved to have Fiji suspended from the Councils of the Commonwealth on 7 June. We now imposed a set of 'smart sanctions' designed to make the maximum impression on Fiji, without injuring the grassroots poor or impeding economic regrowth. Fiji's other international partners—New Zealand, the United Kingdom and France—acted similarly.

With Fiji's Vice President, Ratu Iloilo, after presenting credentials in Suva, 22 July 1999.

At the time I received instructions to convey our decision on smart sanctions to the Fiji authorities, Suva was undergoing a power cut. My deputy and I duly arrived at the nine-storey building that housed the Ministry of Foreign Affairs on its top level. With the lift and airconditioning out of action and the stairwell dark, hot and humid, we climbed the nine flights of stairs by the light of our tiny pocket torches. Struggling not to appear flustered and out of breath, but fanning ourselves madly with our Pacific island fans, we were a sorry delegation as we delivered the news to the impassive Emitai Boladuadua, the permanent secretary.

At times like that, a well-developed sense of the ridiculous helped maintain sanity. In fact, when presenting me for an honorary doctorate at the University of Western Australia in 2002, Vice-Chancellor Deryck Schreuder said that exchanges with me were 'an extraordinary mix of high policy and low humour'.

In the absence of formal endorsement or recognition of Fiji's new, non-elected government, we had to be creative in our efforts to maintain contact with its members to understand what was going on and to try to influence their thinking. We could hardly invite the illegal government, for example, to the official Australia Day reception, but nor did we want to slight the individuals with whom we needed to deal in the pursuit of Australia's interests. These people would probably also emerge, in due course, as Fiji's legitimate leaders. In 2001, we arranged with the Fiji–Australia Business Council that they would formally host the Australia Day function, which we would support financially. They could, of course, invite whom they liked, and of course, we would all attend. The arrangement worked well, and a month later we suggested that, with our support, the Fiji Business Women's Association should host the annual International Women's Day reception in March at the high commissioner's residence, a valuable networking opportunity attended by the most prominent women leaders of Fiji each year.

The interim government's foreign minister, Kaliopate Tavola, an economist and former diplomat, was married to a friend of mine, Helen,

With Bernadette Rounds-Ganilau, Assistant Minister for Women's Affairs and Social Welfare in the Interim Government of Prime Minister Laisenia Qarase, 2000–2001.

with whom I shared early-morning aquarobic classes and membership of a book club. While I could not maintain close contacts officially, it was easy enough to drop around to their house with a good bottle of red whenever we needed to discuss matters.

Australia's efforts to encourage the restoration of good governance suffered a setback in November 2000 when rebel Fiji Military Forces, led by Speightist nationalists, mutinied and attempted to remove Commodore Bainimarama as commander. Loyalist troops retook the barracks within hours, but the aftermath—the 'cleaning out' of the military and bringing the mutineers to justice—took considerable time, finesse and, it was alleged, brute force. Again, Australia supplied specialist resources to assist the military courts martial, and provided ongoing support and advice to the military leadership.

But that was to come later. During the actual mutiny, the high commission chancery, which was a bare two kilometres from the army barracks, had its own share of excitement. Staff, including myself, were outside, listening to the gunfire and watching the flares, when a rain of ammunition clattered out of the sky and onto the roof and the lawn on which we were gathered. Fortunately, none of us was hit. We were not particularly happy to learn later that such ammunition maintains sufficient velocity to maim within a range of five kilometres after firing. (In fact, four civilians were injured in Fiji that evening—one when a bullet entered the bathroom of his home where he was showering and another who was hanging out the washing in the garden.) Such episodes are, of course, traumatic for staff whose families are not within the chancery compound. Our third secretary was about to cycle home to his family, located close to the barracks, and had to be almost physically restrained until the danger was past.

We had another incident involving guns. During the crisis, Joe Browne, official secretary to the President, came to see us in my office. We were discussing personal security when he opened his jacket to reveal a handgun on his hip. At the conclusion of the meeting as she was showing him out, my secretary gave Browne back his mobile phone. I said to her: 'You took his mobile phone off him. Did you also know he had a gun?' 'Oh yes,' she replied, 'but I knew what our policy was on mobile phones—I just wasn't sure what to do about guns!' We sent off a cable to Canberra reporting the discussion with Browne, which we entitled 'Is that a gun in your pocket, or ...?' It was widely read.

In the months that followed, by various means we expressed our official disapproval of the interim arrangements in place since Speight's arrest, while continuing to work creatively to maintain pressure on the non-constituted government for an early return to democracy and constitutionality. Governments that come to power by irregular means commonly seek to perpetuate themselves in power. Australia, with the rest of the international community, used sticks and carrots to discourage this inclination in Fiji. We were successful, and free and fair democratic elections were held in Fiji in August 2001, just fifteen months after the coup. This took considerable persuasion and negotiation, as well as generous practical cooperation with the elections office and with civil society institutions, which were involved in voter education.

Commonwealth and UN election observer missions (which we helped fund and organise) declared Fiji's polls to be free and fair. But life was still not completely back to normal. Prime Minister Qarase, whose party had a majority in Parliament in coalition with the Nationalists, declined to take in former Prime Minister Mahendra Chaudhry's Labour Party, as the constitution provided, even though the FLP had almost half the seats in Parliament. Many countries argued that until this final ambiguity was resolved and the FLP occupied its rightful place within government, full recognition of the Fiji government should be withheld.

I disagreed and argued strongly that this was a matter for the courts of Fiji—not for judgment by any foreign government. Our ministers accepted this advice. Fiji's court system is strong and internationally respected. Prime Minister Qarase gave public guarantees that he would abide by the decision of the court. In these circumstances, I advocated that Australia should remove its smart sanctions and work without any constraint with the Qarase Government for the political, social and economic development of Fiji, as this best served Australian interests.

Other foreign governments, including those of New Zealand, the United States and the countries of the European Union, took a contrary view and decided to maintain pressure and refuse full relations until the constitutional ambiguity was resolved. Though we would have preferred to take others with us, Australia was prepared to stand alone. We certainly benefited from our stance in the access and influence which it gave us and the capacity to move ahead in areas of Australian interest where others remained hampered.

I gave many speeches that were widely reported in the media across Fiji. These public occasions presented excellent opportunities to deliver key messages and through them I urged adherence to the rule of law and the rapid return to constitutionality; explained Australian policies; encouraged the Indo-Fijian community not to be downhearted and not to seek to emigrate from the land of their birth, and the Fijian majority to respect the rights of other citizens; and countered calls from some political quarters that Australia should provide a special humanitarian migration program for dispossessed Indo-Fijian cane farmers. In my position as an outsider, but an accepted friend, I could say some things that the local political players could not. Although some of this contribution to the national debate attracted criticism, there was also positive feedback and encouragement from all sides.

Nor did we neglect our own citizens and throughout all our work, we took pains to keep the Australian community informed, particularly the business community. Where appropriate we enlisted their assistance in putting the Fijian economy back on track, but we also stood firm against those companies whose sole immediate interest was in making money. These firms did not share our conviction that, in the long term, restitution of open, transparent and democratic government would best serve Fiji's and Australia's economic and trade interests. We worked with the Australian trade union movement to remove the trade sanctions they had imposed. But on the other hand, we resisted persistent objections to Australian travel advisories from the travel industry, which they claimed deterred Australian tourists, even from 'safe' areas. Our first priority was the safety of Australian travellers. And when traditional landowners started to invade some of the up-market resorts in the supposedly 'safe' areas, and the traditional landowners threatened to close down Nadi international airport, we knew that our advisories were vindicated.

In August 2002, a year after the elections, Prime Minister John Howard visited Fiji and publicly congratulated Prime Minister Qarase and his ministers on their success in restoring Fiji to the stable and strong position it then enjoyed. Fiji had come a long way since May 2000. Prime Minister Qarase glowed at this accolade from the leader of the country of most importance to Fiji. And—though

At the Pacific Island Forum Leaders' Meeting in Suva, 2002, with the Foreign Minister of Fiji, Kaliopate Tavola, and the Prime Minister of Australia, John Howard, and Mrs Janette Howard.

having decried the Commonwealth's treatment of Fiji—Qarase publicly joined Australia in calls for similar sanctions to be imposed against Zimbabwe.

Nonetheless, I believe that Fiji is a work in progress. As the events of November–December 2006 show, many of the strains and conditions that precipitated the upheaval of May 2000 remain and they will take time to resolve. Australia continues to work with Fiji, helping build social stability, reduce poverty, and promote the conditions necessary for economic growth. We work with its institutions, to strengthen them and equip them to manage evolving challenges and demands. We cooperate increasingly on common threats to our security, particularly transnational crime. And we help Fiji deal with national disasters, such as Cyclone Ami, which hit the northern and eastern parts of the country during my posting, in January 2003.

While for much of my posting the high commission's work focused on Fiji's internal affairs and bilateral issues, we were also engaged on matters that affected the region as a whole. In late 2001, the Norwegian tanker *Tampa* rescued at sea a large group of people from a leaking boat heading for Australia, intent on seeking refugee status. The Australian government decided to ask governments in the Pacific to agree to the use of their territory to establish centres to receive and process the asylum seekers. Australian heads of mission in the region were tasked to negotiate this proposition with their host governments. Nauru, to which I was also accredited, saw the proposal as a way to redress its critical financial situation and agreed immediately, as did Papua New Guinea. After protracted discussions with the government of Fiji, however, it became clear that Fiji had enough problems of its own without taking on more but was finding it hard to say no to Australia. We withdrew the request. Nonetheless, the two governments agreed to work closely together to address the international threats posed by people smuggling and transnational crime. Fiji has played an important, ongoing role in this area.

The 'Pacific Solution' caused considerable disquiet. It was for me personally one of those ethical dilemmas that professional diplomats face from time to time—when the government you serve involves you in the implementation of a policy about which you are deeply unhappy. I had two options: to resign, or to act on the instructions using my skills in such a way that it would do least damage to Australia's overall interests in the Pacific. I was also acutely aware that in the Pacific we were actively advocating democracy, good governance and the responsiveness of governments to the wishes and needs of their people. The 'Pacific Solution' was a policy of the democratically elected government of Australia, and a policy that clearly had wide support in the Australian community.

In my final weeks in Fiji, the Prime Minister of Solomon Islands, Alan Kamikeza, asked Australia to intervene in his country, wracked by civil war, to help restore law and order. The Australian government asked me to seek the opinion of Fiji's Prime Minister Qarase, who was then head both of the Pacific Islands Forum and the EU–ACP grouping, an affiliation of European Union and African, Caribbean and Pacific states. We wanted to know whether Fiji agreed with an Australian intervention, whether Qarase thought that a regional intervention was possible, whether Fiji would commit forces to such a regional initiative, and whether he judged that other Pacific nations would also join. Also, whether he had any advice to offer on the form of assistance to Solomon Islands.

Leading Australia's delegation to the Pacific Islands Forum Regional Security Committee meeting, which approved the Regional Assistance Mission to Solomon Islands (RAMSI) in Nadi, Fiji, June 2003.

Canberra's instruction came on the eve of my departure for the distant island of Vanua Balavu in the Lau group, the Prime Minister's home island, which he and his wife had invited me to visit with them before the end of my posting. The opportunity for the discussion arose as he and I were sipping coconut water, seated under a palm tree on the sand of a pristine beach near his village, waiting for a small boat to collect us for a tour of the island. He was immediate and decisive in his response, supporting the initiative, pledging Fiji troops and police and stressing the importance of engaging civil society, particularly the churches, in the rebuilding of Solomon Islands society. Vanua Balavu is out of mobile phone range, so it was not until our return from the island tour that I had the opportunity to use the only phone in the village—in the Prime Minister's own house—to report back to Canberra.

The following week, at a meeting of the Pacific Islands Forum Regional Security Committee, in Fiji, we were able to support the Solomon Islands delegation as they briefed the other island governments on their predicament and requested regional support. It was important to allay cynicism and suspicions that this was neo-colonial Australian interference. We were at pains to ensure the region understood that Australia was responding to a request from the Solomon Islands government. The Regional Assistance Mission to Solomon Islands formed after this meeting broke new ground in forum politics—it was the first time that the forum secretariat had been so engaged, with leaders agreeing to intervene in a coordinated way in a Pacific island state.

When I left Fiji in July 2003, I was farewelling both a country and a career spanning thirty-four rewarding years in Australia's foreign service and four postings as head of mission.

Publicly at my farewell reception, and privately, Prime Minister Qarase expressed his thanks to the government of Australia, and to me personally, for our role in restoring normality to Fiji. On several occasions Qarase said that he had found our policy discussions extremely helpful and often, he said, his policies and courses of action had been influenced by what I had to say.

Given the active and sometimes tough role Australia played, I took considerable satisfaction that we remained in good standing in Fiji, making a positive contribution to that country while at the same time ensuring that Australian interests were advanced. During the four years of my posting, Australian policy towards the Pacific changed significantly, and became much more hands-on and politically activist. We had judged that this would best serve the interests of the region and of Australia, and events unfolded in ways that vindicated our approach. It was an exciting and rewarding time to be Australia's representative in Fiji and in the Pacific Islands Forum.

The foreign service has changed greatly since I joined in 1970 and the status of women in Australia's diplomatic life has undergone a transformation. I feel immensely gratified to have contributed to these changes in policy and practice. I helped develop the first equal employment opportunity program in the department, which identified many of the causes of the unequal treatment and progression of women, and devised strategies for the department to meet its EEO aspirations. When I joined the then Department of Foreign Affairs in 1970, as one of two women in a group of twenty-three, there were no appropriate female role models. Discriminatory recruitment and staffing practices, the marriage bar in the public service and the absence of maternity leave had prevented women from entering and advancing in the profession. We few

Acting Police Commissioner Moses Driver farewelling me in Suva at the conclusion of my posting in July 2003.

women elbowed, cajoled, charmed and worked tirelessly to resist discrimination, remove barriers and open up opportunities.

And we did this at the same time as doing our day-to-day jobs extremely well. We were constantly under scrutiny in an extremely competitive work environment and we were being judged, not as officers of the department, but as *female* officers of the department. There was no room for mistakes or failing to come up to scratch—we were carrying the reputation of all women officers, and those aspiring to join our ranks. Though we were measured against our male colleagues, we had to formulate our own way of doing things. There were countless irritating barriers to be overcome. For example, though I was clearly the most qualified person available to be sent to East Timor in 1975 at the start of the Timor crisis, I was told that, had I been appointed, it would have been said that the government was not taking the situation seriously, as it was 'only sending a woman'. But changes in traditional outlook were coming, albeit slowly, and it was with great delight that, ten years later in Bangladesh, I could overturn the view that a woman could not succeed as head of mission in a Moslem society.

When I was high commissioner in Bangladesh, I was one of only four Australian female heads of mission. These days there are sufficient women heading Australia's diplomatic missions that the statistics are no longer remarkable for their paucity. It is a great satisfaction to see that women are now better represented in the senior ranks of the department.

Because my career found me among the early contingent of women appointed as head of mission, I became a role model for other women in Australia's foreign service. And in Australian society more broadly, and in international contexts, I have had considerable opportunities as a public figure to exemplify what women could achieve as social attitudes and conventions evolved. I was pleased to be a source of encouragement for other women, in Australia and overseas, in their various endeavours; and I found similarly gratifying the mentoring role that I played for many of my male staff.

But of the many satisfactions of my professional life, the privilege of contributing to Fiji's development and to Australia's relationship with this small but important Pacific neighbour ranks among the highest.

4 Madame l'Ambassadeur

Penny Wensley AO

Consul-General in Hong Kong and Macau, 1986–1988

Ambassador and Permanent Representative to the United Nations, Geneva, 1993–1996

Ambassador for the Environment, 1992–1996

Ambassador and Permanent Representative to the United Nations, New York, 1997–2001

High Commissioner to India, 2001–2004; and Ambassador to Bhutan, 2003–2004

Ambassador to France, accredited to Algeria, Mauritania and Morocco, 2005–

My ambition to be a diplomat was formed just as I entered my teens; through high school and university my career goal was always to join the then Department of External Affairs. At school, as I was considering what course and subjects to take at university, I wrote to the department enquiring about selection procedures and requirements. At university, I went to recruitment presentations, talked to scouting teams, followed the fortunes and took the advice of others who had applied—both those who had succeeded and those who had failed—and in my final year, watched carefully for the annual advertisement and then applied. I was not obsessed or unduly anxious. I simply knew what I wanted to do, was focused on that goal and moved purposefully towards it.

I knew it was difficult to join External Affairs. The recruitment process was reputed to be very competitive, with many applicants and few places available. I had an idea it was more difficult for women, but until I made the 'short list' and travelled to Canberra for the final three-day selection process, I did not appreciate how difficult. The year I applied, there were some 500 applicants

With the President of France, H.E. Jacques Chirac, following the presentation of credentials ceremony at the Elysée Palace in Paris, on 6 June 2005.

Australia-wide. In the final stage, we were three women only in a group of fifty finalists. We stood out in the sea of new, dark suits and by looks, comments and questions were made to feel conspicuous and different. Some said, with a touch of envy, that our competition was only with each other—that it was the department's unwritten policy to take one woman in each intake. The selectors made clear, however, that there were no guarantees for any of us.

So it was with relief that I received the letter offering me a position as a diplomatic cadet, subject to completing my honours degree and necessary security checks. I arrived in Canberra in early 1968 to find I was indeed the only woman, in an intake of nineteen diplomatic trainees. I was twenty-one years old. The average age of the group was twenty-two.

I remember we were asked to sign a form, indicating whether we planned to retire at sixty or sixty-five. I signed up for sixty-five. Although the idea of being either age seemed impossible, it was a logical choice—this was the job I wanted. I was aware that there might be challenges along the way, particularly in relation to marrying and having a family, but I assumed I would be in it for life.

Similarly, I assumed that I would move upwards through the system. I cannot recall, in those early days in the department, forming a specific ambition to be a head of mission, an ambassador. The ambassadors and senior officers we met were distant, intimidating figures. They seemed very old. It was at that stage only an incidental concern to me that they were all men. Likewise, I was not unduly concerned that my male colleagues were paid more than I was, even though my academic qualifications were the equal of, or better than, theirs. I was happy to have been selected. My preoccupation was with the training course, then with my first posting.

When I was told it was to be Paris, I was not surprised: most of the women cadets had been posted to Europe or North America. In the 1960s, women diplomats were rarely posted to Asia, and none were appointed to positions in Africa or the Middle East. But I was not unhappy—Paris matched my skills well. I spoke fluent French, one of the qualifications I had deliberately developed in response to the advice that knowledge of modern languages would enhance my selection prospects. French was still regarded as the language of diplomacy, and my fellow trainees, who did not have this skill, had first to acquire some grounding at the Point Cook language school before they headed for their respective postings. Meanwhile, I packed my new suitcases—a going-away gift from my parents—for Paris with a happy sense of both fulfilment and anticipation.

For the most part, that feeling has lasted throughout my career—as has the sense of logical progression; each posting and placement different and essentially rewarding, each experience building and extending my knowledge and interests, each opening up new opportunities, and each taking me higher up the ladder.

As I climbed the rungs, particularly in the early and middle years, I was not looking at the top. Rather, I was enjoying where I was at the time and managing the particular challenges of each job. I did, however, always have an eye on the next step. These I climbed quite quickly, moving in my first posting between 1969 and 1973 through three ranks—from third to second to first secretary—encouraged by a progressive head of mission who was tough and demanding, but who gave me lots of opportunities to develop. I was also encouraged by his professional wife who gave me definite pushes in the right direction when I was inexperienced and uncertain about my role and place. I remember one reception where she ushered me away from the comfort of a familiar group and propelled me across the room to a cluster of senior men, saying firmly 'this is where you belong' and creating an embarrassing, sudden silence in the group by announcing that I was one of them.

My next posting was as deputy head of mission to Mexico—a deliberate choice on my part, to give me the management experience of being the second in charge, of living and working in a developing country and of learning another mainstream language.

The three years I spent in Mexico, from 1975 to 1977, had an indelible impact. Mexico was driving an ambitious political agenda to lead the Third World and strengthen Third World institutions, bringing to its capital a constant procession of leaders and delegations. Its oil resources, disarmament policies, complex relations with the United States, all provided plenty of scope for reporting and analysis of relevance and interest to Australia. In addition, the post covered Central America, and travel to Costa Rica, Guatemala and Panama added an exciting extra dimension to my work. In all three countries, I had vivid experiences of the value and impact of Australian aid, seeing firsthand the transformation of people's lives achieved from even modest projects, like providing half a dozen sewing machines or digging a well in a remote village.

If the Mexico posting was my introduction to North–South and development issues, it was also my initiation into the dangers and risks of overseas postings. Mexico City was one of the most polluted cities in the world—breathing its air, it was said, was the equivalent of smoking a packet and a half of cigarettes a day. Illness among staff and families was frequent and the risks of serious problems that could affect one for long periods, even a lifetime, were high. Crime, political unrest and violence added further dimensions. Roads—including some major highways—could not be travelled safely; residences were protected by high walls covered with glass and razor wire; kidnappings were carried out by both criminal gangs and dissident groups for both economic and political reasons. Mostly, wealthy Mexican businessmen were the target, but during our time one group, the 24th September Communist League, identified some countries and their diplomats as targets: the young daughter of the Belgian Ambassador was kidnapped on her way to school (happily, her release was secured); shortly after, we received a kidnap threat at our home, which was taken seriously. Fortunately, it was not followed through—perhaps because of the guards the Mexican authorities provided for a period and the other security measures we implemented. Nonetheless, it was an unsettling experience, particularly for my mother in Australia. To my everlasting regret, she was told about it by a journalist waking her up very early one morning, seeking her comment. She was caught off-guard and was naturally distressed. I learned the hard way some important lessons about dealing with the media and about informing families, rather than trying to shield them from worry!

As Ambassador to Bhutan, visiting a Bhutanese school where Australian rice is used for a school lunch program for children in remote rural areas, in cooperation with the World Food Programme.

I had two three-month stints at the United Nations General Assembly during this time, according to the wonderful practice, now sadly abandoned, of giving young officers some experience of multilateral work. This experience confirmed my interest, stimulated first in Paris, in negotiation and multilateral diplomacy, as well as in Asia and Australia's place in Asia. The former came from work in relation to UNESCO, the Organization for Economic Cooperation and

Development and other international organisations based in Paris. The latter sprang from watching Ambassador David Anderson lead Australia's delegation to the Vietnam peace talks in Paris and Ambassador Alan Renouf negotiate the agreement to establish diplomatic relations between Australia and the People's Republic of China. They seemed hugely important processes, defining events for Australian foreign policy.

These two ambassadors gave me strong models to follow. Their styles and approach were very different and I learned much about multilateral diplomacy and engaging with Asia from them, both directly and from watching them in action. At the United Nations I was able to add considerably to this experience, working with Sir Lawrence McIntyre and Sir Ralph Harry, the two ambassadors and permanent representatives to the United Nations in New York, in 1974 and 1975 respectively. As managers, as leaders, as ambassadors, they, too, were utterly different, and although I had moved beyond base camp, at this time, all four still seemed impossibly senior, operating at heights way above a mere first secretary.

I did not act on these burgeoning interests immediately after Mexico. I had my hands more than full trying to manage and balance career, marriage and family in a work and living environment which was not supportive, either in the department or in the wider Canberra community. I had married Stuart McCosker, a veterinarian and fellow graduate from Queensland University in 1974, just before leaving Australia to take up my second posting. We had known one another a long time and from the time we met, he knew of my career choice. He was pleased for me when I was selected to join External Affairs and again when I was posted to Paris. Eventually, we decided we did not wish to be apart, living and working at different ends of the earth, and so he came with me to Mexico, both of us believing—it turned out naively—that he would be able to work.

When, for various reasons, Stuart could not work in his profession in Mexico, we decided to start our family. As I was the first woman policy officer to have a baby while on posting, this initially provoked considerable argument with the department, which wanted to terminate my posting and bring me home. Fired up by the United Nations 1975 International Women's Conference (coincidentally held in Mexico City), I felt it was my right to have my child where I chose, and that it was important that the department accepted that having children was a normal aspect of the life of women officers, not something to be tucked away. In my view, my twelve weeks' maternity leave should be accommodated by the post, in the same way that my twelve weeks' absence in New York for the 1975 General Assembly had been accommodated. Eventually, the department agreed and so we continued in Mexico for the duration of our posting, returning to Australia as originally scheduled in December 1977 with our seven-month-old, Mexico City-born daughter.

Our second daughter was born in Canberra two years later. We have confronted many challenges and difficulties as we have moved around the world together, but we remember those years, when our children were small, as probably the hardest of our lives. We enjoyed being parents but both of us had demanding jobs, with much unpredictable out-of-hours work, and we had virtually no support systems. We simply had to manage and it was exhausting and stressful. I remember vividly, and still with some pain, my immediate boss at the time challenging me one evening as I rushed out of the office at the end of the day to collect our daughters from family day care, saying 'When are you going to make your mind up, Wensley, whether you are a mother or an officer?'

I recall that I retorted 'The day you decide whether you are an officer or a father', but his comment had not been a joke. Nor was it exceptional—there were others. Nonetheless, I never suffered from the marriage bar (which until 1966 required women officers to resign on marriage), and after a few years of discriminatory treatment, I received equal pay with my male colleagues. More women were joining the department, but still there were few in the top positions. The first woman career officer, Ruth Dobson, had been appointed as head of mission in Denmark in 1974, but by the end of the decade, the models were all single women—no one with families and the challenge of managing two careers. The departmental culture surrounding women was still conservative. I, and a few others like me, were in uncharted territory as we tried to move ahead. Some of us tried to form a lobby group to push our cause and concerns. We succeeded in getting girlie magazines removed from the canteen, but failed utterly in our efforts to establish a creche on the premises. Some women officers were reluctant to be identified with activism, fearing it would harm their careers. Others simply could not find the time or energy. I recall one woman colleague, who has now left the department, saying to me quietly that she agreed we should campaign but that she was just too busy surviving.

With two children under five, few countries where my husband could practise his profession, and against the background of the kidnap and bomb threats we had experienced in Mexico, not to mention the legacy of hepatitis picked up there, I opted for a quieter location. It was a posting where my husband could work but one that would still further my career—deputy head of mission in New Zealand, supporting a high commissioner who was a political appointee. In the early 1980s New Zealand was generally not a sought-after posting for young, or even middle-level, Australian diplomats—

perhaps because it was too close to home. However, I calculated rightly that it offered many professional benefits: handling a close, but complex and sensitive relationship; gaining a perspective on the Pacific; being exposed to trade policy work; and also valuable management experience.

But I got more, much more, than I bargained for—underlining the wonderful element of the unexpected in this career. You never know what may happen. Career development and career opportunities cannot always be predicted and shaped. Crises can occur anywhere. For those who like a quiet, conventional, settled life, a crisis or conflict may seem a case of being in the wrong place at the wrong time; for diplomats who have chosen foreign relations and the conduct of business and communication between governments and countries as their career, it is the exact opposite. Crises are what we thrive on: they are exciting professional challenges—testing your skills, your judgment, your capabilities. But you have to get it right. You have to ride the wave and not get dumped by it.

I rode the turbulent waves of my Wellington posting—the ANZUS crisis, the *Rainbow Warrior* affair, the early days of the Closer Economic Relations (CER) agreement, the ongoing fall-out from sporting contacts with South Africa, the notorious underarm bowling incident—straight onto the beach of my first head of mission posting, as Consul-General in Hong Kong.

Before I left to take up my appointment in Wellington, I had been told, by the then secretary of the department, that I had already demonstrated my capacity to manage a post and could expect to have my own post next time

As Australian consul-general in Hong Kong, launching the Australia Koala platinum coin in 1988.

round. I was pleased by this, having by that time become more conscious of what was possible for capable officers, and yet also of the resistance in various quarters to putting women in senior positions, including as heads of mission. I had also quietly, somewhere along the way, been influenced by an article, or press release, I had read about a male officer who had broken records by being appointed a head of mission at a young age. I had formed the ambition to be a head of mission before I turned forty. I assumed, however, given the pattern of past experience for the few first-time women head of mission appointments that had by that time been made, that this would be something modest, a small post on the periphery of Australian policy interests, somewhere to cut my teeth. Hong Kong did not fit that picture. It was a big post, with just over 100 staff, including a large number of attached officers from other departments and agencies. Politically and economically, it was high-profile and important: our fifth-largest trading partner at the time; our largest source of business migrants; and our third-largest source of fee-paying students. Hong Kong also had a sizeable, assertive Australian community; it was on the way to everywhere, with federal and state ministers constantly visiting or transiting the territory; and it offered a host of challenging political issues of direct interest to Australia. These included the fate of the refugees crammed into camps on the outer islands and the negotiation of the transition from British to Chinese sovereignty.

Professionally, it was marvellous: stimulating, absorbing, challenging. Personally, in some aspects, it was difficult, as there was no precedent: I was thirty-nine, the first female head of mission of a large post, married, accompanied by my husband, with small children. I had substantial policy, managerial and representational responsibilities to handle. My household was used to a male head of mission with a wife to manage both it and the staff. Child care was also an issue. The ambassador in a nearby major Asian post, as I understood it, had been provided with expatriate childcare assistance as part of his terms and conditions, as had the deputy head of mission in another major north Asian post—both men. But this assistance was not offered to me prior to my posting. From our first night in Hong Kong, when we were expected to attend a function in our honour, and to leave our two small girls with strangers who spoke little English, it was clear that the domestic arrangements would have to change. As the burden of our situation became daily more evident, I made the case for assistance similar to that offered to my male counterparts in nearby posts. I was told firmly that it would create 'an unacceptable precedent'. We coped, but it cost us a great deal both emotionally and financially over the three years, as we tried to find solutions that gave security to the children and enabled me to meet the responsibilities of my demanding job. Eventually, when we had exhausted local options, we engaged live-in expatriate nannies at substantially our own expense.

Child care is a preoccupation for all officers with children, but is especially so, I would suggest, for people serving overseas in locations where security concerns, language and different cultures have to be taken into account. This should be thought about more seriously as a matter of policy, and career support should be planned, expanding on the excellent in-house facilities on offer to staff in Canberra. Today's increased apprehension about terrorism only adds to this need.

Similarly, the management of official residences, including meeting representational demands that are part of promoting Australia's interests and image overseas, imposes serious pressures on heads of mission. Although others may have a different view, in my experience that pressure is more pronounced for women heads of missions. Having now been head of mission in five major postings—Hong Kong, Geneva, New York, India and France—where sophisticated entertaining is the norm and a significant aspect of doing one's job effectively to achieve Australia's objectives, I can testify to the substantial extra work involved. It is often terribly tedious and time-consuming; it is mostly invisible; but it is absolutely essential. At least among my generation, there is a well-known joke among women heads of mission that our problem is that we do not have wives. The wry observation is not without foundation: diplomatic services around the world, especially when it comes to heads of mission, rely heavily on spouses to do a great deal of work, which is largely unrecognised and taken for granted.

The department ruled in the 1970s that wives (the term spouses had not taken hold) were not obliged to assist with representational work, and it now also pays a small amount to spouses per function to recompense them for time and effort they may have committed to assist. These are welcome changes but there is scope to go further, as other foreign services have done. Much of what Australia achieves through its overseas representatives and missions rests on the willingness of our heads of mission and, when they have them, their spouses, to devote considerable time and effort to organisation of representational activities. This is not reasonable. Nor should there be a double standard. There is a historic sympathy for male heads of mission (and male spouses), and an acknowledgment that they should not be spending time on table plans and guest lists, selecting flowers, planning menus, and holding consultations with the cook. On the other hand, there has been an unspoken assumption that women heads of mission can somehow take this in their stride—and fit it in along with their high-level policy work and their management of the post. We should recognise the true extent and value to Australia of the work involved in managing official residences and their staff and in organising representational functions, and provide all our heads of mission in major posts with the support systems they need to do their job effectively. A professional household manager for the residence, as provided by the French, British and American governments to their senior heads of mission, is a model that could be considered in particular posts—perhaps most logically linked to our post categorisation system.

In making these observations and suggestions, I am conscious that questions of child care, the management of head of mission households and support for representational work pale beside the core policy business of the department. But for all officers, these are significant issues, along with the additional, vital matter of employment opportunities for spouses. The assistance and understanding that the department is prepared to provide in this area are of profound importance. And, although there have been obvious gains for women in recent years, it is still my sense, talking to women officers across the spectrum of ages and levels, that their concerns on these matters are more pronounced than those of their male colleagues and that, for many of them, it is precisely these personal and practical issues, more than their skills and competencies, that they believe will ultimately determine whether they will be able, or will choose, to remain in the service and reach the level of head of mission.

I am conscious, as I make such comparisons, that I am entering awkward territory. Yet at the same time, I feel this is exactly what this chapter, this book,

Visiting an Australian government-funded project in Rajasthan providing library services to Indian women and children when high commissioner to India 2001–2004.

should be about: the awkward territory that women have both to occupy and to manoeuvre their way through to succeed.

Frankly, when I was approached to contribute a chapter to this book, I felt ambivalent and not a little uncomfortable; why not a book on men with a mission? The answer perhaps is obvious: men are not in a minority in the department, at senior levels or as heads of mission. They probably do not need role models or reminders about history or pointers to success to reach the top of the ladder. Arguably, despite considerable gains in recent years, women still do, and therefore it is important—for the department, the government and individuals—to broadcast the message that it is possible, and that there are good career opportunities for women in Australia's diplomatic service.

In the end, I decided I was willing to—and in fact should—help to do that. I have enjoyed a long, interesting and successful career, spanning eight overseas postings: two as deputy head of mission, five as head of mission. I have relished my life and work as a diplomat representing Australia and promoting Australian interests and have derived great stimulation and satisfaction from contributing to Australian foreign policy thinking and advice in a wide range of positions, in Canberra and overseas. I expect to continue to do so for some time to come. I have also been able to combine my career with a marriage of thirty-two years, and a family. (Our two daughters are now in their twenties. They are both accomplished young women, who seem to have benefited, rather than been disadvantaged, by spending most of their lives, until they started university, moving around the world with us.)

It is this combination, this achievement as it appears to some, that seemed to be of most interest—at least when I quizzed colleagues, notably younger women officers, as to what they might want to read about in a book about women heads of mission. A few anticipated I might have some good stories to tell (these will have to wait for a different publication when I am no longer a serving officer). But most confided deep concerns about how they could combine their wish for continuing career advancement and satisfaction with the more personal fulfilment of finding a partner willing to share their unusual life and possibly, almost inevitably, having to make career and financial sacrifices to do so. They worried also about having children (at what age, at what point in their lives and careers) and about the issues that challenge all parents (of child care, choice and quality of schools and teaching, safety, instilling values, providing extra-curricular opportunities). These matters become so much more complicated when moving one's family between postings, countries and cultures.

I understand these concerns well, having confronted most of them, but even while empathising with such preoccupations, I confess to a small, familiar

As Australia's Ambassador for the Environment, chairing negotiations at the UN Global Conference on the Sustainable Development of Small Island Developing States (SIDS), in Barbados, 1994, with departmental officers Dr Peter Howarth (second row, left) and Charles Mott (front row, right).

feeling of disappointment that the initial reaction is to focus on 'the woman angle'—my experience, perspective and advice as a woman, about issues particular to women—rather than my experience with political issues.

As a diplomat, I would rather be asked about my experience with the ANZUS crisis in the 1980s, the Tiananmen Square events of 1989, the Taiwan Straits crisis, the East Timor crisis, or the India–Pakistan confrontation throughout 2001—all major foreign policy issues with which I was closely involved. I would like to talk about my experience representing Australia at the United Nations in Geneva, in New York, and as Ambassador for the Environment, leading Australian delegations to myriad major international meetings, negotiating crucial conventions and agreements. And although I have unique perspectives on chairing the central negotiating process of the UN Conference on the Sustainable Development of Small Island Developing States, the UN Fifth Committee, and the UN General Assembly's special session on HIV/AIDS, gender had no bearing on my appointment or election to these positions.

Similarly, as a head of mission, I would prefer, before being asked about my experience and perspective as a woman, to be asked about my views on building team spirit and staff morale, on motivating officers, about strategies I have used to develop good relations between Australia-based and locally engaged staff, about how to maintain a happy and productive mission, and about juggling competing priorities to deliver outcomes on time and within budget. I would like to provide my insights into what risk management really means, about the challenge of keeping staff and their dependants safe in times of tension and in high-risk locations, about what is actually involved in managing an emergency evacuation of staff, a post closure, bomb threats and an anthrax scare. I have views, born of experience, on how one deals with corruption allegations and the need to investigate and then dismiss staff, and how one responds with sensitivity, compassion and discretion to the personal problems of officers far from home and support systems—a suicide, marital problems, the birth of a handicapped child, a miscarriage, a cancer diagnosis, the death of a loved parent or grandparent, or even worse, the death of a staff member. All these I have dealt with over the years as head of mission, gaining practical, valuable experience as a manager.

But for the diplomats and the heads of mission who happen also to be women, there is, I accept, an extra dimension to our experience which, even if our personal and career histories are distinctive and particular, justifies the idea of defining our 'mission' in a different way—at least until there are many more of us.

Virtually all women who reach senior positions confront this reality, and struggle with the dilemmas it raises. My experience as ambassador in New York exposed the problem probably more clearly than elsewhere—and was shared by my fellow women ambassadors. We were a very small group. In the four years I was there, we were never more than eleven out of a total of 189 member states. Most of us were highly experienced, accomplished professionals, career diplomats who had risen through our respective systems on merit, on a competitive basis. We carried the same responsibilities as our male colleagues, handled the same range of issues across the international agenda, developed our expertise on particular areas of foreign policy according to our governments' strategic and political priorities—and yet were constantly asked for our views 'as women' and expected to be interested in 'women's issues'. For example, in September 1999 I was elected chair of the United Nations' notoriously tough Fifth Committee, which handles administrative

Chairing the UN Fifth Committee (Administrative and Budgetary) with UN Secretary-General Kofi Annan, New York, in 1999–2000, while ambassador and permanent representative to the United Nations.

and budgetary matters. I was steering the member states through a minefield of contentious issues, including that of American arrears to the organisation, and a redesign of the complex contributions system. It was a big story in the media and I was often sought out by journalists tracking the progress of the negotiations. Disappointingly, they almost never asked me about the substance of the issues I was handling, although I knew more perhaps than anyone else they could have interviewed. Mostly, they just wanted to know how it felt to be the first woman to hold the position.

When there was no 'women's angle' to focus on, some journalists seemed to have difficulty seeing us. The situation in East Timor in the late 1990s was a case in point. Australia was in the thick of intense diplomacy and fast-moving action, and journalists scrambled to find out the latest developments. We would emerge from a difficult backroom or late-night session to a barrage of cameras and microphones. Inevitably, Australia's Ambassador to the United Nations was bypassed and the questions were put in the first instance to my male colleagues. Politically, I did not mind, as we were for the most part engaged in intensive 'quiet diplomacy' and it suited Australia to assume a low profile, but there were times when our views and role were pivotal and needed to be articulated—then I would have to insist on being heard.

My experiences were not unique. The Ambassador of Finland, when she was president of the European Union, and the Ambassador of Jamaica, when she chaired a major UN meeting, both had to deal with journalists displaying gender bias: bypassing these women, as the key players and persons best placed to comment on a particular matter, to seek the views of less well-informed male colleagues.

I should emphasise that these experiences, and variations on them played out in other ways, did not blight our lives or cause great distress. Secure in our positions, we got on with our jobs and enjoyed them greatly; but it certainly created a distinctive camaraderie, and, paradoxically, made us more insistent than we may have been previously on having our status recognised and acknowledged. Certainly, in my case, my determination to be accepted as an equal and to have my skills and experience acknowledged has actually become more pronounced in recent years, as I have moved through a succession of senior appointments, than when I was younger and arguably facing greater obstacles and discrimination.

Female heads of mission encounter predictable sexist assumptions, muddled nomenclature, misaddressed invitations, and awkward fumbling and mistakes with greetings and introductions. This can be both irritating and amusing. In Delhi, I was never sure whether to feel pleased or perturbed at being labelled by the Indian media as 'Canberra's man in India, Penny

Visiting the Hyderabad Waste Management project, September 2002, while High Commissioner to India.

Wensley'. Now as Ambassador to France—one of twenty-seven women ambassadors out of 153—I am for the most part entertained by the energy with which French contacts debate the question of whether women ambassadors should be referred to as *Madame l'Ambassadeur* or *Madame l'Ambassadrice*. The issue, as with the form of address for women ministers, has been considered at length and pronounced upon by the highest linguistic authority in the land—the prestigious French Academy. Despite support for the former (which I and my women head of mission colleagues consider is the correct form of address, acknowledging our position and status, not our gender) the arguments seem to roll on ... and on ... and on.

Although, in diplomacy, words matter a great deal and should never be treated too lightly, we all have more serious matters to deal with, including the expectation that women heads of mission should actively champion women's causes. I have encountered this in all my posts, but it was especially the case for the women ambassadors to the United Nations in Geneva and New York. Whatever our private views and personal sympathies, it was not our job to represent women or to focus on women's issues. Our responsibility, as it was for every ambassador, was to represent our countries, to defend and pursue our particular national interests to the best of our ability, across the spectrum of UN activities and the international political agenda. Even if one was so inclined, there was the risk that over-identification with a 'gender agenda' would diminish us professionally, feeding the very stereotypes and assumptions we sought to avoid. At the same time there were strong expectations from women both within and outside the system that we would promote their

With US Secretary of State Madeleine Albright (right) and the Deputy Permanent Representative of the Mission of Trinidad and Tobago, Mrs Yvonne Gittens-Joseph, at a reception hosted by Ms Albright to welcome women ambassadors and delegates to the UN General Assembly in 1997.

interests, using our weight and authority as women ambassadors to make a difference for women.

Finding the right balance was not easy, especially for those among us who had big missions to manage and major political issues to handle. Together and separately, we found different ways of responding to those who looked to us to help make a difference for women. I believe that, without acknowledging it explicitly, we understood that our positions—and the fact that there were so few of us—made us role models and that it was important to a lot of people that we accepted the responsibility that created. We had little choice but to accept the extra burden: we had to perform for our countries and our governments and represent their interests effectively, but we also had, in some way, to represent the country of women, to recognise that what we said and did as women ambassadors undoubtedly could affect the way women were perceived and judged by the community in which we worked. If we underperformed, were indifferent or mediocre, conclusions would be drawn about woman as diplomats; if we did well and were seen to deliver, we could help break down barriers, stereotypes and simplistic assumptions about women's roles and capacities.

This is what I mean by the awkward territory we occupy. I accept that these pressures vary from post to post, in different countries, different cultures. I accept also that in any field or career where women are under-represented there will be similar pressures on women who have reached senior positions to tell their stories and share their experiences, including their pathways to the top. Clearly, there is no one formula for success. For me, hard work, determination, energy, good health and stamina through tough times have all been factors; along with genuine enjoyment, for the most part, of what I do and a strong drive to achieve and keep achieving. Some careful career planning was necessary too, involving both placements in Canberra and positions overseas, consciously developing skills, and looking for ways to acquire experience in particular types of work or regions of importance to Australia.

Although I have never had a mentor, female or male, encouragement and direction-pointing at some critical junctures from some progressive male bosses certainly helped a great deal. I have already spoken of Alan Renouf, my first head of mission throughout my four years in Paris, and who was promoted from there to be secretary of the department. A strong-minded, energetic man, he was forceful but fair, challenging his staff to think independently and to question accepted thinking. As secretary, he pioneered and drove through some key changes for spouses and families. Peter Wilenski, the department's secretary in 1992 and 1993, was an exceptional believer in women's rights and equality, who acted upon his beliefs and instincts to effect changes in the department and wider public service. Peter Henderson, secretary from 1979 to 1984, who led a post liaison visit to Mexico City during my posting and with whom I worked in the Executive Secretariat in 1978 and 1979, was of a decidedly different generation in relation to women working. Yet he was sensitive, sympathetic and supportive when I was a new mother, trying to prove that I could manage everything—he helped me accept that it was all right to admit that I was tired and that I did not need to be perfect to succeed. Robin Ashwin was a truly inspiring role model. I worked with him at the First International Women's Conference in Mexico City in 1975, and he was my Division Head from 1980 to 1982, when I headed the Central and Southern Africa Section. This was a demanding time for the division, with Australia hosting the Commonwealth Heads of Government meeting and the Commonwealth Games and the issue of sporting contacts with South Africa running hot. Ashwin's absolute command of all the issues we were handling, his assured manner at Senate Estimates and Parliamentary Committee hearings, his quiet but effective negotiating techniques at international meetings and patient good humour in dealing with demanding VIPs, all provided invaluable lessons. He was simply a great boss, generous in giving credit to younger officers, male and female alike, allowing us space and opportunity to develop, and pointing us towards new capabilities and experiences.

Beyond the deliberate, calculated career decisions, there was the unexpected—political events, crises, policy shifts—that suddenly created exciting opportunities. And supporting it all there was, and is, the bedrock of my husband and family. I would not wish to have pursued this career alone. It

Talking to the president of the French chapter of the Australian Business in Europe (ABIE) Network, Mr Jean Georges Malcor (centre) and Mr Steve Bishop, Office of the Premier of Queensland, the Hon. Peter Beattie, following a luncheon hosted at the residence for the premier and delegation during their visit to Europe, May 2006.

is, I believe, a life to be shared. With all its difficulties it brings great personal rewards through living in and experiencing, as a family, different countries and cultures. I have been fortunate to have with me a strong and generous partner who has shown extraordinary selflessness and strength, enduring long periods of not working, and the serious financial loss and myriad indignities that involves. For such partners, men and women alike, the department needs to redouble its efforts to reduce the barriers to work overseas, to negotiate more reciprocal work agreements, to achieve recognition of professional qualifications. There have been spurts of effort on this, but progress has been slow. Many officers and their spouses have suffered, are suffering, and will continue to suffer, the consequences until more resources are committed and a sustained effort made to bring about real change.

I have seen, over the years, gradual changes and improvements in the conditions and opportunities for women officers in the department. Some, like the childcare centre in Canberra, came too late to benefit me, but I am glad to see the progress that has been achieved. I look forward to further enhancements in our conditions of service and, as long as they are needed, continuing efforts to recognise the particular challenges that women confront in pursuing a successful career in the Department of Foreign Affairs and Trade. I hope that many more of my women colleagues will achieve happy and fulfilled lives representing Australia.

5 Fractured paradise

Tonia Shand AM

High Commissioner to Sri Lanka, accredited to The Maldives, 1988–1992

In early 1988, I was advised that my name as high commissioner had been put forward and accepted by the governments of Sri Lanka and the Maldives, subject to the normal protocol procedures. It was a moment of profound professional delight and one for which I was well prepared. I had, by this time, served with the department for twenty-seven years and was then head of the South Asia, Africa and Middle East Branch in Canberra. This branch had responsibility for a complex and broad spread of countries and issues in those regions. My credentials for the Sri Lankan appointment were strengthened by two previous postings in Asia—as first secretary, later counsellor, in New Delhi (1973–1975), and as deputy high commissioner in Kuala Lumpur (1979–1982).

Professionally, this appointment was the culmination of a lifetime of service in Australia's external affairs. I had joined the department in 1961 but had to resign when I married in 1963. I soon secured temporary employment with the department but, on pregnancy, had to resign yet again. After the birth of my daughter, I again rejoined as a temporary officer and continued in that

Making a prepared statement as a member of the Australian delegation to the UN General Assembly in New York in 1962.

capacity until the passage of legislation enabling permanent employment for married women in the Public Service in 1966. At the time, many within the most senior levels of the department believed that married women were unsuitable candidates for diplomatic postings, and it was several years before those with a more liberal view of the role of women prevailed.

Personally, it deepened my interest in a country that had been ignited when I stopped in Colombo on my return voyage to Australia after twelve months' postgraduate study in Bonn in 1960. At the time I had been entranced by its beauty and the charm and warmth of its people—characteristics that are as seductive now as they were then. I also made a return visit in 1975 at the end of my three-year posting in New Delhi. Almost thirteen years later, as the plane pierced the monsoon clouds over the central highlands, I felt that a cycle was about to be completed.

Colombo—an old fashioned and intimate South Asian capital city—had changed little since my first trip in 1960. It remained a port city, well known to generations of Australians travelling by ship to and from Europe. There were still relatively few high-rise buildings. The city was famous for its old hotels, its winding streets and labyrinthine lanes, and its urban sprawl.

Australia has a well-established profile in Sri Lanka, and its interests have been well served through the efforts of its diplomats since the establishment of relations with then Ceylon in 1947. The bilateral relationship has been reinforced through the close contacts maintained by Sri Lankan migrants in Australia and through educational, cultural and sporting links. (Many Australians may be surprised to discover that every Australian cricket team from 1884 to 1956—with the exception of the 1921 side, whose ship arrived too late for the scheduled match—played in Colombo en route either to or from England.) At the time of my appointment, these links had been impressively researched in a beautiful book, *Links between Sri Lanka and Australia*, by Dr Wickrema Weerasooriya, the then Sri Lankan high commissioner to Australia.

The strength of the bilateral relationship and my existing familiarity with Sri Lankan affairs provided a firm foundation on which to begin my posting as head of mission. Nevertheless, the Sri Lanka I landed in was in the midst of a political crisis and I knew there were testing times ahead. With the commencement the previous year of a violent insurrection by the Sinhalese Janatha Vimukthi Peramuna (JVP), the People's Liberation Front, against the elected United National Party (UNP), Sri Lanka was facing one of the most turbulent periods in its post-independence history. Similarly, the Maldives presented issues of concern and opportunities to develop further in my capacity as Australia's accredited representative there.

Diplomats are expected to be prepared to start work immediately, but the settling in and familiarisation process necessarily requires some attention. I was fortunate to be working with a small but close-knit team of professional staff who were devoted to their work. But knowing the challenges that the high commission might face in the near future, I set about gauging how well it was equipped to deal with these, given the existing responsibilities of the officers and their relative workloads. As with all incoming heads of mission, I had my own views on staff management and performance and wanted to try my ideas and hopefully gain their acceptance. In the brief period between arriving in Colombo and being formally recognised as head of mission, with the presentation of my letters of accreditation to the Sri Lankan President, J.R. Jayewardene, on 13 June, I had a little time to reflect and act on these 'domestic' issues. It was a useful period for me to talk to the high commission's Australia-based and locally engaged staff and generally familiarise myself with my new workplace and living quarters.

I had inherited an elegant, spacious two-storey residence with a superbly designed and landscaped garden. Much of a diplomat's official representational

A corner of the wonderful garden at the residence in Colombo.

work is conducted at home. Social occasions can be as useful for pursuing national interests as formal appointments in offices during business hours. My residence and its grounds were the venue for many representational events, including Australia Day receptions, other official functions and children's Christmas parties. During my term it was chosen as a location for the filming of a number of scenes for the successful Australian–British television miniseries *Shadow of the Cobra*, starring Art Malik and Rachel Ward. I also opened the garden to Sri Lankan charities to raise funds for worthy causes.

These were troubled times for Sri Lanka and I needed to give high priority to increasing personal security arrangements for the expatriate Australian community and high commission staff. In the deteriorating political climate, a warden system had been established for the expatriate community. We divided up Colombo and appointed wardens to coordinate security activities for their locales. The high commission regularly briefed wardens on the security situation and liaised with them regarding contingency planning for evacuation if and when such a situation was deemed necessary. We installed emergency radio communication for Australia-based staff in case of a breakdown in normal communications and assigned security guards to the chancery and staff residences. Subsequent events were to prove the worth of such precautions and contingency planning.

Once accreditation was behind me, I commenced my calls on the Prime Minister (later President), Ranasinghe Premadasa, appropriate ministers, key heads of departments and senior officials in the Ministry of External Affairs. My level of access to ministers and senior officials was commensurate with the warmth of the bilateral relationship. Given the uncertain political situation, even these early meetings, which in other countries might have been driven more by protocol than by substance, were specific opportunities to present Australia's interests and concerns.

With government-to-government contacts established, I began calling on my diplomatic counterparts and acquainting myself with the Sri Lankan community at large: local newspaper editors and journalists, opposition spokespersons, leading university experts, and other groups and individuals with an interest in Australia.

With the President of Sri Lanka, J.R. Jayewardene, at the presentation of credentials ceremony in Colombo, June 1988.

The diplomatic community in Colombo was small compared with

those of Kuala Lumpur and New Delhi, but I quickly discovered an impressive reservoir of talent and goodwill. Traditionally, the British, Canadian, US and Australian representatives met once a month over lunch to review key political developments and to share perceptions and experiences. These meetings served as a barometer of the political and economic climate in Sri Lanka. I was delighted to find that my Canadian counterpart was also a woman, as were the Cuban and Thai representatives. The diplomatic community was a close-knit one within which I made strong friendships.

Unusually, I returned to Australia within a month of my accreditation, accompanying Prime Minister Premadasa and his wife and daughter who were visiting Brisbane to open the Sri Lankan pavilion at Expo '88 in July that year. It is the custom for heads of mission to join heads of host governments on such trips which, although invariably hard work, provide invaluable opportunities to cement productive relations at the highest level. In addition to his official engagements, Premadasa's itinerary was hardly conventional. Included among the sites of purely practical interest we visited were the Sewerage Farm at Werribee (Colombo was suffering the inadequacies of an ancient waste disposal system dating back to Dutch times); and the Melbourne Cricket Ground to inspect the new lighting system installed for one-day cricket (he was exploring such a system for a stadium in Colombo). For me, the visit was a unique chance to get close to the Sri Lankan Prime Minister and appreciate his priorities. He greatly impressed me with his commitment to seeking practical solutions to problems that restricted the living standards of the Sri Lankan people, his long working hours, strict adherence to business and punctuality, and his personal charm and warmth.

A major responsibility of any diplomatic mission is political reporting, and during my tenure, I and my staff kept Canberra well informed about Sri Lanka's December 1988 presidential elections, the subsequent general and provincial council elections, and a number of complicated constitutional issues. Given the nature of Sri Lankan politics, this proved a complex task requiring close attention on a daily basis.

After the visit to Australia, two issues took centre stage, both of which were familiar to me before the posting. The first was the JVP insurrection, a violent terrorist campaign emanating from the south of the country. Essentially a radical Sinhala Buddhist Marxist group, the JVP aimed to overthrow the Sri Lankan government and put ownership in the hands of the people, drive upper and middle classes into the countryside, and ban multinational companies. The second critical issue was the continuing separatist movement for the creation of a Tamil Eelam (homeland) in the north and east. Both claimed thousands of lives on each side and wrought devastation in towns and countryside.

Political violence had begun in Sri Lanka soon after independence with the assassination of Prime Minister Solomon Bandaranaike in September 1959. The two issues facing the government in May 1988 when I arrived had their foundations in earlier crises. In 1971, a JVP insurgency (the first) was put down by the then Prime Minister, Mrs Sirimavo Bandaranaike, and an estimated 10,000 people were killed. Then, in July 1983, communal violence between Sinhalese and Tamils killed 3,000 Tamils (by 1993, 25,000 more would die in the war in the north and east).

When I took up my position, the government was bracing itself against a renewed onslaught from the JVP. This second insurgency was to be more insidious and far more deadly than the first—two and a half years of unparalleled ferocity and bloodletting. Often compared to the ruthless Khmer Rouge in Cambodia, the JVP created an atmosphere of fear and tension—a veritable war of nerves—so that where its posters appeared on the walls of buildings declaring a *hartal* or strike, Colombo and the cities of its heartland in the Sinhalese south effectively became ghost towns.

Relying on indoctrination and fear, the JVP found support among the disaffected underemployed and unemployed in both urban and rural areas and among those who saw the democratic system as culturally and politically bankrupt—dominated by greedy and corrupt politicians and administrators whose only interests were to secure the continuing superiority of their own community, caste and clan.

The JVP waged a guerrilla war of such intensity that at some points it seemed the government could possibly collapse. By September 1989, the JVP had closed in on Colombo and the city was gripped by fear. Threats against politicians, businessmen, prominent personalities, bureaucrats and the public caused the administration of the city to falter. Posters, death threats conveyed by phone or letter and *hartals* paralysed the administrative structure. Offices, business houses

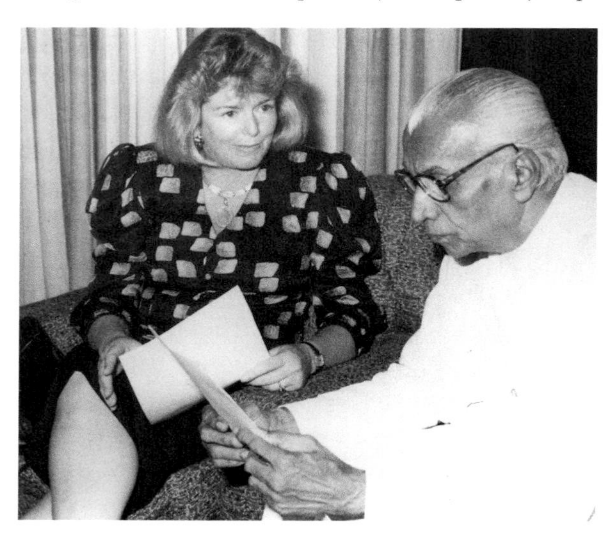

Making a call on the Sri Lankan Prime Minister, Dingiri Banda Wijetunga.

interests, gave support for specific promotional activities, and sought out trade and investment opportunities.

When I arrived in Sri Lanka, this function was still in its infancy. Until 1977, Sri Lanka was one of the most regulated and closed economies in the developing world, with a poor record of growth and development. In 1977, the Jayewardene government broke with the past and decided to open the economy. It gave priority to export-oriented manufacturing and encouraged foreign investment. Foreign investors responded enthusiastically to the new opportunities until the mid-1980s, when the civil disturbances became a serious deterrent. Despite the war in the north and east, foreign investment figures began to rise again from 1990.

Participating in the opening of the Ansell Lanka Latex Production Facility at Mawanella, Sri Lanka, in August 1990.

Australian business investment was slow to enter the country initially, with the first manufacturing firm only commencing operation in 1985. In the first year of my tenure, despite the security situation and its effect on the Sri Lankan economy, several large Australian firms made sizeable investments in the country. By 1990, Australia contributed a relatively high 15 per cent share of overall foreign investment, second only to the Republic of Korea. This was almost entirely due to the contribution of one company, Ansell Lanka, which produced surgical gloves and condoms.

In 1989, together with the local Austrade representative, I set up the Business Interest Group of Australia (BIGA). The objective was to provide a framework through which the high commission could support the growing Australian business community in a period of civil turmoil. Through BIGA, we briefed Australian investors on political and security developments and established business contacts at ministerial and official levels of government. We held monthly meetings, inviting Sri Lankan officials to speak on their areas of expertise. Adopting an informal approach in these meetings, on the advice of businessman and former Sri Lankan high commissioner to Australia, General Denis Perera, BIGA functioned in a relaxed, candid and flexible manner. I believe BIGA was influential in this early and difficult period of Australian investment and helped our small business community to remain steadfast in the face of a threatening investment climate.

One of the busiest events with which a head of mission must deal is a ministerial visit. Such visits require careful planning, close liaison with the host nation and assiduous attention to detail. Ministerial visits to foreign countries are usually brief and intended to accomplish a range of specific purposes in a short time. Even in the most conducive environments this can be stressful; slight hitches in the daily program or a small lapse in the provision of information on the local situation could produce effects out of all proportion to their cause. On the other hand, these are times when you might be witness to an important episode that can change the complexion of an otherwise standard ministerial visit.

One such occasion was the high commission's hosting of a three-day ministerial visit by the then Minister for Foreign Affairs, Senator Gareth Evans, in August 1990. Crammed into those three days were calls on the President, the Foreign Minister, the Minister for Trade and Commerce and the Leader of the Opposition; an official visit to the ancient city of Kandy; a press conference; and an official dinner. During one of the calls, the matter of external mediation in the ongoing hostilities between the Sri Lankan government and the LTTE was raised. Several offers from other governments had been declined, and Evans now brought an offer from the Australian Prime Minister, Bob Hawke, to act as a broker on behalf of the Commonwealth. The bid to assist the Sri Lankan government, in fact, had its roots in an idea that was floated by Senator Robert Hill, then the Australian shadow minister for Foreign Affairs, and the Hawke government pursued the objective energetically. With this initiative, Evans' visit took on special significance. Australia was indicating its willingness to participate in an area of foreign policy outside its immediate interests. The offer was subsequently declined but, as a step forward, a Sri Lankan Parliamentary Select Committee comprising all parties was established to look into the ethnic issue. Although Australia's initiative was not taken forward, I was proud to have witnessed such a fine example of Australian bipartisanship in our efforts to resolve a complex and tragic situation and to strengthen a bilateral relationship.

The ministerial visit was well behind us when two incidents occurred that ensured that I did not forget the proximity and intensity of the ongoing war with the LTTE. Both these took place close to the Australian residence and the chancery. Early in the morning of 2 March 1991, our peace was shattered by a huge explosion that resonated throughout the residence. Although we did not know it, at that moment the Deputy Minister for Defence, Ranjan Wijeratne, had been killed by a car bomb only a street away. Whether it was the work of the LTTE or the remnants of the JVP and its sympathisers was never clear, although most in the capital believed it was the work of the former.

The second incident was a terrorist suicide attack on the military's Joint Operations Command headquarters in June 1991. This headquarters had been set up three months earlier, when the armed services were given a free hand to control security following the collapse of the ceasefire. It was only 400 metres from the high commission and in the heart of the busy residential area of Colombo. The headquarters was charred beyond recognition and many other buildings close by were severely damaged, including a school. Anxious parents from the high commission rushed to this and other schools to check on the safety of their children. Fortunately, none of their children was in the direct path of the explosion.

Being close to the blast, the high commission was also affected, although not as severely as might have been expected. A prominent Sri Lankan community leader was calling on me at the time of the incident. The huge explosion shattered the chancery's windows and was followed by a tremor that shook the foundations of the building. My secretary was thrown out of her chair by the blast, fortunately suffering only minor injury. In many traumatic incidents there is a bizarre detail that one recalls wryly. In this case, my guest's bodyguard had been stationed in the courtyard of the chancery at the time. Thinking that the explosion had occurred within the chancery, he burst in, brandishing an AK-47 and demanding assurances of his charge's safety.

Immediately after the explosion, the high commission staff responded magnificently as we assembled downstairs within the compound to the sounds of the sirens of the ambulances ferrying away the maimed and the dead; fatalities numbered close to a hundred. Our staff had escaped largely unscathed. An Australian swimming coach on an official visit to coach the Sri Lankan swimming team had had a lucky escape. She had been travelling to the high commission by taxi and had just passed the headquarters when the bomb exploded. Her taxi was thrown some distance down the street, but miraculously she was not injured. She was, however, badly shaken—all the more so when she realised that a taxi travelling behind her had not been so lucky.

We later learned that an LTTE suicide van had driven to the gate of the headquarters and the driver, on receiving the usual request for identity, had detonated the explosives packed in the truck. The attack had been planned against the senior military leaders who normally met at that time. On this day—for whatever reason—they had cancelled the scheduled meeting.

The climate of fear and anxiety engendered by such episodes was to a significant degree counteracted by the warmth and hospitality that characterised much of my contact with Sri Lankan community groups. I was invited to participate in many public events as Chief Guest. Often they were arranged by non-government organisations which, despite the hindrances of the security situation, were pursuing inspiring programs to help local communities. On average I attended at least one such function every weekend. The position of Chief Guest carried a special ceremonial significance. Each occasion included

Presenting medals to high school students at an athletics carnival in Colombo.

a ritual that began with the lighting of a lamp or the boiling of milk and an introductory speech from the local agency, followed by a short speech in reply by me. This custom enabled me to meet a broad spectrum of interesting and distinguished Sri Lankans in diverse fields. Among these were the profusion of contemporary Sri Lankan artists, architects and inventors, in whose work I quickly became absorbed. I was pleased to be able to organise visits to Australia for some of them, such as Tilak Samarawickrema, the gifted architect and artist.

I was also able to engage with grassroots communities through our broad development assistance program and the Head of Mission Discretionary Aid Program. I set up a small sub-committee in the high commission to develop recommendations on the disbursements of these funds. We were inundated with requests for causes worthy of a contribution, but some stood out. One was the construction of a students' hostel at the University of Colombo: as many as twenty students were occupying a single room with one toilet.

My simultaneous accreditation to the Maldives took me to this beautiful group of atolls on a number of occasions. I found each of my visits to be memorable in its own way; not surprisingly, they were a sharp contrast to the hectic work schedule in Colombo. With a population of roughly 216,000 people, of whom 40 per cent were estimated to be under the age of thirty, the Maldives comprises twenty-six atolls made up of almost 1,200 islets. Only 200 of these are inhabited, although some of the uninhabited islands are used as tourist resorts. Tourism and fishing are the major export earners for this small Islamic nation. I have fond memories of the first time I flew into the Maldives, early in the evening of 23 July 1988. Looking from the cockpit of the aircraft it seemed as though the heavens had been inverted—a constellation of twinkling lights emanated from the many tiny atolls.

My journey, the following morning, to present credentials was unique and exhilarating. Accompanied by several Maldivian protocol officers, I was taken by speedboat to the capital, Malé, to be presented to President Maumoon Abdul Gayoom. With the formalities completed, the President's conversation turned immediately to business and his concerns about the environment, particularly the threat to small island states of global warming and rising sea levels. The Maldives is one of the most vulnerable countries in the world to the latter, the islands' average height above sea level being 1.5 metres.

Over the following few days I made the customary round of introductory calls on those Maldivian ministers with whom I could expect to have professional contact over the term of my accreditation. Australia and the Maldives have always enjoyed friendly relations and share a common interest in international environmental issues, particularly through the United Nations. In the bilateral relationship trade has played only a small role, the most important component being Australia's ongoing development assistance program. Australia is the Maldives' second-largest aid donor (after Japan). Australian aid in 1991–1992 amounted to around $2.4 million and consisted of commodity assistance, food aid, training, and the upgrading of the international airport at Ghan on the southernmost atoll. Australia also upgraded the navigational and communication facilities at the gateway airport in the north, to assist the tourist and commercial development of the Maldives.

Our assistance with education and training through scholarships was highly appreciated by the Maldivian government, which has high regard for the quality of Australian education. The scholarship winners, according to my Maldivian interlocutors, reintegrated and performed well on return, particularly in the government and teaching sectors. The government consistently sought an increase in the number of student scholarships. When I left in January 1992, thirty-three Maldivians were studying on scholarships in Australia, which I understand was a record at that time.

With the President of Republic of Maldives, Maumoon Abdul Gayoom, after presenting credentials in Malé, July 1988.

The Maldivians also valued the role played by Australian volunteers in the development of the country, particularly in writing an English curriculum for schools and in teacher training. I met a number of these volunteers and was greatly impressed by their professionalism, their dedication and the way they had integrated with the local population.

Although the Maldives seemed to exist in a calm, tropical idyll, I knew that appearances could be deceptive. There had been two coup attempts against President Gayoom, in 1980 and 1983, but I was not unduly concerned: I did not have anxious Australian investors seeking my advice about the political and security climate. Australian interests, as I have said, lay primarily in aid-related activities and in strengthening the friendly relations that already existed. I did not think that the Maldives would require a strong focus from me as the Australian representative—but I was wrong.

On the night of 3 November, less than five months after my first visit, I was awakened by an urgent call from an Australian volunteer nurse in Malé with the news that she and some of her fellow volunteers were witnessing a gun battle on the streets. I could hear the conflict in the background as she spoke. The volunteers were in fact witnessing a third attempted coup. After alerting Canberra, from Colombo we set up a relay communications system. My contact on Malé kept in touch by phone with the other volunteers; at regular intervals throughout the night she rang through developments to me, which I passed on to Canberra. Our primary concern was the safety of the volunteers. Fortunately, the coup was short-lived. President Gayoom evaded capture, and the rebel mercenaries were soon overpowered by Indian paratroopers, flown in following a request by the Maldivian foreign ministry to the Indian government.

On a happier occasion, I attended the celebrations to commemorate twenty-five years of independence for the Republic of the Maldives, on 26 July 1990. The Maldives had been a protectorate of Portugal (1558), the Netherlands (1654) and Britain (1887–1965). The independence celebrations were a wonderfully festive occasion held over three days. Again, I was struck by the goodwill expressed by Maldivian ministers and officials towards Australia. Internal events may have belied the image of a tropical idyll, but our positive bilateral relationship remained on track.

Although my posting as Australian high commissioner to Sri Lanka and the Maldives was not without difficulties, given the political situations of the two countries, it was nonetheless a special and memorable time due to the warmth and hospitality that I encountered wherever I went. My mission finished in January 1992, but the country and the friendships have retained their hold and I regularly return.

6 Thinking Australia in the Middle East

Victoria Owen

Ambassador to Syria and Lebanon, 1990–1992

Ambassador to the Arab Republic of Egypt, accredited to Sudan and Tunisia, 1998–2001

There are no ambassadors in there! barked the Egyptian security guard, waving his gun at our driver as he looked at my Ethiopian friend and me in the back of the car. We spent the next half hour persuading him that indeed we were ambassadors—despite our gender—and that was why we were in a diplomatic car and should be allowed to proceed into a restricted customs area of Port Said, a city in north-eastern Egypt at the entrance to the Suez Canal. We were two of only five female heads of mission among the overwhelmingly male contingent heading 150 or so embassies in Cairo at that time, and the guard took a lot of convincing.

But that was rare. For the odd occasions when being a woman seemed to mean I could not possibly be my country's representative to whichever Arab country I was visiting or living in, there were many more times when I was reminded of the benefits of being a female diplomat. As Australia's ambassador to Egypt, Syria, Lebanon, Tunisia and Sudan (and earlier chargé d'affaires in Jordan), I was a privileged guest, able to promote my country's interests as effectively as if I wore the grey suits of most of my colleagues. What counted were energy, commitment and understanding of the country, not my gender. I had ready access to male-dominated circles in society—government leaders and officials, businessmen, the media, and academia. And my gender also gave me entrée to women's networks, with their particular insights into the twists and turns of domestic politics and their knowledge of the complicated familial networks that affected the making of political and commercial deals.

I had my first taste of the Middle East in early 1974 when I was sent to Tehran as third secretary on a short-term mission. It was my first experience of living in a Muslim country and I rapidly learnt a great deal about Islamic belief and practice. My three months there whetted my appetite for that part of the world.

In the early 1980s, I returned to the region when I was posted to Amman as second, then first, secretary. I served in Jordan for a little over two years, including one year (1982) as chargé d'affaires. (At that time, the Australian ambassador in Damascus was responsible also for Lebanon and Jordan. He visited regularly, but the day-to-day running of the embassies in Beirut and Amman was in the hands of their respective chargés d'affaires.) Regional events, including Israel's invasion of Lebanon in June 1982, were testing Jordan's stability and lending urgency to the country's desire for an Arab–Israeli peace settlement. It was a challenging and invigorating year as well as a most enjoyable one. The Jordanian countryside is beautiful and my family and I spent many happy weekends exploring the rich archaeological remains there, sometimes guided by Australian archaeologists in charge of important digs. When a resident ambassador was appointed in November 1982, I handed over responsibility for the mission with some regret.

Speaking with President Hafez al Asad of Syria, during the presentation of credentials ceremony in Damascus, 1990.

The opportunity to run a mission again came less than eight years later, in 1990, when I was appointed to Syria, with accreditation to Lebanon—Australia's first female ambassador to a Middle Eastern country. I was gratified—and fortunate—that by then the Department of Foreign Affairs and Trade was pleased to recommend to the government appointments as head of mission that were based on officers' capabilities rather than their gender. I arrived

Preparing to inspect the Guard of Honour during the presentation of credentials ceremony in Beirut, Lebanon, 1990.

in Damascus in June of 1990. Less than two months later, President Saddam Hussein of Iraq invaded Kuwait, following his contention that Kuwait was illegally slant-drilling petroleum across the border with Iraq. The invasion precipitated a war that, though short-lived in terms of actual hostilities, was to rule the life and work of my mission for a large part of my two-year posting.

After Iraq's invasion of Kuwait, the United Nations immediately demanded the withdrawal of Iraqi troops and imposed economic sanctions. The international community then spent several months determining what other action to take. The credibility of the coalition to free Kuwait turned in part on the participation of Arab countries, and Syria's role was especially important. Syria (unlike Egypt and Jordan) had not concluded a peace treaty with Israel, and it was regarded as less inclined to bow to any pressure from the West. As the former US Secretary of State, Henry Kissinger, had observed more than a decade earlier, 'You can't make war in the Middle East without Egypt and you can't make peace without Syria.' Syrian policy on most issues involving inter-Arab relations, and in particular on one as complex and sensitive as this, flowed from the top. It was extremely difficult to follow the development of their thinking and to report accurately on it to Canberra. But in a country where access as a Western diplomat was never easy, and in a region where Australia had no natural standing, and therefore no easy entrée, I felt I had an advantage as a woman. Particular courtesies were extended to me that were less likely to be enjoyed by my male counterparts at other missions. Doors opened readily, interlocutors were generous and welcoming, even when we did not agree. I had a sense of the respect with which Syrians regarded professional women.

Syria's eventual decision to participate in a US-led multinational coalition against Saddam marked a striking departure from its traditional relationships both with other Arab states and with the West. We did not know how Saddam would react to coalition intervention, nor to Syrian participation in that coalition. There was a widespread expectation that Iraq might use non-conventional weapons against its neighbours, of which Syria was one. At the end of November 1990, the United Nations set 15 January 1991 as the deadline for Iraq to leave Kuwait or be forced out by military means (UN Security Council Resolution 678). As this date approached, I increasingly turned my attention to the security and evacuation plans for the embassy's staff—something that had been a constant preoccupation. I now spent many hours supervising the evacuation of family members and non-essential staff, stripping the embassy down to a skeleton staff who could evacuate promptly if necessary. The ambassador's residence was equipped with additional communications facilities and emergency supplies (food, water purification tablets, first aid kits) so that it could operate as a temporary office and accommodation for the few remaining staff in the event we could not travel to the embassy. Satellite phones gave us uninterrupted communication to Canberra. Many embassies in Damascus engaged in the same exercise in the run-up to the 15 January deadline, and we were a small band left just before the coalition intervention in Kuwait.

Visiting the Khan Danoun camp for Palestinian refugees in Syria.

Shortly after the deadline had passed, on 17 January, the coalition launched a massive air campaign, Operation Desert Storm; in late February it began its formal ground campaign, Operation Desert Sabre. Soon after, a ceasefire was declared and on 27 February Kuwait was pronounced liberated. Syria, fortunately, had been spared any reprisal from Saddam, although Iraq did launch missile attacks on coalition bases in Saudi Arabia and on Israel. As the tensions eased and the ceasefire proved enduring, the embassy's staff and families gratefully returned to Damascus. And I could start getting home from work in time for dinner.

Syria was a difficult place for male spouses at that time. It had a limited foreign community and there were few, if any, job opportunities for those who were not fluent in Arabic. The economy was still rather closed and international organisations had only small offices in Damascus. My husband, on leave without pay from a busy job in Canberra, found it hard to fill his days in any meaningful way. He lacked the ready-made group of acquaintances who ease newly arrived ambassadors' wives into a new posting, and he discovered that writing the great Australian novel was less of a preoccupation than we had anticipated. It was even hard to find a male tennis partner. Many of the networks and opportunities that have evolved over decades to support the female spouses of a head of mission are not as readily available to the husband of a female ambassador. My husband did not share my passion for the Middle East. He endured the situation for my sake but was keen to return home as soon as possible.

So in 1992 we returned to Australia where I spent several years working on multilateral environment issues and then promotion of Australia's international image before I returned to the work I really loved, the Middle East, in 1996. It was another two years before a posting opportunity came up that I could not resist. After long and hard thought, in 1998, my husband and I agreed that I should apply for the position of Australia's ambassador to Egypt, also responsible for Tunisia, Algeria and Sudan (and later Syria). He would visit for several months each year but would continue to work in Australia. It was far from ideal, but it was a sensible approach after our experience in Syria and a workable compromise. My children similarly were less than impressed at my choice of the Middle East as my home for the next four years over places they regarded as more promising for exotic and luxurious holidays.

From my own point of view, the posting to Egypt was the pick of all head of mission positions in the Middle East at that time in my career. Egypt, while not central to Australia's foreign policy concerns, was influential on a range of international issues that affected us. Egypt's voice was heard with respect throughout the Middle East, and it mattered for Australia's views to be understood in Cairo at suitably senior levels. Cairo was the seat of the League of Arab States, a forum to which all its members attached considerable weight, even if they did not always agree on how to advance its interests. It was for sound national interest reasons that the United States had its biggest embassy in the world in Cairo. Cairo was certainly another step up from my previous head of mission experience and one which at the beginning I found daunting. My predecessors were a long list of distinguished representatives, including Sir Roden Cutler, stretching back to 1950. And the ambassador I was replacing was a fine Arabist with long experience in the region, who had done a top-rate job. I left Australia for Egypt feeling somewhat intimidated by the shoes I had to fill.

On arrival I saw the dusty brown sand hills encircling Cairo airport and I knew that I would enjoy my posting. It smelt good. And sounded good—the call to prayer, marking as it does the passage of the Islamic day, is pervasive in Cairo and one of the things I miss most about life in the Middle East.

I was fortunate to have an excellent team at the embassy. All the Australians loved being in Egypt and were determined to make the most of its opportunities. Not all foreigners do. Some find Cairo's crazy energy confronting and enervating, and some would simply prefer to live in a more orderly society. On my husband's first visit to Egypt, I took him to my favourite part of the city, medieval Cairo, where majestic Islamic monuments mingle comfortably with modern chaos. It was hot and dusty down at Bab el-Futuh, the Gate of Conquests (commonly known these days as Souk al-Limoon). The donkeys were braying, young hawkers were noisily touting their wares, and the odour rising from the debris along the streets was richly pungent. I was in heaven, yet for my husband the experience served to confirm that he had made the right decision to remain in Australia.

But the embassy was filled with enthusiasts revelling in the culture of their posting and eager to promote the country they represented. We set about developing a work program designed to impress upon Egyptian decision-makers—in government, business, universities, the press—all the good things about Australia and what we could share with Egypt. We established a Think Australia program. My predecessors had, of course, done a superb job in showcasing Australia—but Egypt is huge (with a population of 66 million in 1998) and most Egyptians were inclined to look to the United States and Europe as sources of new ideas, technologies and sophisticated products. We felt we were still confronting the relics of Australia's 'girl-bites-crocodile' image.

By the end of my posting, we had made some inroads. During a seminar on Australia that the embassy arranged for senior government officials, a senior Egyptian minister looked up at our Think Australia logo and declared that indeed everyone was now thinking Australia. We wanted Australia's interests and views to be in the minds of leaders—in government and commerce—when they were making decisions about political and strategic issues and also about sourcing goods and services.

The Sydney Olympics did a great deal to turn around local misconceptions about Australia. The opening ceremony was on a Friday (the first day of the Egyptian weekend), and I was at home, hoping to indulge in watching television. A visiting Australian guest and I settled down in the study with mugs of tea as the ceremony began. Fifteen minutes later the phone rang for the first time. It did not stop. Egyptian friends and acquaintances just kept calling, in their delightfully warm and effusive way, to congratulate Australia on the brilliance of it all. They seemed genuinely amazed that this distant country of wheat and kangaroos could deliver such sparkling, sophisticated perfection. I unashamedly revelled in the praise for Australia.

Senior Egyptians whose visits to Australia we arranged returned to Cairo similarly enthused, declaring that now they understood what we had been talking about all this time. Australia really was the best place in the world (after Egypt, of course).

The reaction of our Egyptian hosts to official Australian visits was also positive. Under our Think Australia program we arranged visits to Egypt by significant Australian figures including Alan Fels, Chair of the Australian Competition and Consumer Commission, and, separately, Alaistair Nicholson, Chief Justice of the Family Court of Australia. In both cases, our Egyptian contacts were hugely impressed that we had developed in Australia institutions designed to meet current Australian needs. The Egyptians' genuine interest in adapting and replicating these institutions in Egypt was immensely satisfying both as affirmation of Australia's particular strengths in these arenas and also as confirmation of the value of our program of visits.

The embassy staff worked hard to ensure that we took every opportunity to publicise Australia. They arranged briefings for journalists on specialised subjects; wrote and sent press releases to appropriate publications; and organised for important visitors to appear on prime-time television and to do radio interviews. By the time I left Cairo, I had participated in so many breakfast television programs that I had mostly overcome my anxiety about live interviews. We tried always to work with journalists, regarding them as our collaborators in getting publicity for Australia. They did not let us down.

But the job of ambassador of course went far beyond the exhilarating business of showing off Australia. There was the familiar grind of day-to-day paperwork, as well as the accounts, property issues and security scares. The days in the office were long, interspersed with time-consuming expeditions through

The amazing pyramids of Egypt.

Cairo's frenetic traffic. I frequently found myself doing one of my favourite tasks—political reporting on regional developments, on which there was a wide range of information and expertise in Cairo—late at night when all the other staff had gone home and blessed peace reigned in my office overlooking the Nile.

Within this schedule of predictable, regular tasks, the mission also responded to the unexpected crises that emerged from time to time, often in the form of consular cases outside Cairo. Effective advocacy of Australia's interests is the most obvious of the responsibilities of Australian heads of mission. From time to time, though, advocacy on behalf of individual Australians in difficulty overseas becomes their most important task. Consular work is probably the most emotionally compelling responsibility carried by all embassy staff.

On one longed-for spring weekend, I was wandering in awe through the Karnak Temple in Luxor, in Upper Egypt. I was succeeding rather better this time in impressing my reluctant husband with the glory that was, and is, Egypt—even he had gasped in amazement at the tombs in the Valley of the Kings. The magic was interrupted by the sharp ringing of my mobile phone. It was our consul in Cairo asking me to go to the Luxor hospital to visit a young Australian woman about whom the Egyptian police had just rung him.

After some prolonged negotiations at the hospital's front desk with an official who found it hard to believe that this dusty, sweaty, middle-aged tourist was indeed an ambassador, I was taken into the woman's room. There I found a young bipolar sufferer in great distress and in serious need of a sympathetic figure from home. I was pleased to have been able to get to her quickly and to listen to her concerns. She was one of a small number of young Australians who think that, while on holiday and away from the stresses of everyday life at home, they no longer need their medication. We were able to contact this woman's family in Australia and persuade them to travel to Egypt to provide reassurance and to take her back to Australia where her condition could be treated in familiar surroundings. I was silently grateful that my own daughters had never been through such a torrid experience.

Another desperately sad, and all-too-frequent, consular problem involved young Australian women who had married Egyptian men and then found their marriages less than happy. These women discovered to their distress that they had limited rights in relation to their children while they were in Egypt and could not take them to Australia without the father's permission, which was usually withheld. We did all we could to help (including the negotiation and signature of a Child Protection Agreement with the Egyptian Government), but often it was less than we would have liked, and much less than the women deserved.

In contrast with the intractable problems that the embassy's consular work sometimes presented, I derived great satisfaction from promoting and seeing positive developments in Australia's important commercial interests in Egypt. We spent much time and energy on protecting and advancing Australia's trade and investment, often working through the confusing Egyptian bureaucracy to find a solution that met both Australia's interests and the disparate concerns of the numerous officials.

Egypt has been a major market for Australian wheat for many years. Our sales there were healthy, won through open tender in the world market. A former Egyptian Prime Minister always knew he could please me with his story about 1973. He said that in the lead-up to, and during, the October 1973 War, at a time when Egypt was having a great deal of trouble sourcing supplies, only Australia would provide him with what he needed to feed his people. The US Ambassador in Cairo (whose friendship I treasured for his warmth and wisdom) found little to disagree about with me—except our strong wheat trade.

Other commodities also presented challenges well beyond the usual round of diplomatic activity. The embassy's excellent counsellor, who could turn his hand with ease from economic reporting to ensuring embassy security, spent one miserable weekend in Port Said assessing the teeth of a shipload of Australian cattle with Australian veterinary experts. A dispute over the alleged age of the livestock was jeopardising acceptance of the entire consignment. Cows one day, pulses and dairy produce the next. Over the course of our postings, we all learnt more than we had ever planned about the best breeds of cattle for hot climates; the virtues of the Australian faba bean (widely used in the famous Egyptian *foul*) and lentils; and the shelf life of various Australian cheeses. Australia's capacity to provide a wide range of foodstuffs and Egypt's large population, whose domestic supply was virtually confined to the long, narrow strip of the Nile, made us natural partners in the food commodity trade. I was always pleased to remind Egyptian audiences the trade was not just one way: Egypt now exports to Australia its wonderful cotton products, fresh oranges, fruit for jam and olives for pizzas.

Life in Cairo extended well beyond the office and home. The social life could have become a full-time occupation and I often gazed longingly at my bed in the morning, tempted to spend just a few more hours gathering my strength. The Egyptians love a party and have a flexible start to their working day. I would socialise late into the evening with them and end up paying the consequences. But partying for me was not about chatting and dancing and dining. Late at night the 'big boys', including ministers, other politicians, businessmen, academics, journalists, would gather in dark corners with cigars and Black Label scotch and discuss the major issues of the day. The gossip was often commercial, frequently political, sometimes wonderful, all intriguing and all shedding light on the huge complexity of the country and its interests and politics. It was an important part of my work and I needed to be well connected with those able to advance Australia's interests. Often they were hard to contact during the day but were there at parties. I had to be there too—but I did miss my sleep.

One of the most moving duties I had, in both Syria and Egypt, was to represent Australia at services to remember our servicemen and women who had died in war. Local officials were always moved and impressed that Australians had been prepared to travel to such distant destinations in defence of freedom. They were also familiar with the reputation of our soldiers as tough and headstrong characters who carried with them, wherever they went, the finest Australian traditions of mateship and a fair go for all. At the sand dunes of El Alamein and the eerie dawn services at the Commonwealth War Graves cemetery in Damascus for Armistice and Anzac Day commemorations, I always found it difficult to deliver my speeches with calm composure, having wandered past the gravestones of those young Australians who had lost their lives in such unfamiliar surroundings, so far from home.

During my posting, Australian soldiers were again in the region and serving with great distinction. But this time, they were engaged in peacekeeping rather than military action. Australia has participated, almost continuously, in the Multinational Force and Observers (MFO) in the Sinai, a peacekeeping operation established to ensure both Israel and Egypt abided by the provisions of the 1979 Israel–Egypt peace treaty regarding their respective military presences along the common border. It has become something of a tradition for the Australian ambassadors in Israel and Egypt to spend Australia Day hosted by our MFO contingent at their base in the northern Sinai, often cold and wet at the end of January. It was always a treat to enjoy military hospitality while watching hard-fought sporting events from indoor cricket to consumption of Vegemite sandwiches. The Australians, being Australians, did all the organising and so could ensure that the playing field was at least level. Few apart from the Australians could stomach the Vegemite.

About a year and a half after I arrived in Cairo, the Australian government decided to close our embassy in Damascus in 1999 for financial reasons—a cause of some sadness to all those of us who had been posted in that ancient city with its easy access to Syria's archaeological treasures. When consideration was given to which Australian embassy in the region should take over responsibility for Syria, my hand shot up, but I was not alone. Ultimately Canberra decided that Cairo was indeed the most suitable place from which to cover our interests in Syria and that I would become Australia's non-resident ambassador. I was delighted.

One of my first duties was to represent Australia at the funeral of President Hafez al Assad, to whom I had presented my credentials a decade earlier. At the time of my posting to Syria in 1990, President Assad had a daunting reputation as a tough and wily leader, well able to manipulate the vagaries of the region's politics to Syria's advantage. I had found him a thoughtful and engaging interlocutor when, after the formalities, we sat discussing the importance of promoting the role of women in public life as well as Australia's and Syria's shared commercial and economic interests.

President Assad's funeral was a sombre occasion for the people of Syria, who had been ruled by this man for thirty years. There was an eerie sense of uncertainty during those days in Damascus as the international community watched to see how the Syrians would move on to the next generation of leadership. During the official mourning period the streets of Damascus were draped in black, and muffled drums echoed from different parts of the ancient city. The President's body lay in state in the massive marble presidential palace looking out over Damascus. Hundreds of dignitaries from Syria, the region and many other countries mingled in the forecourt and were slowly ushered past the coffin. As I paused to pay Australia's respects, I was struck by the historic significance of the moment and my enormous good fortune in being able to participate in it.

My early trepidation about my head of mission posting to Cairo had rapidly dissipated. I revelled in the job and the life, and part of me will always miss it. I came quickly to feel that my grand house in elegant Zamalek was part of a neighbourhood where I could always feel safe. The old, chain-smoking *boab* (doorman) at my neighbour's house, the boys trying to sell plastic bags of prickly pear on the street who yelled out *ya australia* when I was out walking, the devout owner of the corner shop who seemed permanently to be saying his prayers and the newsagent who sold the *Egyptian Gazette* in a perfect Oxbridge accent all made me feel welcomed and at home. I did not once feel that my personal security was under threat.

Being ambassador puts you in the privileged position of being able to meet and get to know all the Australians in the region. I can think of none who did not bring credit to Australia: Sister Narelle, the Franciscan nun from New South Wales who worked for years with intellectually disabled children in the old city of Damascus; the teachers in Khartoum living in most difficult circumstances and thoroughly enjoying their interaction with the Sudanese children; the world-class archaeologists working from the eastern desert of Syria to upper Egypt who would delight in showing you over their dig.

Relaxing on the Nile.

I was extremely fortunate to spend so many years living and working in Arab countries. I learnt a great deal about Islam and the way it influences the lives, now, of many Australian Muslims. The practice of the religion differed in many ways among the various countries in which I lived, but its essential elements were, of course, the same. I was privileged to witness the evolving practices of Islam in Egypt. During my time there, a large number of middle-class women decided to start wearing the head-scarf, often in defiance of the strong wishes of their families. For those I knew, adopting the scarf was not related to what is loosely called Islamic fundamentalism. It reflected, rather, a deepened spirituality and heightened commitment to principles beyond the material and had no political, let alone antagonistic, dimension.

Islam pervades Muslims' days and lives in a way which Christianity, at least as generally practised in Australia, tends not to. In Egypt I was perpetually conscious of living in an Islamic society and always respected my hosts' beliefs. Now, years later, I still find myself silently adding *Insha'allah* ('if God wills it') when referring to the future; and thanking God for a safe return from a journey. And having lived within the Muslim world over many years—observing

Islam practised with calm, gentle dignity—it is especially painful to see the distortions that have surfaced in the current geopolitical climate.

Ramadan, the holy month of fasting, was respected and observed throughout Egypt. The pattern of Cairo's daily life changed entirely. Just before sunset, when the day's fasting was broken by the meal of Iftar, the streets would empty as the whole Muslim population (90 per cent of the country's people) gathered with their families to pray and then eat. The wonderful Egyptian warmth and habit of hospitality meant that I was sometimes invited to family Iftars, an experience I cherished. I was treated to delicious feasts, served in festive circumstances where the wish to share culture, to commune around a common table, overcame differences in faith, geography and heritage. Dates and apricot juice were offered first to quench thirst and take the edge off gnawing hunger. The clamorous streets of Cairo were filled with long trestle tables laden with food, quietly provided by those who could afford it for those whose means did not stretch to a proper meal. Those tables gave a profound insight into a society bound together by bonds of charity and humility. I have been delighted recently to see Muslim groups in Australia inviting non-Muslims to Iftar to share that experience and gain a deeper understanding of Islam.

I developed a deep and lasting fondness for the Arab Middle East as a result both of living in the region and also working on it in the department in Canberra, where I often had the pleasure of interacting with representatives of Arab embassies. It saddens me now that after so many years the region is torn by strife and that a comprehensive settlement of the Arab–Israel dispute continues to elude the parties and the international community. It distresses me that the children of the region are growing up with continuing resentment against those they regard as their enemies and will find it all but impossible to put their disputes behind them in this generation. It pains me too that the economies of many of the countries of the region may be held back by their distraction from the development to which their resources, both human and material, entitle them. I wish the nightly television news did not have to show the pictures of violence and destruction that deter tourists from visiting those exhilarating places that gave me so much pleasure. Were more visitors to see those sights and feel the warmth of Arab charm and hospitality there might be less tension within our own societies.

I have had a most fulfilling career and owe a great debt of gratitude to the Department of Foreign Affairs and Trade. I cannot speak for my women colleagues. I would guess, though, they might share my view that we have been offered every opportunity to show we can perform the demanding and privileged duties of Australian ambassador at least as well as our male colleagues. And we've done it.

7 A singular and plural life

Ruth Pearce

High Commissioner to Solomon Islands, 1992–1994

Ambassador to Russia, accredited to Armenia Azerbaijan, Belarus, Georgia, Kazakhstan, Kyrgyzstan, Moldova, Tajikistan, Turkmenistan, Ukraine and Uzbekistan, 1999–2002

Ambassador to the Philippines, 2002–2005

My road to diplomacy was set early in my life. This may seem curious, given my upbringing. As a child, I lived in the relative remoteness of a tiny farming district of Victoria. But from the outset my grandfather expanded my childhood horizons, inspiring my unwavering attention and curiosity with his tales of Palestine and France as a young soldier in World War I. This sole encounter with the outside world (apart from a holiday many years later in New Zealand), shaped my grandfather's life to an extraordinary extent, and through him, mine. As a 16-year-old, I then relished my first direct experience with the world beyond home, when I spent a year in the United States as an American Field Service scholar. This year saw me determined to seek a career that offered the opportunity to combine Australia and international life.

In the early 1970s, Australia's diplomatic service stood out as the best available option through which I could pursue my dream. With much excitement I set out for university, the first in my family to do so. I carefully chose studies suited to my goal, combining law and international relations

106

degrees. There remained the hurdle of the graduate trainee selection process of the Department of Foreign Affairs (as it was at that time). With this successfully negotiated in late 1973, I headed to Canberra to begin my diplomatic journey, from Wycheproof in the Mallee to Manila in the Philippines, via many extraordinary places and events.

Two early experiences were instrumental in setting a framework for my career. One of my initial professional roles was that of liaison officer for Australia's first professional career woman ambassador—Ruth Dobson. Her historic appointment as ambassador to Denmark had only recently been announced and coincided fittingly with the United Nations' preparations to celebrate 1975 as International Women's Year. Dobson had entered the department as a research officer, accommodating and overcoming the challenges and frustrations of a very male culture to reach the level that now saw her head of mission. Today, it is difficult to accept that if she had married earlier in her career, this achievement would have been denied her. She would have been obliged to resign under the marriage bar—legislation preventing married women working in the public service—which was not removed until 1966. Fortunately, as I set out in Ruth's footsteps, there was a growing sense, both within the recently elected government and more broadly, that the 'women and diplomacy' relationship deserved more support and encouragement. Indeed, the secretary of the department, in his welcoming address to the six women and thirty-five men commencing

Presentation of credentials in Manila to President Gloria Macapagal Arroyo of the Philippines, May 2002.

our diplomatic careers at this time, challenged us all to aspire to a career that promised the honour and responsibility of becoming head of mission.

The second experience occurred later that same year, during the first week of my first overseas posting. This was as third secretary to the Australian High Commission in Dhaka. At the time, Bangladesh was in the throes of a severe famine and Australian emergency food aid was being shipped in. There were, however, allegations of misappropriation. Together with other high commission colleagues, I was tasked to monitor the distribution and use of the aid in the many camps set up throughout the northern regions of the country. It was here that I learned an invaluable lesson in the practice of diplomacy. I had struck up a conversation with a woman in one of the food queues. (Mothers and daughters dominated these queues, their male relatives left to protect properties and belongings.) The woman was clutching several young children whom I took to be her grandchildren. As we talked, I quickly learnt otherwise. This Bangladeshi woman was not in her fifties, as I had assumed from her appearance, but only in her early thirties. She had been married at fifteen, experienced twelve pregnancies with only three children surviving, and indeed she herself would be very lucky to live beyond the average mid-forties life expectancy for a woman in Bangladesh. In response to her queries, I told her that I was twenty-four, unmarried, childless and just starting an exciting career. The depth of her expressions of pity and concern at my sad and even humiliating status completely disoriented me and left me somewhat chastened. On later reflection, I saw this encounter as a powerful reminder of the need for constant sensitivity, curiosity, openness and wit if my diplomatic career was to be successful and fulfilling. The memories of this Bangladeshi woman have often appeared on my many diplomatic horizons throughout thirty years of working in a wonderful assortment of countries, positions and among new friends and colleagues. She has been my best guide.

Although these two encounters are part of the framework of my diplomatic service, many elements contributed to its substance. The diplomat's essential role is that of advocate, persuading a wide range of interlocutors of the relevance and value of his or her country's views and positions. In fulfilling this role, I believe that Australian diplomats are greatly advantaged by the special qualities of the Australian personality and culture, and I often reflect on how different my experience and practice of diplomacy might have been had I been representing a country other than Australia. Representing a small–middle power, without a natural international constituency, the typically Australian qualities of friendliness, fairness, directness, professionalism, cultural diversity and ingenuity all make for a strong diplomatic mix and have proven both distinctive and persuasive in most of my diplomatic experiences.

The department's Diplomatic Training Program in the 1970s effectively promoted and developed these skills and attitudes and sought to broaden the outlook of the trainees. As diplomatic cadets, we shared part of our training program with a wide range of young diplomats from many other countries, recipients of Australian development assistance. These early encounters with fellow foreign representatives were invaluable learning and networking experiences. Throughout my career, I have continued to meet up with my '1974' colleagues, often now in influential, even powerful, positions, across their governments and beyond. The cadet training program was enhanced through travel around Australia, meeting various community groups, which enabled us to understand and, in turn, explain how our chosen career related to the broader community.

For me, the effectiveness of this training was soon obvious. In Bangladesh, I was able to call on these qualities and skills to engage a government and wider society unfamiliar with, and sometimes negative towards, professional women. To have responded too formally and negatively to the sometimes offhand, even rude, and often reserved, approach of my interlocutors, would have rendered me ineffective. This was also the case many years later when I was posted to Solomon Islands as high commissioner. As part of my representational role, I had to visit isolated villages, meeting villagers who had never seen a white woman before. In Israel—my second overseas posting, as second secretary from 1979 to 1982—I faced comparable difficulties in undertaking my responsibilities. These required that I develop contacts with Arabs influential in the Occupied Territories and Israelis influential in the conservative Begin government, including orthodox Jewish groups unfamiliar with outsiders, especially women.

When I moved into the arena of multilateral diplomacy as a member of Australia's delegations to the United Nations in Geneva and New York during the 1980s, I also found that Australian diplomats had an advantage over many of our counterparts, who practised a more formal, hierarchical style of diplomacy.

In the mid to late 1980s the United Nations and the wider multilateral system were beginning to feel the impact of the decline of the Cold War, with a more fluid political context in which to protect and promote national and international interests. The emerging new international order inspired renewed optimism and confidence in the international system. Australia was a dynamic middle power, determined to punch above our weight and innovative in promoting our objectives. In this UN world of the mid-1980s, I was pursuing an expanded multilateral agenda that actively advanced Australia's priorities at that time. Australia's interests in promoting human rights, the rights of indigenous peoples and the status of women broadly matched the UN focus in that period. As did many countries, Australia welcomed the emerging opportunities to further its interests, and the region's, through the UN system.

Australia's Western history, its expanding multiculturalism and its Asia–Pacific geography, all lent a uniqueness to our multilateral approach and obliged our representatives in international forums to be innovative on both issues and alliances. Our success in this regard resulted in Australia's influence exceeding its international weight. To give an example, I was involved in promoting a more educative and preventive approach to human rights violations at the Commission on Human Rights sessions. The intention was to balance the perceived 'Western, punitive' flavour of the resolutions condemning specific governments for specific violations with a more constructive 'capacity-building' focus. The balance was invariably difficult to achieve, the politics and practicalities of each situation varying greatly. But our Asia–Pacific experience and links enabled us to influence the Western Group's ongoing traditional focus on condemnation (applied year after year, often with little practical, but considerable political, impact) and broaden the range of responses to human rights issues. It took intense networking to garner support for Australia's National Institutions Resolution, which sought to assist governments to set up their own human rights bodies to enhance national awareness and local response to such problems. A more comprehensive manifesto for managing human rights issues is now the international norm, although its application still requires considerable and sensitive effort.

With Chris Gallus, Parliamentary Secretary for Foreign Affairs (centre) and beneficiaries of AusAID education programs in Mindanao, the Philippines, January 2005.

Inevitably my multilateral work exposed me to the dynamics of coalitions, large ones like the Cairns Group and the Western and Others Group (WEOG) and small ones like the Canada, Australia, New Zealand and the United States (CANZUS) grouping and the South Pacific group. These coalitions placed a premium on the diplomatic skills of communication, negotiation and flexibility without compromising priorities. Here again, Australia's status as one of the 'Others' of the WEOG, together with its unusual mix of history and geography, compelled its diplomats to be more creative and active in seeking 'friends' across complicated international agendas. The Cairns Group in the international trade arena has emerged as a successful coalition achievement on Australia's part, but it is certainly not the only one.

Working to implement Australian foreign policy overseas is an exciting and fulfilling experience, but equally so is the time that a diplomatic officer spends in Canberra, the hub of the foreign-policy-making process. I returned to Australia in 1987 from my UN position to a newly restructured department. The government's foreign affairs and trade portfolios were merged that year, creating the Department of Foreign Affairs and Trade. The merger broadened the range of opportunities and challenges open to departmental officers and I was to be part of the seam binding the two previously separated functions, working on issues arising from the General Agreement on Tariffs and Trade (GATT).

I believe I was one of the first Foreign Affairs officers to move into the trade side of the new portfolio. In Geneva I had been co-located with Trade colleagues working on GATT issues in Australia's Geneva mission. This had exposed me directly to the importance of the trade agenda to our overall international policy objectives. But my new position in Canberra thrust me into the deep end of a strategic policy and operational shift, one which challenged the more traditional diplomatic agenda with the sharp edge of trade and business priorities. This was particularly true of the ambitious Uruguay Round of talks, with both old and new reform issues at play, and which served to reinforce the historically radical economic reform program of Australian governments during the 1980s. Managing the GATT Rules Section, I was engaged across the entire spectrum of Uruguay Round priorities, dealing with both new issues and new clients, in Geneva and across the Australian business community. This distinctive kind of multilateralism, practised in the rarefied GATT environment, most definitely challenged and broadened my diplomatic skills.

During a particularly busy period of the Uruguay Round negotiations, some of my staff discovered a copy of the government's 1960 Dillon Round brief in a dusty office cupboard. It was a stark reminder of the extent of change in the conduct of international relations that had taken place in the intervening thirty years. The Dillon Round trade negotiators travelled to Europe by ship for talks that began in Geneva in May 1961, taking with them a brief that was to cover the entire round, from beginning to end. Legend has it that they were not seen again in Canberra until they returned at the end of the round, which concluded in March 1962. (Among the papers was a report that the delegation did at least make one telephone call to Canberra from Colombo, while in transit.) On occasions, facing overnight requests for new briefs from our delegation in Geneva, I felt envious of my predecessors. The ease of communications during my Uruguay Round experience in the late 1980s, including regular trips to Geneva, highlighted for me both the benefits and drawbacks of instant communications. Only a few years earlier in Geneva, our delegation's endless speeches to the many UN meetings required labour-intensive typing, each amendment necessitating a complete, new speech. The communications revolution has certainly tilted the balance of power in Canberra's favour. It has changed departmental processes beyond recognition, and broadened opportunities for, and expectations that there will be, consultation on just about every issue.

Another new influence was emerging to shape my diplomatic experience. The Uruguay Round negotiations were being conducted in the context of increasing concern about global dynamics. The term 'globalisation' was not yet common, but the issues and mood of the multilateral trade round were largely shaped by developments that had a global dimension. The Uruguay agenda included new areas of interest, such as trade in services and intellectual property. But the real challenge to the international trade system came from agriculture, a 'new' agenda item but probably the most traditional of trading activities. It remained one of the most divisive negotiations, especially, but not exclusively, dividing the developed and the developing economies. Australia was pivotal in managing this conflict, initiating the Cairns Group to connect more effectively developed and developing countries' aspirations. Our engagement on these issues prepared us well for the emerging globalisation agenda. The issues that have continued to confront the Doha Trade Round were unfolding then, such as proposals to develop international norms for environment and investment trade and the continuing restraints on agricultural trade.

For me there was a striking contrast between my GATT experiences and my previous UN work: the absence of non-government organisations as direct players in the negotiations. The failure of the Uruguay Round to engage NGO interests properly, especially those of the business community, was rectified in the Doha Development Round whose processes recognise that globalisation requires more than governments as direct players in the negotiation of fairer and freer trade rules.

My UN and GATT experiences increasingly exposed the irrelevant demarcation between foreign and domestic policy agendas. Over more than three decades representing Australia, this interdependency has become compelling, with diplomats having to engage more actively with domestic constituencies—local interest groups, politicians and lobbyists, organisations as diverse as the National Farmers Federation or the Human Rights and Equal Opportunity Commission. Our advocacy is as much focused on the domestic, as the foreign, arena. The issues that international systems address were once the sole responsibility of national authorities. But as international trade priorities moved beyond border issues such as tariffs and quotas to non-tariff trade barriers such as internal subsidies, the distinctions became less real. And the same trend has shaped the international human rights agenda, with attention shifting to internal institutions and domestic policy-making environments.

My first posting as head of mission was to the South Pacific, to Solomon Islands, which in my time (1992–1994) was already showing clear signs of what it has sadly become, a failing state. The Australian mission was the most engaged of the small diplomatic community, so for the first time in my diplomatic career I was representing the local and regional 'major power'. Because of our extensive civilian and defence assistance programs and active business community I had a high profile, a sensitive and influential position. Furthermore, the daunting agenda of interests we were pursuing in Solomon Islands was complicated by regional politics. Australia's support for the unity and integrity of Papua New Guinea drew criticism from the Government of Solomon Islands,

With Australia's Prime Minister, Paul Keating, and Solomon Islands Minister for Foreign Affairs and Trade, Job Dudley Tausiga, on Mr Keating's arrival at the 23rd South Pacific Forum in Honiara, 8 July 1992.

which quietly and determinedly supported the separatist aspirations of the Bougainville Revolutionary Army. The western region of Solomon Islands was ethnically and culturally linked to Bougainville; but colonial borders did not recognise this. Border tensions challenged the high commission's defence cooperation program and I was frequently required, in sensitive circumstances, to reinforce Australia's support for Papua New Guinea's territorial integrity without feeding local perceptions that Australia sought to undermine historical ties between Solomon Islands and Bougainville.

Perhaps the most difficult challenge of my posting to Honiara was of an 'unofficial' nature. Then Solomon Islands Prime Minister, Mamaloni, was seriously insulted that the government of Australia, upon which his country depended and which he both loved and disliked, had sent him a female high commissioner. Managing Mamaloni's umbrage was not easy. He refused to address me by my official Pidgin title, Big Fella Mary, Boss B'long Australia, and instead was often heard to ask how 'his girlfriend up the road' was managing relations between Australia and his government. On many occasions the Prime Minister refused to deal with me. Indeed, early in my posting he sent a handwritten letter to Prime Minister Paul Keating requesting that I be recalled. This was apparently ignored—I stayed the full course and managed, in the main, to enjoy extraordinary experiences in the beautiful 'Happy Isles'.

Against the awkward backdrop of the Prime Minister's offence at my appointment, I maintained friendly, open and cooperative relations with most cabinet members and all the key civil society leaders. I was careful never to complain, criticise, or even seem uncomfortable, about Mamaloni's public efforts to compromise my effectiveness. I travelled widely around the islands, enjoying local hospitality and promoting Australia's extensive development assistance programs in a practical environment. As a female diplomat I was an oddity and I used this to my advantage; I worked hard to engage the women, who quietly ran the place and were the best agents for change.

Australia's over-arching interest in Solomon Islands was to assist it to become a viable, modern nation-state. This demanded constant review and evaluation of the quality and kind of development assistance we and other donors were delivering. Governance was an emerging priority, as were programs to rescue the badly degraded forests and fisheries. A relatively well-resourced country, Solomon Islands proved incapable of protecting the extensive natural resources that were the mainstay of its socio-economic life. Its ethnic diversity, compounded by colonial and post-colonial pressures, rather than maturing to become a distinctive advantage, turned violently against the country's unity. As concerned as I was about this beautiful country's future, I never then imagined the violence and disorder that was to follow.

The fiftieth anniversary of the Battle of Guadalcanal was celebrated during my Honiara appointment. The anniversary of this turning-point in World War II provoked considerable thought about the kind of threats that confront our Asia–Pacific region today. Transnational crimes (mafia organisations, even from distant Russia, were active in the region), environmental exploitation, lack of international competitiveness were all preoccupations during my time in the Pacific. Symbolically, the US Embassy in Honiara closed soon after the fiftieth anniversary, reinforcing the expectations of Australia's role in the region. Responsibility for Solomon Islands' secure and prosperous future shifted more heavily towards Australia, New Zealand and our other Pacific neighbours. Our exceptional role in the Pacific continues.

My next posting as head of mission, four years later, could not have seemed a more striking contrast to Solomon Islands—in climate, ambience, culture and politics. But in many ways the challenges for both nations were similar. The Russia to which I was appointed in 1999 was still struggling with the Soviet collapse, managing acute and widespread expectations of social and economic progress and political accountability. I presented credentials in the magnificence of the golden Kremlin Palace to a fragile Boris Yeltsin. The grandeur of this ceremony was repeated in various manifestations as I presented twelve sets of credentials to the former Soviet Republics, from Belarus in the west to Kyrgyzstan in the east. The blend of colourful local custom and persistent remnants of the grey Soviet protocol made for a unique series of ceremonies. For example, in Moldova, I was required to shout a greeting in the local language to the presidential honour guard, magnificently costumed and strategically positioned on a steep golden stairway that would lead me to the waiting head of state.

With Boris Yeltsin, President of the Russian Federation, after the presentation of credentials ceremony in the Kremlin's Golden Palace in Moscow, February 1999.

The post-Soviet revolution, in fact, was not complete until President Yeltsin's resignation nearly a year later. His successor, Vladimir Putin, sought to shock Russians into understanding the magnitude of the modernisation challenge their country faced. A brutal pragmatist, Putin outlined unequivocally what Russia had to do to avoid what he described as permanent socio-economic degradation. Despite a steady decline in living standards since the mid-1960s, there had been no official acknowledgment of the challenges faced by the new Russian state. The task of becoming globally competitive was for Russia different to, but no more daunting than, that facing countries as diverse as Solomon Islands and the Philippines. The threats to Russia's international competitiveness that preoccupied President Putin's government included Russia's continued reliance on oil and energy exports, with concern that the level of such dependence risked Russia remaining an 'old' economy; depopulation, particularly in the far east regions; dysfunctional health and education sectors; and a brain drain.

Russia's Asia–Pacific status and its vast resources and communications opportunities in the Far East underscored it as a country of regional and bilateral relevance to Australia. Russia, however, persisted with a 'Soviet' approach to foreign relations for most of my time—making power, rather than mutual interests, the cornerstone of its foreign policy. Its continued focus on major capitals in Europe and Asia and its preoccupation with the United States left little room for the development of comprehensive relations with Australia. But obviously the conduct of Russia's international strategic agenda had an impact on Australia and the region's security interests. Its extensive border with China, its long-standing territorial dispute with Japan, the vast energy resources of its Far East regions, were several of the issues that affected our region's security and stability, and accordingly filled my days.

The World Trade Centre tragedy on 11 September 2001 was a dramatic climax to my posting. In the post-9/11 security environment, Europe and Russia (and its former Soviet republics in central Asia especially), with NATO and UN agendas, faced complex future directions, including more flexible coalitions of interests. President Putin was one of the first leaders to support President Bush's War Against Terrorism. This 'new' threat offered Russia the opportunity to move beyond its residual Cold War preoccupation with NATO and its expansion. Ultimately however, Russia's primary imperative was, and continues to be, overcoming what President Putin described as the threat of 'permanent socio-economic degradation'.

The year 2002 found me in the Philippines, once again in the broad Asia–Pacific region, but managing Australia's relations with a close neighbour and one comprehensively relevant to our national interests, especially after September 11. Regional security, economic integration, transnational crime, including international terrorism, and the demands of global competitiveness, were all mutual concerns that directed much of the bilateral relationship, including Australia's long-standing development assistance and defence cooperation programs. The security environment regularly demanded my attention, on occasion in the most personal of ways.

Following a specific and credible bomb threat, our embassy was swiftly closed in Manila in late 2002. Staff worked from my residence for several weeks until temporary security reinforcement allowed us to return to the embassy pending the acquisition of a new permanent location. The threat inspired a strong team spirit across the embassy that I felt proud to be part of. It also prompted a strengthening of my personal security; for the rest of my posting I was accompanied by personal security guards wherever I went.

In July 2003, Prime Minister John Howard visited Manila and opened Australia's new embassy. He spoke about the changed security environment and the challenges this presented to staff in our diplomatic missions around the world. Ironically, a week later, I managed to be in the wrong place at the wrong time and was taken hostage during an attempted military coup in the centre of Manila's business district, where I was living temporarily while the residence was being upgraded. For half a day I became the focus of much attention, both good and bad, one of a number of hostages in a building taken over by armed soldiers who were busily lacing the building and its surrounds with sophisticated explosives. The mutineers refused the demands of the government that I be released before the other hostages to avoid the international implications of the attempted coup d'état, but after eight hours of negotiations the entire group was released without harm. For the rest of my Manila posting, I was often recognised in shops and streets by local residents who apologised for the offence I had suffered. Filipinos are a warm and generous people.

With Australia's Prime Minister, John Howard, and Australian embassy staff at the official opening of the new Chancery in Manila during the Prime Minister's state visit to the Philippines in July 2003.

In Manila my role in directing effective advocacy and public diplomacy programs was especially relevant given Australia's considerable, and at times complex, role in the region. Australia promoted its engagement in the Philippines in a number of practical ways: policy seminars; media visits; extensive training activities; capacity-building programs; education assistance; and partnerships with local organisations in government, the science and technology community, non-government organisations, business groups and cultural organisations. This agenda is a big one for the head of mission and the embassy team but crucial to Australia's credibility and effectiveness across our strategic priorities.

I have tended in these reflections to concentrate on the plurality of my diplomatic life. I have been privileged to experience personally significant international milestones—events that have changed the course of history. My Bangladesh posting saw the assassination of its founding father, Sheikh Mujibur Rahman, and the country's efforts to reach a balance of history and geography between its ties to Islam and Pakistan on the one hand, and India and its Bengali identity on the other. In Israel, I witnessed President Sadat's historic Jerusalem visit, the return of the Sinai to Egypt, and the entrenchment of Jewish settlements in the Occupied Territories. I was engaged in perhaps the golden age of multilateralism with my UN and GATT experiences, when the agendas were ambitious and the mood confident of international cooperation. This was especially so with the arrival on the scene of Mikhail Gorbachev and the beginning of the end of the Cold War. While the challenges in the early 1990s were obvious for the Pacific

Visiting the Lapu-Lapu Community Centre operated by the Cebu Missionary Foundation with Australian government assistance in Cebu, the Philippines, September 2004. Embassy funding was used to provide educational materials for the children living with their squatter families at five waste disposal sites in Cebu.

island states like Solomon Islands, the extent of the threat of irrelevance in an increasingly competitive global economy was not yet imaginable. And in Russia and the Philippines too, I was witness to the way the opportunities and challenges of globalisation—rapid technological change, brain drain, the economic irrelevance of political borders, a changed security environment—were beginning to bite.

Many of these events, these changes, are still being played out, and in some ways, little has altered. The reports I read today of the UN agenda on many issues, I would have written twenty years ago as a UN delegate. The dynamics shaping Bangladesh's future remind me of issues we confronted nearly thirty years ago, and Russia's choices are almost perennial. Significantly also, there has been a constant framework for Australia's foreign and trade policy: protecting and promoting our security and prosperity. What has, however, changed in my personal diplomatic history has been the means, the tools of diplomacy.

The dynamic of strongest impact on the way diplomacy is conducted has been globalisation. It challenges the very concept upon which diplomacy has been based, namely, the nation-state. The countries I have lived and worked in, a diverse cross-section of nation-states, are experiencing the demands of international competitiveness in a variety of ways. How does Russia respond to its brain drain? How can the Philippines reinvent its 20-year-old Overseas Filipino Worker scheme to ensure it remains a globally competitive labour force? How does Solomon Islands recover from its exclusion from the global village? And Australia's response—the imperative to secure a niche for ourselves, and to remain innovative and internationally and regionally engaged—is the essence of our diplomatic brief.

As the international environment has become more complex, it has required a different level of diplomatic sophistication. It is no coincidence that corporate governance and corporate reform became a greater priority for the Department of Foreign Affairs and Trade in the 1990s as the demands of global competitiveness sharpened. In 1997, as the newly appointed head of the department's Corporate Management Division (CMD), I was directly involved in introducing dramatic changes to the way the department, as part of government, manages its business in Canberra and overseas. In my early diplomatic experiences, codified departmental and post priorities, formal performance management systems, post evaluation programs, transparent and accountable promotion rounds, did not exist. Changes commenced in the late 1980s, but the shift after 1996 was formidable. Across the board, public sector reforms brought severe resource cuts; greater departmental autonomy, especially in the area of management and staff-negotiated conditions of service agreements; and the lifting of security of tenure and implementation of a performance-based management system that included upward assessment.

Presenting the first M-series passports issued in Manila to two young Australians, December 2003.

As the head of CMD, the 'change' agenda involved me in consultations across public sector agencies and intensively across the department's various constituencies—in Canberra, at state offices, posts, and with staff associations and unions—all with different perspectives and priorities. My CMD experience was, in many ways, my most important contribution to a new departmental culture.

Reform presents particular challenges to a policy department like Foreign Affairs and Trade that is not profit-based and that has unique overheads, namely our overseas network. Negotiating and applying the change agenda in this department's context reinforced my strong sense that its most important client is the domestic constituency in all its plurality: civil society, parliamentary committees, audit agencies and, of course, the Australian taxpayer. It also reminded me that this constituency does not necessarily have a good understanding of the department's work. We need to be proactive in promoting wider public awareness of diplomacy's relevance to Australia's continuing security and wellbeing. This is especially necessary given the persistent public image of diplomacy as one long cocktail party.

Leadership, both its style and substance, has changed significantly over my diplomatic life. The singular authority of the head of mission—the role's apparent omnipotence—has been transformed by accountable and transparent decision-making. The changing composition of the department in terms of gender and ethnic diversity has also improved the quality of leadership, and the influences of a broader demographic have enhanced overall governance throughout the department.

Far from being a small group of each annual intake of diplomats, women are now more likely to be in the majority. And there is more than one female head of mission, more than one Ruth Dobson, for a diplomatic novice to look up to. The skills and attributes that modern diplomacy demands—perception, networking, sensitivity, teamwork, cleverness, preparation and engagement of diversity and difference—are all strongly demonstrated by our female colleagues. The world, and the face of Australian diplomacy, has changed significantly since I joined the service in 1974.

8 Witness to change

Margaret Adamson

Consul-General in Berlin, 1993–1996

Ambassador to Poland, accredited to the Czech Republic, 1998–2002

My choice of a career focused on public service and international affairs was shaped by my extended family. My great-grandfather Hugo von Alpen migrated to Australia from Schleswig-Holstein in northern Germany in the nineteenth century. A composer and then Director of Musical Education, he played an active part in Australia's Federation celebrations in 1901 by conducting a choir of schoolchildren in Sydney's Centennial Park. Two of Hugo's children returned to Europe: Eileen, a journalist, settled in newly independent Poland, in Cracow, where she lent active support to the cause of Polish sovereignty in the years before World War II; and George, who worked for British intelligence. George married a Belgian veteran of World War I, finally returning with his family to Australia at the outbreak of World War II. His son Paul served in the Australian army and later joined the Department of External Affairs.

The dramatic events of that period, and the narrative of our relations' personal experiences, attracted my curiosity about the wider world. My 'foreigner' relations were instrumental in my career path, providing a vivid

With President Vaclav Havel after presenting credentials at Prague Castle in Prague, the Czech Republic, 1999.

introduction to foreign cultures and languages, as well as to the complexities of international relations and diplomacy. And that path led me to my spouse, who has shared my ongoing interest in international issues and an enthusiasm for the first-hand exposure to other cultures we have experienced through our travels.

I joined the Department of Foreign Affairs as a graduate trainee in 1975. In the years that followed, a common thread to my five overseas assignments has been unification and reconciliation in the aftermath of conflict and the Cold War. I have been posted in two countries, Vietnam and Germany, at the time of their reunification, and in Poland as it joined the North Atlantic Treaty Organisation and prepared for membership of the European Union. A number of my postings closed geopolitical and also historical circles spanning several generations of my forebears.

In 1976, I was posted to Hanoi, following intensive Vietnamese language training at the Point Cook RAAF School of Languages. I was the sole student of Vietnamese at the school that year, apart from an occasional influx of civilian and military personnel for refresher courses. As veterans of the Vietnam War, most were hostile to my posting on what had been the 'enemy' side of the 17th parallel. The teacher–student ratio of two to one ensured rapid progress in this totally new linguistic environment. My teachers also introduced me to the intricacies of Vietnamese culture which, once in-country, equipped me to communicate with the local people on a level beyond the superficial exchanges favoured by the orthodox communist regime. In subsequent postings I placed a similar emphasis on mastering the local language, achieving fluency in German and Polish.

Hanoi remains for me a watershed: my first posting and my first exposure to a non-English-speaking country. The timing of the posting, so soon after the end of the Vietnam War and coinciding with the reunification of the country, etched the experience on my memory. Shortages were endemic—food and clothing were rationed and private ownership of cars and other property was banned. Extensive physical damage was still obvious. Very few bridges had been restored, making river crossings tortuous, via a series of overloaded ferries or pontoon bridges. The people were conditioned to hardship but, with the exception of Party officials, were openly curious about the outside world and frank about their aspirations for a better life. Apart from young men, who continued to wear their army fatigues after discharge from active service, the people dressed in a uniform of black trousers and white shirt. It was a welcome relief for the senses to see young women in the traditional *ao dai* with its smooth-fitting silk bodice and floating panels lightening the sombre black trousers—a treat reserved for private wedding parties glimpsed behind closed doors.

Australia recognised the Government of the Democratic Republic of Vietnam and opened an embassy in Hanoi in 1973. Following the end of the Vietnam War in 1975, the Australian government decided to pursue an active bilateral relationship to encourage the unified country out of its international isolation. During my posting Australia commenced an aid program to help Vietnam improve its beef and dairy production, and for students to undertake English language courses in Australia. My duties included assisting the delegations associated with the beef and dairy projects, accompanying them to meetings in relevant ministries and to project locations in rural Vietnam. I also administered language aptitude tests for students applying to study in Australia. My reporting responsibilities required me to keep abreast of developments in Vietnam and in its relations with neighbouring countries.

Dealing with the Vietnamese bureaucracy at this time had its complexities and frustrations. We jokingly decided that it exhibited the best and the worst traits of the country's Confucian, French and socialist legacies. Banking was a particularly complicated science, requiring patience, perseverance and time if transactions were to be completed satisfactorily. Western diplomats were treated differently from those of the fraternal socialist countries. We were not given access to the generously stocked diplomatic commissary reserved for our socialist colleagues, and the market reserved for Western officials was so poorly supplied that we preferred to shop at the open market. Our accommodation, in the Hotel Reunification, was a far cry from its predecessor, the French colonial-era Metropole. The physical infrastructure remained but now it offered broken plumbing and intermittent electricity, formidable rats (though their existence was officially denied) and enormous cockroaches. We preferred cooking in our rooms to eating in the hotel restaurant, where yoghurt and eggs were often the only edible items on an unvarying menu.

Nonetheless, we fared quite well as we were able to supplement market produce with canned goods brought back from the courier runs.

Communications in the 1970s were rudimentary compared with today's sophisticated networks. Some classified material had to be transported around the region and back to Australia by 'safe-hand' couriers—with embassy staff rostered as couriers in and out of Hanoi. In addition to acquiring supplementary food supplies, our courier runs from Hanoi to Vientiane, and less frequently to Bangkok, gave us some respite from conditions of life at post. Although the political climate in Laos mirrored that in Vietnam, the change of scenery, and of expatriate company, was welcome.

Travel within Vietnam too, although strictly monitored by local authorities, was an antidote to the irritations of day-to-day professional life. More importantly, our experiences in rural and regional Vietnam were essential for the mission's understanding of, and capacity to report back to Australia on, the political, social and economic developments. We explored as much as we could within the constraints of the government's strict system of travel permits for movement outside Hanoi. We visited what have now become heavily promoted tourist destinations, such as the breathtakingly beautiful Ha Long Bay, but also more remote locations redolent of Vietnam's colonial and Ho Chi Minh eras: the cool and misty mountain retreat of the French colonials at Tam Dao; and the mountain cave hideaway of Ho abutting the Chinese border, Lang Son, deep inside the traditional territory of Vietnam's mountain tribes, not far from the site of France's defeat at Dien Bien Phu. We searched out Buddhist pagodas, partly out of curiosity and partly to demonstrate our support for religious freedom in what was then a strictly orthodox communist state. On my only visit to Thanh Pho Ho Chi Minh (Saigon), among other meetings, the ambassador and I called on the Women's Committee, an organ of the Communist Party of Vietnam, to discuss the situation of women and families in the southern part of the country. We were surprised to be served tea in crockery bearing the official Australian crest, left behind when the embassy was evacuated in April 1975.

As the sole Vietnamese-speaking Australian member of the Hanoi embassy, and one of the few Europeans in the diplomatic community speaking Vietnamese, I was granted insights unavailable to my colleagues. I was invited by the Vietnamese Government to assist with the preparation of a new Vietnamese–English dictionary. I was also the object of much curiosity on the part of Vietnamese thirsty for contact with the outside world. Although private contact with foreigners was proscribed, conversation was possible at noodle stands where we ordered chicken *pho*, tangy with coriander, and endless cups of green tea. Cycling on the crowded Hanoi streets on my bicycle with its diplomatic number plates also provided plenty of scope to explain that I was not a Soviet citizen (the assumption made of all white Europeans in the north of the country), but from Australia.

My second posting took me to Vienna in December 1977. I would leave, three years later, married, and with new professional expertise in multilateral diplomacy, specialising in non-proliferation and disarmament. In addition to my bilateral role in the embassy, I was a member of Australia's mission to the International Atomic Energy Agency (IAEA), the United Nations Industrial Development Organization (UNIDO) and the other UN agencies located in Vienna. As a permanent member of the Board of Governors of the IAEA, Australia—then, as now—played an active role to extend the reach and effectiveness of the international nuclear non-proliferation regime. During the 1970s, nuclear technology was sought after not only as a potential source of power generation but, for non-signatories to the Nuclear Non-Proliferation Treaty (NPT), also as a potential deterrent. In the IAEA, Australia, together with other NPT members of the board, encouraged non-signatories to join, or alternatively to accept, comprehensive IAEA safeguards as a confidence-building measure for neighbouring countries. Technical assistance in the peaceful applications of nuclear energy was offered in return for good non-proliferation behaviour.

Buying live crabs with one of the embassy's staff, Huong, in Haiphong, Vietnam, 1977.

Our work with the other major UN institution located in Vienna, UNIDO, was punctuated by the pressure-cooker atmosphere of the regular meetings of the executive organs. Here, more starkly than in the IAEA, the dynamics of the North–South divide were played out, as developing countries pushed for a larger share of global prosperity via technical assistance in the form of industrial technology transfer. All-night negotiating sessions and haze-filled rooms were a reality, as well as a cliche, for the diplomacy of the time. Australia was already concerned about the standards of governance in developing countries and rejected the proposition that the developed world was 'responsible' for delivering economic transformation in these countries.

In 1979, still on posting in Vienna, I travelled to New York to join Australia's delegation to the UN General Assembly. A key task for me was the negotiation of the final language of the Convention on the Elimination of all Forms of Discrimination Against Women (CEDAW), adopted by the United Nations on 18 December. The negotiation of this landmark for women's rights was complicated by different definitions of 'equality' in different cultures, religions and political ideologies. Australia took a firm approach, consistent with the government's national commitment to cement gains for women's equality internationally.

The following year, I was a member of the Australian delegation at the Second World Conference on Women at the mid-point of the UN Decade for Women (1975–1985), held in Copenhagen. The conference was a memorable failure; its objectives sidelined by the then standard exchanges between East and West, and North and South, that permeated the international conference landscape at the height of the Cold War. Delegates from socialist and non-aligned delegations routinely attributed blame for shortcomings to the West, particularly the United States. I recall, for example an intervention by a (male) socialist representative insisting that domestic violence was an exclusively Western phenomenon, unknown in the civilised, freedom-loving socialist world where women were treated with respect and enjoyed complete equality. Such statements lent an element of the surreal to conference proceedings. In addition to deep divisions over the status of women, the conference provided a stage for socialist, non-aligned and Arab states to maintain their attack on Israel, linking the 'Zionist entity' to South Africa's then apartheid regime. It was a vote on a resolution on those extraneous issues that brought the conference to a disorderly end, shattering hopes that CEDAW would lead to an active international consensus on a minimum set of standards for combating discrimination against women and girls.

While the global order at the end of the 1970s was dominated by the Cold War and Vienna was itself an important centre of Cold War diplomacy, the city revealed a fascinating juxtaposition of its early history and Hapsburg Empire past. It was a cosmopolitan city, its central and eastern European communities a living reminder of Austria's lost empire and a statement of Austria's openness to citizens from beyond the Iron Curtain. One of these was my husband Marek, through whom I became acquainted with this section of the Cold War's Polish diaspora.

Living in Vienna afforded endless opportunities to enjoy music. I fell under the spell of opera and the sacred music performed in the acoustic treasures of the myriad Vienna churches. I managed just one of the traditional New Year's concerts at the Musikverein but attended many other concerts, including one memorable Christmas oratorio where the icy coldness of the wooden seating seeped through layers of warmest Aussie wool. Art and architecture, the living culture of the Viennese coffee house and wine tastings in the outlying villages were other favourite leisure activities. We enjoyed weekend excursions to the Wachau, a World Heritage-listed stretch of the Danube Valley, for historic discovery, fine white wine, and ambrosial apricots in the summer time.

We returned to Canberra in 1980, where we remained for almost seven years. I worked initially on nuclear non-proliferation issues before returning to management, from the Canberra end, of Australia's relations with the countries of Indochina. Meanwhile Marek established himself in the civil engineering scene as one of the first engineers on the site of the New Parliament House Project. Following the birth of our daughter Ursula in 1987, we were ready to move again, and I was posted as first secretary and then counsellor in Bonn.

Bonn was true to its character as a 'small town in Germany', depicted in John le Carré's novel of that name. We were also struck by the similarities to life in Canberra. Certainly Bonn was an easy environment for family life and it was also close to a much larger city (Cologne) that offered a diverse, vibrant cultural scene, much like the role Sydney plays relative to Canberra. But there were also important differences in ambience: Bonn was a temporary capital, and it was already a university town of considerable antiquity when selected after World War II to host the seat of government while Berlin remained out of bounds. Bonn's selection had much to do with the fact that the first postwar German Chancellor, Konrad Adenauer, hailed from a small village on the banks of the Rhine River, close to Bonn.

Our son Nicholas was born in May 1989, during Bonn's 2000th anniversary celebrations and shortly before the official visit to Germany by Prime Minister Bob Hawke. (My colleagues in the embassy joked that I had planned the baby's arrival to escape all that a prime ministerial visit entails!) From the hospital balcony, Nicholas and I watched the spectacular fireworks display, China's birthday gift to Bonn, lighting up the breadth of the Rhine River. Proof of the department's family-friendly approach, Nick was my frequent office companion in the embassy following my return to work.

My work in Bonn spanned Germany's foreign relations within the European Union as well as with central and eastern Europe. With the advent of *glasnost* these relationships had become infused with a momentum and

In the garden of the ambassador's residence in Warsaw with my husband, Marek Krol, and our children, Nicholas, Ursula and Anastasia.

expectation of change, although in its divided state Germany seemed impervious to these external developments. Even as peaceful, democratic revolution got under way in Poland, Hungary and then Czechoslovakia, one week before the fall of the Berlin Wall analysts in Berlin were unwilling to make the mental leap to a unified Germany.

The final fourteen months of my posting were dominated by the drama of the fall of the Berlin Wall in November 1989, precipitating the end of the Cold War and the reunification of Germany the following year. It was an extraordinary experience to be in Germany to witness this turning point in European history, and its global repercussions. I visited Berlin as the Wall was being breached, passing through a gaping hole near the Brandenburg Gate, in the company of a throng of people similarly aware of witnessing the unravelling of history. The East German guards who ushered us along had already shed their characteristic menacing demeanour and behaved like benign traffic policemen. We bought some souvenir lumps of mortar, hacked from the Wall by enterprising citizens wielding hammers. I still have my piece of Wall; it looks harmless, and odd, in our Australian home. But I keep it as a tangible reminder of our having been there at the time, and for all that it symbolises.

The reunification of Germany and the end of the Cold War were welcomed in Australia, as in other Western countries, as a victory for democracy over totalitarianism. The collapse of the Soviet Union meant that Europe could emerge from the uneasy stability that had been based on equality of destructive military capacity between West and East, and concentrate its energies on consolidating democracy and economic prosperity. Australia had multiple interests in this process: on behalf of its first and second generation European-origin citizens, as well as economic and strategic interests. Many Australians had close family ties in Germany and eastern Europe; our exporters and investors saw commercial opportunities to exploit in the 'new' Europe; and a stable and prosperous Europe was expected to yield a positive dividend globally.

German reunification paved the way for the disintegration of the Warsaw Pact and the subsequent enlargements of NATO and the European Union, taking in the nations of former Soviet-dominated eastern Europe. German Foreign Minister Hans-Dietrich Genscher, himself of East German origin, had articulated his vision of *European House* long before the Iron Curtain was drawn back. The largest yet enlargement of the European Union, in May 2004, which included eight of the former Soviet satellites of central and eastern Europe, represented the realisation of Genscher's concept and the fulfilment of the determined ambition of these countries.

At a personal level, too, these developments were welcome. Marek underscored for me the significance to Polish people in particular of the opportunity to enjoy normalised relations with Germany and to rejoin democratic Europe.

Our family connections to Poland also brought some exposure to the realities of life in eastern Europe during the pre-unification period. My career had returned us to the broad neighbourhood of my husband's family. Our proximity from Bonn to Marek's Warsaw-based parents offered the prospect of family reunions. Early in our posting, we booked to travel by train from Cologne to Warsaw to spend Christmas with Marek's family. Our train was bound ultimately for Moscow and, as it slid into the dimly lit platform, crowds surged from the shadows for the carriages. Marek was swept aboard, leaving me with baby Ursula, asleep in her pram. The pram proved too wide for the carriage door, and Marek was nowhere to be seen. A reluctant conductor finally agreed to assist, and wrestled the pram—at a precarious angle—aboard, at which point the train lurched into motion. The narrow carriage corridor was chaotic: bulky, fur-clad people jostled each other in an effort to find their compartments, but the compartment numbers bore no relation to the numbers on our tickets. In a further twist, most compartments were already full to the brim with large boxes containing western white goods and television sets bound for sale in Russia. Against the odds, Marek and I tracked each other down, solved the riddle of the compartments and cleared ours of the white goods. Mercifully, Ursula slept through the entire ordeal.

I returned to Canberra in 1991 to resume work on international nuclear non-proliferation. The non-proliferation regime was under threat from the activities of states, both within and outside the NPT, which were attracted to the nuclear option. Non-signatories India and Pakistan have since joined the ranks of nuclear weapon states, and Iran and North Korea remain the subject of intense international efforts to persuade them to honour their NPT undertakings. Australia continues to work actively within the international community to strengthen the non-proliferation regime. With some 40 per cent of the world's known uranium resources, and as a member of the NPT, Australia has a special responsibility to prevent the spread of nuclear weapons. Australia has a long-standing policy of requiring a treaty-level agreement with any customer for its uranium, to guarantee that our uranium is used exclusively for peaceful, non-explosive purposes. Australia's international credentials are further buttressed by our permanent seat on the governing board of the IAEA.

In early 1992, accompanied by new baby daughter Anastasia, I travelled to Warsaw as a member of Australia's delegation at the Nuclear Suppliers Group (NSG) meeting. The NSG binds together a number of countries with a common commitment to reducing nuclear proliferation by ensuring that any nuclear material, equipment or technology that they export goes only to countries that have accepted so-called full-scope safeguards applied by the IAEA on their entire nuclear activities, and will only export under the same IAEA conditions. A major focus of the meeting was the ongoing issue of dual-use equipment. The NSG in 1991 had finally agreed on a list of such equipment, which would require the same safeguards as exports of nuclear items directly relevant to proliferation, and the list was published in 1992. Australia had worked for a wide interpretation of what should be considered dual-use, and for publication of the list to maximise transparency.

Following the NSG meeting in Warsaw, I joined a delegation of G7 countries plus Australia to travel to the capitals of eight of the newly independent former constituent republics of the Soviet Union. Australia had been invited to participate in this G7 initiative in recognition of our role in support of global non-proliferation efforts. Ana stayed in Warsaw with Marek, who had travelled across to support me during my recall to duty from maternity leave.

The purpose of the 'G7 plus 1' mission was to encourage host states to embrace the letter, as well as the spirit, of the international non-proliferation regime. We presented our message in Belarus, Ukraine, Russia, Kazakhstan, Azerbaijan, Armenia, Georgia and Moldova. The discussions were in most respects premature: these states had neither the necessary governance structures nor sufficient political stability to respond to our messages. In Azerbaijan and Armenia, our meetings were held during ongoing hostilities between the two countries, and a military coup seized power one day after we departed from Baku. Deteriorating stability forced the cancellation of the itinerary in the central Asian republics other than Kazakhstan. Although the mission failed to achieve all its objectives, the urgency of our message was confirmed by our encounters in the same capitals of delegations peddling a different message. Political and profit-driven motives were attracting a range of purveyors of proliferation-sensitive material and knowhow in these newly independent states.

In 1993 I received my first head of post appointment as Australian Consul-General in Berlin. Much of the euphoria of the end of the Cold War had given way to the 'hangover' of actually realising a united Europe in more than name. Berlin was dubbed *Werkstatt Europas* (Workshop Europe, where Europe was being joined together again, with some experimentation in the process), to denote its physical, as well as symbolic, role in this process. Spectacular buildings have healed the the scar where the Wall once ran. But the task provoked an uneven social and political response, as the populations on both sides of the former Wall confronted the realisation that living the dream of German, and European, reunification would involve more than physical transformation.

Following the decision in 1991 by Germany's Bundestag (lower house of parliament) to make Berlin the seat of the national government, government agencies and foreign diplomatic missions began preparing to relocate from Bonn, culminating in a formal transition on 1 September 1999. My role as Consul-General in Berlin was largely shaped by this process. I was to re-establish Australia's presence in Berlin in advance of the move of the government, to lift Australia's profile in the new German federal states, and to support Australian trade and investment activities in Berlin and eastern Germany.

A major focus for the post was the search for suitable accommodation for the future Australian embassy chancery in Berlin. I also supported efforts to establish an Australia Centre to promote Australia's profile in Germany, and Europe more broadly, as a leader in science and technology and higher education—a first for Australia in continental Europe. The Australia Centre was officially launched by Prime Minister Keating in 1995, and the premises were opened by Senate President, Senator Margaret Reid, during her visit to Germany with an Australian parliamentary delegation in 1996. Having recommended and then signed the purchase documents for the heritage building approved for the embassy chancery, I was pleased to close the circle by accompanying the Minister for Foreign Affairs, Alexander Downer, during his visit to Germany in January 2003, when he officially opened the embassy.

Watching the presentation to the Director of the Australia Centre by Patron of the Centre, Senate President Margaret Reid, in the presence of Brandenburg Premier Manfred Stolpe (right).

My posting once again coincided with major change, as Berlin underwent its transition to a unified Germany's capital. I witnessed the ceremonies to farewell the troops of the Four Powers (the United States, the United Kingdom, France and the former Soviet Union) in 1994 and President Yeltsin receiving the keys to the unified city of Berlin at the City Hall (located in former East Berlin). President Clinton visited in the same year. He delivered a speech to an audience packed into the square at the foot of the restored Brandenburg Gate—just inside the former Berlin Wall and close to the site of the prewar US Embassy. In celebrating Germany's unification, Clinton referred to the messages of Western solidarity with divided Berlin delivered by his predecessors John Kennedy ('*Ich bin ein Berliner*') and Ronald Reagan ('Mr Gorbachev, tear down this wall'), which had helped West Berliners (and many others trapped on the eastern side of the Wall) to dare to hope that the Cold War would end.

Visits to Berlin by Pope John Paul II and President Nelson Mandela of South Africa also attracted wide attention. In 1996, the Pope celebrated mass and beatified two German saints in the 1936 Olympic stadium that had witnessed Hitler's preference for the 'Aryan' race. The ceremony was heavily overlaid with spiritual symbolism and characterised by many as a type of exorcism of the past evils of the Nazi era. President Mandela launched an African cultural festival, opened by the Soweto String Quartet—another potent reminder of the impermanence of racist and totalitarian regimes.

The visit by controversial installation artists Christo and Jeanne-Claude in 1995 to wrap Berlin's Reichstag — the original parliament of the German Empire and a symbol of democracy for Germany — was the climax of twenty-four years of work by the artists. The Reichstag project was so fiercely debated that a vote had to be taken in the Bundestag. The normally green swathe of lawn in front of the building turned to dust under the feet of the millions of viewers who visited during the two weeks it was shrouded in fabric. As the building was unwrapped, the Reichstag's ghosts were dispelled, in readiness for its transformation by British architect Sir Norman Foster to become the permanent seat of the German parliament in 1999, for the first time since 1938.

In recognition of contemporary Germany's emphasis on culture and the arts, our public diplomacy strategies often featured Australian artists or performers, to help sell Australia's policy messages. The Australian Youth Orchestra, Australian Chamber Orchestra under Richard Tognetti and the Sydney Symphony Orchestra conducted by Edo de Waart all performed in Germany during my time there, at such iconic theatres as Berlin's Schauspielhaus and the Gewandhaus in Leipzig. Simone Young was already acclaimed internationally by the time of my posting to Berlin. She gave generously of her time to assist our public diplomacy efforts, from attending Prime Minister Paul Keating's reception following Wagner's *Tristan and Isolde*

During the visit by Minister for Immigration and Multicultural and Indigenous Affairs, Philip Ruddock, to Prague in August 2002. L–R: Barbara Day, member Prague Society for International Cooperation, Mr Ruddock, Professor Marc Ellenbogen, Managing Director, Prague Society for International Cooperation, Mrs Ruddock, Margaret Adamson. In the background, the Moldau River about to burst its banks in the disastrous floods of that year.

conducted by Simone at the Staatsoper, to her guest appearance at our post's International Women's Day events.

In May 1997, I returned to Canberra as assistant secretary of the Pacific Islands Branch. For the first time in my career I was responsible for developing policy options in relation to Australia's immediate neighbourhood. During my time in this position, I visited many of the Pacific island nations—participating in regional meetings, including the Pacific Islands Forum. The beauty of the islands, and the friendliness and hospitality of their peoples belied the economic, social, environmental and governance challenges confronting these countries. In Canberra I established and led an interagency task force preparing the policy and logistical preparations for the fiftieth anniversary of the South Pacific Commission.

After one year, I left this active focus of Australian foreign policy for an assignment distant from our immediate foreign and trade policy priorities as Ambassador to Poland and the Czech Republic, a position I would hold from 1998 to 2002. Although a leader of the resistance that precipitated the end of the Cold War, this increasingly active, large European country barely registered on Australia's geopolitical radar. Why did I accept the appointment? There were clear personal reasons: Marek's elderly parents were alone and longed to spend time with their only child and to get to know their grandchildren better. But there were professional rewards too. A posting in Poland at this juncture offered a chance to deepen my acquaintance with Europe as the continent prepared to assume a larger global role, with implications for Australia's interests.

Poland's primary foreign policy goal upon regaining its soveriegnty was membership of NATO, rapidly achieved in 1999. Poland then set its sights on membership of the European Union, which it joined in 2004. Poland's emerging significance as a regional player was positively evaluated by its new political and security partners. Senior EU and NATO ambassadors were appointed to serve in Warsaw, and Poland played host to a stream of high-level visitors: President Bush, the Emperor of Japan, Latin American as well as European heads of state and the Pope.

I was not the only female head of mission in Poland. At one point eight women ambassadors were serving in Warsaw. We were frequently called upon to give our perspectives on gender issues in a society where women were strongly represented in non-traditional sectors, but continued to carry an unequal domestic burden.

For all that diplomacy operates at the level of global issues and the 'big picture', at the core of any bilateral relationship are crucial people-to-people links. Developing a firmer foundation of such ties between Australia and Poland was therefore a focus of my posting. In 1999, I established what has become an annual observance of Anzac Day in Warsaw, drawing on the comradeship of Anzacs and Polish soldiers and airmen during World War II. Individual Australians of Polish and Polish–Jewish descent, especially leading sociologists Professors George Zubrzycki and George Smolicz, lent strong support also to my other initiatives, including a promotion of Australia's successful experience of multiculturalism.

Laying a wreath on the tomb of the Unknown Soldier at the annual Anzac Day service in Warsaw, 25 April 2002.

In Warsaw and Prague I was greatly assisted by two other women with significant diplomatic experience: the former Polish and Czech ambassadors to Australia, Agnieszka Morawinska and Jara Moserova. These women were also leaders in their respective societies. Both were well-connected to the key players in the two countries' democratic transformation and had been sent to Australia as the first Polish and Czech envoys following democratisation. Their connections delivered me excellent access to register Australia's perspectives on global and bilateral issues at the highest levels. Their efforts as ambassadors to Australia in turn delivered me ready access to the elites in the government and intellectual circles in Poland and the Czech Republic, and their friendship provided me with excellent connections in the wider society of both countries. During my posting, Morawinska was appointed head of Poland's National Gallery for Contemporary Art, and Moserova was a veteran senator in the Czech parliament. I am indebted to them both.

The coincidence of my close association with ambassadors Morawinska and Moserova provokes the question whether there is something distinctive about a female in comparison to a male head of mission. In my view there is no greater gender distinction in this profession than in any other that has traditionally been regarded as a male preserve. One minor advantage for a female ambassador is that she can exploit opportunities to meet the wives of the host country's leaders, picking up insights not always available from the official contacts I maintained with their husbands. At the same time, the greater numbers of women now pursuing their own careers has, happily, displaced the 'exceptional' label with which women ambassadors have been tagged in the past. But if women are no longer automatically relegated to the role of accompanying spouse, paradoxically, accompanying male partners all to frequently find themselves positioned awkwardly in 'ladies' programs when activities are planned for spouses. This relic of past assumptions needs to change.

At the conclusion of my posting to Warsaw, President Kwasniewski presented me with a Polish order, the Commanders Cross, in recognition of my contribution to strengthening bilateral relations, a first for Australia in Poland. By the time I left, high-level bilateral visits had recommenced after a lengthy gap, stimulating closer ties. Poland had become Australia's fastest-growing market for education exports, and our wine exports were increasing at an exponential rate. Over the same period the Czech Republic had become Australia's

Speaking with the ambassador of South Africa to Poland, Sikose Ntombazana Mji, after the Anzac Day service in Warsaw, 2002.

major trading partner in central Europe, including as a source of European students. The strong transatlantic orientation of the two countries has reinforced their contemporary value to Australia as like-minded partners within the broader Western alliance in addressing global security and other contemporary challenges.

I feel privileged to have represented Australia internationally. Beyond the stimulation and sense of achievement the experience has brought to me as I have strived to excel in my professional mission, I have been conscious of the challenges and opportunities our postings have presented to our children. An appropriate balance between professional and personal commitments is at times difficult to achieve, but the rewards are immense when the line between the two is well drawn. My diplomatic career has provided a unique context in which to foster in our children qualities of open-mindedness, awareness of global issues, a lively quest for knowledge and values firmly based on fairness, democracy and respect for all peoples, cultures and religions. We have had to work hard simultaneously to nurture a sense of stability and constancy in our family life, but all in all I have found my professional choice has enriched rather than detracted from my other key mission in life: my family.

Promoting the Sydney 2000 Olympic Games at Międzyzdroje on the Baltic Coast.

9 Embajadora de Australia

Susan Tanner

Ambassador to Chile, accredited to Peru and Bolivia, 1997–1999

Ambassador to Spain, accredited to Andorra, 2003–2006

I joined the Department of Foreign Affairs in January 1974—one of six female graduates in an intake of forty-four diplomatic trainees. I had just graduated from Flinders University in South Australia with an honours degree in European languages (Spanish, Portuguese and French). In March of that year, Australia's first career female ambassador was appointed: Ruth Dobson to Denmark. To mark the occasion, female officers were invited to a modest lunch in her honour held in the department.

As we lunched, I idly wondered when the first Australian female career ambassador might be appointed to an embassy in what I saw at the time as 'my' part of the world, Latin America. (My first placement in the department was in the Americas Section, working on Latin American issues.) Twenty-three years later, in 1997, I became that ambassador, appointed to the Australian Embassy in Santiago de Chile, and concurrently accredited to Peru and Bolivia.

In addition to being the first female Australian ambassador in Latin America (and there were still many such 'firsts' among my female colleagues in the 1990s), my posting to Chile as head of mission had particular significance for me. I had previously been posted there from 1988 to 1991 as first secretary, later counsellor, during the final turbulent years of the Pinochet regime and the early days of the country's return to democratic government. The government of President Eduardo Frei (to whom I presented credentials in July 1997) was the second democratically elected administration since the end of Pinochet's seventeen years of military rule. I found it both professionally and personally rewarding to observe the changes that had occurred since 1991 and to have the job of identifying and promoting Australia's interests in this new Chile.

I felt extremely fortunate in having had a prior posting in Chile—in addition to developing my language skills, it gave me the wonderful advantage of knowing, personally or by reputation, many of the key players in government, politics and civil society, and a feel for the complexities and sensitivities of Chile's recent history. With reasonable fluency in Spanish, the full support of a sympathetic spouse (himself an experienced diplomat) and assisted by a team of very capable colleagues in the embassy, I was able to settle in quickly and adjust to my new role.

Australia's relations with Chile had developed significantly since the late 1980s and early 1990s, the most notable change being the country's increased focus on the dynamic Asia–Pacific region. Chile and Australia now shared a much broader multilateral and regional agenda, not only through Chilean membership of the Asia–Pacific Economic Co-operation (APEC) group, but also through our common participation in coalitions on priority issues, including the environment, disarmament and, as members of the Cairns Group, on agricultural trade liberalisation.

Reviewing the honour guard at the entrance to the Moneda Palace in Santiago de Chile, prior to presenting credentials, July 1997.

There had also been tremendous growth in Australia's investment in Chile; it was then ranked sixth among the largest foreign investors, largely due to the Australian mining giant BHP's significant stake in the Escondida copper mine in the country's north. This investment base underpinned the economic relationship and made Australia a country of some influence in the Chilean mining sector. There were around thirty Australian companies providing mining services and equipment in Chile, as well as a small but growing number of Australian business and investment interests in finance, entertainment, energy and wine.

The modest trading relationship between Australia and Chile was dominated by commodities and constrained in potential by the similarity and small market size of our respective economies. But there were important niches that Australian companies could develop in areas such as services, goods and technology for the mining sector. The embassy saw it as a major challenge to promote Australian opportunities and confidence in the Chilean market through encouraging Australian companies to view Chile both as a business destination and as a base for expansion elsewhere in Latin America.

The embassy's activities focused on promoting Australian trade and investment in our three countries of accreditation—Chile, Peru and Bolivia—and about two-thirds of my advocacy and representational efforts were devoted to trade and commercial matters. In this I was ably assisted by the head of the Austrade office in Santiago and his staff, in addition to my own departmental staff. Many of the embassy-assisted visits undertaken by Australians—both official and private sector representatives—to our countries of accreditation were related to achieving Australia's trade and economic objectives. Our contribution to these visits was the embassy's extensive and targeted network of contacts, our thorough research of the matters to be addressed during the visit and, where official visits were concerned, meticulous planning of every aspect, including back-up for contingencies.

Briefing Australian business representatives at EXPOMIN in May 1998, Santiago de Chile.

Australian participation in EXPOMIN, the biennial mining fair held in Chile, in May 1998, was a case in point. The Austrade staff were kept busy organising and managing the Australian contingent of sixty-four companies. They provided a series of briefings to the Australian exhibitors on opportunities for business in the mining sector in Latin America, and to other exhibitors on Australian capabilities in that field. As well as taking part in the EXPOMIN program, I participated in a subsequent Austrade-organised mining mission of eleven Australian companies to Peru, where we received briefings from government officials and made presentations to representatives of the mining sector on the equipment and services that these companies offered. My credentials as ambassador opened the right doors in an environment in which Australia and its capabilities were not well known, and also oiled the wheels of commerce through the social interaction so important in Latin American societies. Often I was invited to 'say a few words' (in Spanish) on behalf of the relevant Australian interest, and I quickly learned how to respond when handed a microphone at short notice.

The mining industry and the business opportunities it presented for Australian companies were of such magnitude that I and embassy staff had to develop a solid understanding of the mining exploration and extractive industries. I followed developments in the Australian mining industry closely, and my Spanish vocabulary began to encompass technical mining terminology as I daily read the mining pages in the Chilean press and discussed opportunities with our contacts in Australian mining companies. Embassy staff developed a wide range of capital-based contacts in the mining sector and visited the mining regions where Australian companies were doing business. As well as learning about the operating environment in which these companies worked and demonstrating to the local authorities our support for their capability, we offered consular services, such as help with passport renewal, to resident Australian citizens who could not travel to Santiago.

An important event during my time in Chile was the first ministerial-level meeting of the Bilateral Trade and Investment Commission, a body designed to provide a focus and work program for advancing the economic and investment relationship between Australia and Chile. The meeting was held in November 1998 to coincide with a planned visit by the Deputy Prime Minister and Minister for Trade, Tim Fischer, which was to prove hectic and eventful.

Mr Fischer was a champion of developing relations between Australia and the countries of Latin America, and he was respected locally for his efforts to encourage interchange between Chile and Australia. During a visit to the Escondida mine at the beginning of his stay, the news broke that the British House of Lords had ruled against the release of ex-President Pinochet in London (Pinochet had been arrested, at the request of a Spanish judge, in October 1998 during a private visit to London for medical treatment). The arrest reopened old divisions in Chilean society, threatening to undermine the difficult process of national reconciliation. When we returned to Santiago we found a tense atmosphere, with Pinochet supporters staging rowdy demonstrations outside the residences of the British and Spanish ambassadors—in the same street as the Australian embassy chancery. Although the official party was escorted from the airport by *carabineros* (police) on motorcycles, there was always the possibility that the Australian flag might be mistaken for the Union Jack by the demonstrators and our cavalcade would suddenly become a target. Mr Fischer took all this in his stride, however.

The Deputy Prime Minister's brief program in Santiago included a meeting with President Eduardo Frei at the Moneda Palace (the presidential office) and although the President clearly had urgent issues to attend to as a result of developments in the Pinochet case, the meeting proceeded. When Mr Fischer arrived at the entrance to the Moneda Palace, however, he was disappointed to find that it was not the custom in Chile for the media to be in attendance before such calls. Mr Fischer had hoped for the opportunity to tell Chileans about the gift of a leather stockman's whip he had brought for the President made by Mick's Whips of Noonamah in the Northern Territory, an Australian e-commerce export success. Mr Fischer briefly sketched the origin and significance of these particular whips for President Frei, who listened attentively, although the serious situation with which he was contending was perhaps not far from his thoughts. In thanking the Deputy Prime Minister for his gift, President Frei smilingly made as if to crack the whip and wryly noted that it would come in handy at the cabinet meeting he had called for that afternoon.

A great pleasure I had on returning to Santiago as an ambassador was the company of my distinguished female colleagues in the diplomatic corps. Eight years earlier there had not been a single female head of mission resident in the Chilean capital. By the time I left at the end of 1999, there were six female ambassadors in a resident corps of sixty-eight, with the Asia–Pacific region well represented—Australia, Malaysia, the Philippines, Thailand—as well as the United Kingdom and Costa Rica. Because there were so few female ambassadors in the resident diplomatic corps, we stood out at most official gatherings. The innate Chilean courtesy and respect for diplomatic representatives was doubly evident in the treatment of female heads of mission; in all our official contacts we were made to feel especially welcome, both personally and professionally.

Early in my term four of the five Australian departmental officers of the embassy were female (ambassador, counsellor, senior administrative officer and second secretary), which generated some light-hearted and affectionate ribbing from our Chilean colleagues in the foreign ministry. We were also well known elsewhere in the Chilean government. In particular, the young agriculture minister, with whom we worked closely, always made a point of commenting on the superior abilities of the fair sex in diplomacy when I had occasion to call accompanied by one or more of my female colleagues. Although there were advantages in having such a profile, we worked hard to ensure that our reputation in government and other circles derived from respect for our competence and professionalism, not the novelty of our gender. Still, the interest generated by Australia's predominantly female presence in Santiago enabled us to advance Australia's interests in the wide range of issues relevant to the bilateral relationship.

With local Mapuche children at the Colegio Australia in Traiguén, southern Chile, October 1999.

Subtle cultural expectations regarding the role of professional women in Latin America affected the way in which female heads of mission were viewed and treated in Chile. One of these related to marital status: the single professional woman was an accepted phenomenon, but a married woman whose husband had put his own career on hold to support her generated some curiosity. In the Spanish-speaking world of diplomacy this was complicated by the fact that *embajadora* was the word for both a female ambassador and the wife of an ambassador. It was not uncommon for the assumption to be made, when I introduced myself at social gatherings as the *embajadora de Australia*, that my husband was the ambassador and I his accompanying spouse. This misunderstanding was easily sorted out but it could become tiresome when the explanation had to be given several times at the same function. My good humour was sometimes tested by the surprised and amused look on the face of my interlocutor (usually male) on contemplating the prospect of a professional man accompanying his wife on her head of mission posting. Of the six female heads of mission in Santiago, I was the only one at post accompanied by a spouse. My husband, who had taken leave from his job and was working on a PhD in history during our posting, over time came to appreciate the 'student' label that gave him an acceptable answer to the frequently asked question 'But what do you *do*?'

As elsewhere in Latin America, in Chile there was considerable emphasis on traditional feminine attributes such as attention to personal grooming and fashion. Professional women were expected to be clever but also to look the part, to be sharp but stylishly feminine at the same time. As ambassador, I knew I could never go to my local supermarket on a weekend dressed as casually as I might in Australia—I was on duty twenty-four hours a day, and local community expectations of an ambassador, particularly a female ambassador, were high.

In 1997, before my appointment to Chile, Peru and Bolivia, I attended a departmental seminar in Canberra that focused on the challenges and opportunities for female heads of mission and post. The event was designed to encourage more women to apply for future vacancies at that level. During the seminar it was noted that one of the particular advantages of being a woman in these positions was that we were able to gain access to women's networks not open to male counterparts and to individual women who were influential in their own right. This access offered us a broader range of contacts than our male counterparts.

Once in Santiago, I found that being a female head of mission gave me a particular interest in and sympathy with women and their place in the societies of the countries of my accreditation. In addition to establishing contacts with female decision-makers in senior positions, I also took an interest in the prominent role of women in development projects in these countries. (The embassy was able to support these projects in a modest way through its Direct Aid Program.) The opportunity to pursue personal contacts such as these was welcome as there are restraints on friendships and relationships, both personal and professional, imposed by the role of a head of mission.

Embassy functions were ideal opportunities to interact with women's groups. In 1997, I hosted a lunch in honour of the young women of the Chilean Diplomatic Academy Andrés Bello and their director, Don Eduardo Ortiz, to help celebrate the Academy's achievement in accepting an equal number of female diplomatic cadets for the first time in its 71-year history. In conversation with this impressive group of young women, we noted the many similarities

Participating with local school children in the Clean up Chile campaign in northern Chile, sponsored by the Australian embassy, October 1999.

with our own female graduates—the same personal and professional concerns about combining a foreign service career with family, about opportunities for career development and general management practices within their workplace related to gender equity.

As an embassy, we were also able to demonstrate publicly Australia's commitment to gender equality by hosting an event to mark International Women's Day in March each year. The Department of Foreign Affairs and Trade actively encouraged all Australian posts to celebrate this anniversary.

During my first International Women's Day in 1998, I hosted a lunch at the residence to which I invited a group of eighteen women, representing the mainstream political spectrum in the country. The guest of honour was the Minister for the National Service for Women, Josefina Bilbao, and others included a governor of the Central Bank, the head of the National Audit Office, a mayor, members of the Chilean Congress, a senior member of the police force and my female ambassadorial colleagues.

At the suggestion of the deputy head of mission, the following year the embassy's celebration of International Women's Day focused on women in the mining industry. Unfortunately mining practitioners were primarily based at the mines located in northern Chile, but again I hosted a lunch at the residence for women from a number of walks of life associated with the industry—Senator Carmen Frei (sister of President Frei), who represented a mining region in the Chilean Senate, senior women from the state copper company CODELCO, representatives from the Ministry of Mining, the National

Geological and Mining Service, private mining companies, lawyers specialising in mining matters and journalists covering the mining sector.

As these were not only celebrations of International Women's Day but events in the embassy's public diplomacy program, it was also important that they were covered by the main national daily, *El Mercurio*—a significant influence in the life of the national capital (and beyond). In a professional life where profile is important, coverage such as this provides soft avenues for public diplomacy that can be surprisingly effective in promoting one's country and its interests. The published photographs of the lunches generated a lot of positive interest and attention, not only for International Women's Day but also for the embassy's objective of demonstrating support for the contribution of Chilean women to the service of their country.

Another of the potential challenges identified by some former female heads of mission at the 1997 departmental seminar was having to contend with the outdated opinions of Australian expatriates who had not caught up with contemporary social attitudes in Australia, let alone in their country of residence. In the case of Chile, the local Australian expatriate community was mostly made up of men from the mining companies, accustomed to and more comfortable with an exclusively male environment.

Throughout my term as head of mission, however, I found only one minor example of sexism in my contact with members of the Australian expatriate community. The majority were always most courteous and cooperative in working with me and others in the embassy. Indeed, we received much positive feedback from Australian companies on our efforts to improve liaison and consultation with them. We furthered these aims through a series of regular business breakfasts held at the residence; production of a guide to the services offered by the embassy; and advice, briefing and country assessments for resident Australian personnel and visiting senior company representatives. The local Chile–Australia Chamber of Commerce was also particularly helpful in reinforcing the projection of a distinctive Australian business identity in Chile.

During my three previous overseas postings I had never had the opportunity to participate in the credentials ceremony of any of my heads of mission, so it was with some curiosity and trepidation that I faced my own credentials ceremonies in Chile, Peru and Bolivia. It seemed like a formal and somewhat old-fashioned rite of passage in this era of modern diplomacy. In the event, each of the ceremonies, including a review of the respective presidential guard, was conducted with great dignity and reinforced the strong sense of pride I felt in representing Australia overseas at such a senior level. The presentation of letters of credence to the three heads of state also served to remind me of the heavy responsibilities of a head of mission.

It was usual for an ambassador-designate to present credentials in the country of resident accreditation before those of non-resident accreditation. As it happened, my credentials ceremony in Chile was delayed by the absence of President Frei from Santiago for some weeks—he was touring regions of Chile devastated by winter flooding. The Peruvian government, however, advised that a credentials ceremony had been scheduled for myself and the Chilean ambassador-designate, who happened to be the current deputy chief of protocol in the Chilean Foreign Ministry. It was agreed that I would present credentials in Lima with my Chilean colleague and then join the other ambassadors waiting in Santiago for the Chilean ceremony.

The credentials ceremony in Lima was extremely well organised and conducted with due pomp and ceremony at the Presidential Palace. Afterwards I spent a good thirty minutes discussing a range of issues relevant to the state of the bilateral relationship with Peru's President Fujimori and his foreign minister, Francisco Tudela. Australia's relations with Peru had been strengthened by steadily increasing Australian investment in the mining sector (including by BHP) and by Peru's recent admission to membership of APEC. Australia's decision to open a consulate-general in Lima, in mid-1999, to provide both consular and commercial services to the growing Australian community in Peru, was strongly welcomed by the Peruvian government. President Fujimori took the opportunity to meet the Minister for Trade during the latter's visit to Lima to open the consulate.

In discussion with President Fujimori of Peru and Foreign Minister Tudela at the Presidential Palace in Lima, July 1997, following presentation of credentials.

The timing of the ceremony in Bolivia was determined by the need to present my credentials to the outgoing Bolivian President, Gonzalo Sanchez de Lozada, and to represent the Australian government at the inauguration in La Paz of President-elect Hugo Banzer, scheduled to take place one week later.

La Paz, at 3,600 metres above sea level, is the highest capital in the world, and soon after my arrival I began to suffer from the severe headache that accompanies *soroche*, or altitude sickness. (The problem increases with age, and several visiting older ambassadors had, over the years, suffered heart attacks due to over-exertion in their first few days in La Paz. The homely advice given to newcomers by local wits was: *andar despacito, comer poquito y dormir solito*—walk slowly, eat little and sleep alone.) With the symptoms of *soroche* more or less under control, I managed to enjoy my credentials ceremony with the President, a simple but dignified event given colour by the traditional uniforms of the presidential guard.

During the week between the two presidential ceremonies, I visited other cities in Bolivia where Australia had commercial interests and had some respite from the constant headache at the lower altitude. I then returned to La Paz and the *soroche*, the effects of which were compounded by the liveliness of Bolivian politics at that time.

My return to the capital coincided with the need for the Bolivian Congress to schedule a late afternoon session to formally elect the President as none of the candidates had obtained an absolute majority in the elections. Both the Congress and the Presidential Palace were situated on the Plaza Murillo, as was our hotel. Thoughtfully, the hotel management had allocated me a front room overlooking the square. But the congressional session turned into a filibuster and dragged on into the small hours of the morning. Hundreds of supporters of the respective presidential candidates congregated in the plaza chanting slogans; bands played traditional Andean flute and drum music; helmeted police patrolled surrounding streets. Every now and again a group of miners, a political force to be reckoned with in Bolivia, would let off a round of dynamite to express their displeasure at the events unfolding in the Congress building. Needless to say, no one staying at the Gran Hotel París got much sleep that night!

I finished my term as head of mission in Santiago late in 1999 with mixed feelings. I was pleased to be able to re-establish our home in Canberra for my two sons, who had not wholly enjoyed their experience in boarding school, but I regretted leaving an embassy team that had accomplished a great deal in advancing Australia's interests in Chile, Peru and Bolivia, and which had an active and interesting agenda of issues still to be pursued. By this time I was not the only Australian female head of mission in Latin America—I had a colleague in Buenos Aires who was herself succeeded by another female ambassador. And, subsequently, another female head of mission was appointed to the Australian embassy in Santiago.

Following three and a half years back in Canberra working on Australia's relations with Europe and the European Union, and then on trade and business issues, I was delighted, in August 2003, to be appointed Ambassador to Spain, with non-resident accreditation to Andorra. In career terms, the new appointment seemed a natural progression from my earlier postings in Latin America and from my recent experience with EU matters. My husband had generously offered to remain in Canberra for three months to run the family home and provide support for my younger son who was studying for his final school examinations, so I initially settled into the post on my own. Even though there were significant differences between the work of the embassies in Chile and Spain, and the diplomatic corps in Madrid was nearly double the size of that in Santiago, I found that my earlier experience as head of mission (not to mention my language skills) had equipped me to adapt quickly to my new role in the Kingdom of Spain. I also enjoyed having a larger group of female ambassadorial colleagues in Madrid; the number ranged between twelve and sixteen as ambassadors came and went during my three-year term.

Being received by His Majesty King Juan Carlos of Spain, Her Majesty Queen Sofia and His Royal Highness the Prince of Asturias at the royal reception for the Diplomatic Corps in Madrid, January 2004.

At the Elysée Palace in Paris on 17 March 2005, with the Foreign Minister of Andorra, Juli Minoves Triquell, and the French Co-Prince of Andorra, H.E. Jacques Chirac, during the presentation of credentials for the Principality.

Following the presentation of credentials as Ambassador to Andorra to the Bishop Co-Prince of Andorra, H.E. Joan Enric Vives i Sicília, Bishop of La Seu d'Urgell on 28 November 2003 at the Bishop's Palace, Andorra.

The ceremony for presentation of credentials to His Majesty King Juan Carlos one month after I arrived was a memorable occasion, full of pomp and pageantry. Although the usual custom was for the presenting head of mission to be conveyed to the royal palace in the horse-drawn carriage reserved for state occasions, it rained on the day I presented my credentials and I was duly transported to the palace in the magnificent black Rolls-Royce originally used by General Franco. As I was also accredited, on a non-resident basis, to the Principality of Andorra, I subsequently presented credentials to the two Co-Princes of Andorra—in Spain, to the Bishop of La Seu d'Urgell (a small town in Catalonia) and in France, to the President of the Republic. This arrangement reflected the fascinating history of small, mountainous Andorra, ruled since 1607 by the French head of state and the Spanish Bishop of La Seu d'Urgell, with both positions retaining their titular responsibilities after a parliamentary democracy was formally established in 1993.

With Spain's national elections due to be held in first half of 2004, political commentary and profiling were readily available during my first six months in Madrid. This provided a useful introduction to the Spanish political scene and pointers to the likely outcome of the election; the consensus was that the government would be returned to power with a much reduced majority.

In the event, the terrorist attacks on the Madrid suburban train network that took place on 11 March 2004, three days before the elections, profoundly affected Spain's political future, generating various controversial hypotheses about the unexpected electoral result. For embassies based in Madrid, the terrorist attacks were both a consular emergency to be managed and a crisis with political implications to be analysed and reported on in great detail.

Seven bombs exploded on commuter trains at three train stations in Madrid between 7.35 am and 8 am that Thursday, killing 191 people and injuring nearly 1,500. The Australian consul, who lived near one of the stations in downtown Madrid, rang me at the embassy at eight o'clock to report the explosions. I began monitoring local television and radio as other staff arrived, by which time the scale of the disaster was clearer. As head of mission, my first responsibility, once all embassy staff and families were accounted for, was to confirm that there were no Australians among the dead or injured. Although we judged that there were unlikely to be significant tourist casualties due to the timing and location of the bombings, we needed to do everything possible with the local authorities and with our consular colleagues in other embassies to investigate thoroughly the involvement of any Australian citizens. As it turned out, there were forty-seven foreigners of fourteen nationalities among the dead, but no Australians.

Madrid's local authorities were understandably overwhelmed by the scale of the tragedy at first, but emergency services were soon operating at full capacity. Two hours after the first bomb had exploded, 291 ambulances were working to take the injured to nineteen hospitals in greater Madrid; they attended to 1,430 patients in the first nine hours and performed ninety-five surgical operations. Within an hour of the blasts, six mobile clinics were operating to process the thousands of Madrid citizens who lined up to donate blood. Eighty-three forensic surgeons from Madrid, plus additional volunteers from elsewhere in Spain, identified 120 bodies in the first twenty-four hours.

The consul and her assistant were fully engaged from the outset in their work of liaison and gathering information; this was complicated initially by the collapse of the mobile phone network and the overload of emergency telephone numbers. As the day wore on, increasingly detailed information became available from the local authorities and we became more confident that no Australians were among the casualties.

The attacks took place around 6 pm Australian time. Within two hours, the embassy began to receive enquiries from Australian representatives of television, radio and print based both in Australia and in London. Persistent media interest lasted for approximately forty-eight hours. Following helpful guidance by the media liaison staff in the department in Canberra, I gave a joint on-camera interview in the embassy to three television stations and subsequent telephone interviews to ABC radio, the *Sunrise* program, Skynews, the *Today Show*, SBS news and John Laws (an interview which took place from my kitchen at home approaching midnight). Generally, the initial media enquiries focused on consular issues; when it became evident there were no Australian casualties and speculation increased about the perpetrators of the terrorist attacks, media questioning focused on this angle, making it more difficult for me to respond in any detail.

Once the immediate crisis had passed, embassy staff began to analyse the impact of the attacks, especially in relation to the forthcoming national elections on 14 March. We reported on developments relating to the blasts and on wider terrorism issues. As police investigations into the bomb attacks continued, with mounting evidence that the perpetrators were Islamist extremists rather than from the Basque terrorist group ETA (originally identified by the government as the likely perpetrators), the government cancelled all election campaigning and convened a public march with the theme 'With the victims, with the Constitution, for the defeat of terrorism'.

The Spanish foreign ministry had agreed to coordinate a meeting point for those embassy representatives wishing to take part and so, on a wet and cold Friday evening, my husband and I joined two million *madrileños* in marching through the streets of Madrid towards the Atocha station in a silent protest against terrorism. It was a never-to-be-forgotten experience, with the cries of *who did it?* from the crowds lining the route periodically breaking the sombre silence maintained by the marchers, led by members of the royal family, the Prime Minister and other foreign dignitaries who had flown to Madrid especially for the occasion.

On 14 March 2004 the Spanish people elected a socialist government to replace the previous conservative Partido Popular administration. The impact of the 11 March terrorist attacks on the elections has continued to be the subject of much speculation and analysis. For me and the staff at the embassy, the change of government signalled a new stage of our work in Spain.

Since emerging from its relative isolation during the Franco era, joining NATO in 1982 and becoming a member of the European Union in 1986, Spain has played an increasingly important role in international affairs. Although Europe is at the heart of Spanish foreign policy, it also has close historical and cultural ties with the countries of Latin America and with the Philippines, its former colony in the Pacific, as well as important political and economic links with Middle Eastern and Mediterranean rim countries. Over the past few years, respective governments have recognised the need to add substance to Spain's relations with the Asia–Pacific region

Giving a presentation on Australia to students of international relations at a course organised by the Society for International Studies in Madrid, June 2006.

Putting Australia on the map in Spain has long been a challenge for our diplomatic representatives in Madrid—Australia suffers from a somewhat outdated image, with a positive but modest profile in Spanish society. Australia is regarded as an exotic but friendly location for a long holiday and the home of world-class sports representatives. In terms of commercial interaction, the value of two-way trade has been rising steadily but Australia brand awareness is still generally underdeveloped in Spain, reflecting the practical difficulties caused by distance, language and differences in business culture. During the preparations for my new position in Madrid, I noted the frequent reference to the unfulfilled potential of the bilateral relationship—not just in trade and investment, but in other fields such as high-level visits, cultural exchanges, education and tourism.

The forging of links between countries can be a slow process, requiring the contribution of a wide range of people and organisations. Embassies do not, of course, make business nor indeed manage all elements of a bilateral relationship. Our role is to assist by providing knowledge and resources, by lending support where needed and using our official status and access to promote connections, projects and business opportunities.

I worked closely with my experienced Austrade colleague in Madrid on an active trade promotion program that helped Australian companies export to and/or establish themselves in the Spanish market. We also encouraged further Spanish investment in Australia, working with the Invest Australia representatives based in Frankfurt and Paris. There had been several cases of significant Spanish direct investment in Australia in recent years and evidence of potential interest by some large Spanish multinational companies in construction and infrastructure. But apart from a small group of globally focused executives, it was a challenge to convince sceptical Spanish business people with little experience in the Asia–Pacific region that a 24-hour flight to Australia would be worth the effort. It was much easier to promote Australia to Spanish youth looking for international study opportunities. The number of Spanish students travelling to Australia for language and university-related courses continued to grow, slowly but steadily.

The job of promoting Australia as a worthwhile trade and investment partner was helped by the activities of the three branches of the small Australia–Spain Business Association—in Madrid, Barcelona (Catalonia) and La Coruña (Galicia). It was always rewarding to visit the latter two regional areas to promote Australian business, culture or specific projects. The success of these events owed much to the enthusiasm and creativity of the Australian representatives there. The embassy was also fortunate to have the support of the University of Barcelona's Australian Studies Centre, whose dedicated and hard-working director achieved extraordinary results with limited resources.

Our public diplomacy work was facilitated in practical ways by Casa Asia—a joint venture between the Spanish government, the regional government of Catalonia, and the Barcelona City Council. Casa Asia's mandate was to promote Spain's relations with the countries of the Asia–Pacific, particularly in institutional, economic, academic and cultural spheres. We used the impressive headquarters of this organisation in Barcelona for a range of Australian promotional events; the staff there, and in the small branch office in Madrid, were knowledgeable and helpful.

With the acting Lord Mayor of La Coruña, signing the visitors book at the Town Hall during a visit to the autonomous community of Galicia, Spain, in June 2004.

During my time in Spain, the bilateral relationship expanded with the establishment in Madrid of a project team from the Australian Department of Defence. The Spanish arm of the European Aeronautic

Defence and Space Company (EADS CASA) had won a $1.4 billion contract to provide the Royal Australian Air Force with five new air-to-air refuelling aircraft. The Defence Department had arranged good relocation support through a private contractor to help the staff and their families settle in, and the embassy provided additional support: arranging visas and residence permits, signing residential leases, and processing ongoing administrative functions such as organising payment of staff salaries.

Although the workload of the embassy (and particularly of the senior administrative officer) increased significantly as a result of the presence of the Defence team and their families, we appreciated the contribution the newcomers made to the small official Australian community in Madrid. The EADS CASA senior executives and Defence team management maintained regular contact with the embassy and, shortly before my departure, I was delighted to attend the ceremony, held in an enormous, purpose-built hangar, to mark the arrival from France of the first A330 aircraft, which were to be fitted out in Madrid. The range of defence contacts between Australia and Spain also grew as the result of the participation by the Spanish naval shipbuilding company, Navantia, in tenders for major projects for the Royal Australian Navy. During my appointment we hosted two visits to Spain by the Australian Minister for Defence, and assisted in arrangements for a series of visits by senior Defence personnel and technical experts. My knowledge of naval shipbuilding expanded considerably following several visits to the Navantia shipyards in Ferrol (northern Spain) and attendance at the ceremony to launch one of the series of frigates built by Navantia for the Spanish navy.

The principal role of head of mission lies in the external sphere—representing Australia both formally and informally, protecting and advancing the interests of Australia and Australian citizens, and informing the authorities in Canberra about relevant developments. But none of these tasks is possible unless the embassy itself is working effectively and its staff, both Australian and local, are motivated and well equipped to do their job. The head of mission is responsible not only for the smooth and efficient running of the mission, including key personnel and financial management functions, but also for the conduct and welfare of all the Australia-based staff and their families. Overseas, there are increasing challenges in efficiently managing large budgets according to strict rules of accountability, in carefully observing both local regulations (such as local labour laws) and relevant Australian legislation, and in ensuring the safety and security of staff in uncertain times.

In practice, this 24-hours-a-day, seven-days-a-week set of responsibilities was the biggest difference between my management role in the department itself in

At work in the Australian embassy in Madrid, March 2005. [AR-La revista de Ana Rosa magazine, Madrid]

Canberra and that at my two posts. I was fortunate in both Santiago de Chile and Madrid to have extremely capable officers in the positions of deputy head of mission and senior administrative officer—key roles in an overseas mission—and I appreciated the dedicated and professional way in which the majority of embassy staff carried out their duties. There were, of course, some exceptions over the years involving difficult situations that required firm handling but, in general, I found staff responded well to a fair and consistent approach and clearly articulated expectations.

My two assignments as head of mission stand out as valuable professional and personal experiences in my thirty-two years and five postings with the Department of Foreign Affairs and Trade. As an increasing number of women have been recruited to the department, it is now no longer unusual to see women appointed as heads of mission, although of course there is still some way to go before complete gender equity is achieved. Overseas, female heads of mission are still a rarity in most countries and a competent woman in the position can utilise her higher profile to advantage in representing her country's interests. Perhaps because women are still in the minority as heads of mission, an element of solidarity characterises the interaction between female ambassadors in various diplomatic corps.

Reflecting on my career, I occasionally think of the male departmental officer who, when I announced in my first year as a diplomatic trainee that I was to be married, told a colleague that it obviously would not be long before I left the department; he was articulating an anachronistic assumption that for women, marriage and a foreign service career were incompatible. As it turns out, four of the six female trainees in the 1974 graduate intake of forty-four have successfully combined the demands of professional and personal lives, winning merit-based promotions into the department's Senior Executive Service and appointments to represent Australia at the highest level as head of mission.

10 Into Africa

Denise Fisher

High Commissioner to Zimbabwe, accredited to Angola, Malawi, Mozambique, and Zambia, 1998–2001

Consul-General in Noumea, 2001–2004

It was an honour to be appointed as Australia's high commissioner in Harare, Zimbabwe, from May 1998 to May 2001. As the world becomes smaller and ever-improving communication and transport links bring countries closer, many Australians represent Australia in myriad ways—through sport, cultural events, science, education and business. But still today, the head of an Australian diplomatic mission represents Australia in a unique, formal way across the entire range of government activities. As a high commissioner, that is an ambassador to a Commonwealth country, a diplomat reinforces and draws upon the special values and connections—from parliamentary systems to sporting and linguistic links—that are unique to the Commonwealth.

Having embarked on a career in foreign affairs as a trainee in 1976, my first overseas posting in December 1977 had been to Nairobi, Kenya, so I knew that our diplomatic missions in Africa offer a rare experience. The five Australian missions on the African continent are typically small, but each covers a number of additional countries. Thus, even as a junior officer in one of these posts, an Australian diplomat has a rich variety of responsibility and

Presentation of credentials to the President of the Republic of Zimbabwe, Robert Mugabe, 17 June 1998. L–R: Secretary, Zimbabwean Ministry of Foreign Affairs, Denise Fisher, President Mugabe and Denis Fisher.

experience in what is still an exotic part of the world. The posting not only requires travel to different countries and into remote areas, but also provides valuable exposure to the broad range of mission tasks—consular assistance to Australians; promoting trade; political and economic analysis and development cooperation; and the domestic tasks of tight budget administration and mission management. Then there is the all too frequent involvement with natural disasters and civil disturbances.

Twenty years after my first African posting, I returned as Australia's high commissioner to Zimbabwe based in Harare—I was accredited as well to Zambia, Malawi and Mozambique as high commissioner and to Angola as ambassador. I also covered the Democratic Republic of the Congo without accreditation.

Australia's diplomatic mission in Harare was set up in the heady days of post-colonial Africa. Zimbabwe, formerly Rhodesia, was one of the last African countries to achieve independence, which it finally did in April 1980 following an abortive effort by the minority white regime under Ian Smith to claim independence unilaterally in 1965. Australia did not have a diplomatic mission in Rhodesia in 1965, but it did have a trade office. This was suspended when Smith made his Unilateral Declaration of Independence and ushered in the dark days of isolation aimed at preserving the white-dominated political system. The Australian government strongly supported the anti-apartheid movement in southern Africa and in the ensuing years played a behind-the-scenes role within the Commonwealth in the development of the Lancaster House Agreement, which laid the ground for Zimbabwe's independence. Australia showed its support for the new nation when, less than a month after independence, we were one of the first Western governments to establish a mission there in May 1980.

The high commission was initially set up in the Monomotapa Hotel, where I am told the toilet in one of the suite's bathrooms served as the communicator's office chair. We then moved across the road to a bleak 1960s office building but, by the time I arrived in May 1998, we had been ensconced in the nearby multi-storey Karagamombi Centre for some years. Even though the mission was only a medium-sized one by the standards of the time—seven Australian and sixteen local staff—I took one look at the cramped office premises and, with excellent support from Canberra, promised staff we would soon move to a better chancery. In the event, with the slowness of the local bureaucracy and building contractors, it took eighteen months for us to improve our working environment and move to a new light and spacious chancery in a leafy inner suburb. By the time I left in May 2001, however, the changes that had taken place in Zimbabwe itself, along with streamlining of our technology and management, resulted in the mission being reduced to four Australian and eleven local staff.

Harare, on my arrival, was a stimulating place. Dating from its status as a front-line state during the apartheid years in South Africa, Western governments, the United Nations and other international organisations saw

With the CEO BHP Hartley, John Grubb (left), and my son, Jonathan Fisher, during a visit to the BHP Hartley Platinum Mine, Zimbabwe, in August 1998.

the Zimbabwean capital as a regional hub in southern Africa. This status survived during the 1990s because Zimbabwe warmly welcomed international diplomats. It was a comfortable, inexpensive and tolerant place to live. Its good communications and air links offered every opportunity to fulfill professional tasks efficiently, while at the same time to experience some of the world's most exciting scenery and wildlife. Governments and organisations therefore found it easy to attract high-quality expatriate staff. The United Nations alone had eighteen agencies with their headquarters in Zimbabwe. In all, the country played host to more than eighty diplomatic missions.

These were increasingly unsettled times, however, and my work as Australia's representative in Harare changed dramatically during my posting. On arrival in 1998, I was promoting Australia's growing economic interests there. By 2001, I was expressing our concern at the Mugabe government's human rights policies, and assisting Australian companies to wind down as those policies led to the destruction of investor and donor confidence.

Elsewhere, however, things were more positive. I was fortunate to be involved in supporting the strengthening democracy and economic prosperity in Mozambique, both through development cooperation and promoting our Australian business engagement in the massive Mozal aluminium project in southern Mozambique. Beginning in July 1998, soon after my arrival, the smelter was the first major development project in Mozambique for thirty years and the country's largest private investment ever. I also visited Angola regularly to support our mining companies operating there, and by the end of my tour was beginning to do the same in Zambia, where copper mining had been revived. In Malawi, we operated a tiny but well-targeted aid program that focused on health and on good governance.

As for all heads of Australian diplomatic missions, my most important job was to look after the interests of distressed Australians, who seemed to be remarkably numerous, adventurous and ingenious in finding trouble in just about any part of my large parish. Two particular consular cases exemplified the excitement, frustrations and challenge of operating as a professional female diplomat in southern Africa. These cases highlighted the utility of the diplomatic network, where friendly governments help one another, usually in a spirit of great camaraderie. They also demonstrated the collegial character of our own Australian diplomatic network.

The first took me to the seething, grey, desperate world of Kinshasa, capital of the Democratic Republic of the Congo (DRC). Because Australia had no accredited diplomatic representation there, it was the job of the Harare mission to follow what went on to the extent we could, and to assist Australians in difficulty. In fact, my very first job in Harare, the weekend after I arrived, had involved the Democratic Republic of the Congo. I had received a phone call late at night from our consular office in Canberra advising me that a British overland tour truck full of young tourists from London—including a number of Australians—had been detained by the Congolese authorities for entering a forbidden border area. Unlike Australia, the United Kingdom had a resident diplomatic mission in Kinshasa. I immediately contacted the British ambassador there and he agreed to include our Australians with his British nationals when he sought information about the travellers from local government authorities. Fortunately, it was a problem that was fairly promptly sorted out and within a few days the tourists were freed. But this was an early and sobering lesson about the heavy-handed nature of the local Congolese authorities and the sometimes blithe insouciance of our compatriots.

I thought of this incident as I boarded a plane for Kinshasa for the first time three months later, in early August 1998, to meet with senior representatives of an Australian mining company that had the concession to a gold mine at Bunia in the far north of the country. They were having problems with a competing illegal claim to their concession, which emerged only after they had invested heavily in developing the site. They wanted me to be present as they sought to secure the support of President Kabila and of various Congolese ministers to ensure the company's claim.

I landed in Kinshasa and still remember vividly the images of the trip from the airport into the city. I had served all over the world and had seen the extremes of poverty but Kinshasa's outskirts at the time surpassed many of my previous experiences—an intense, grey mass of humanity housed in extensive suburbs of small houses of concrete blocks and corrugated iron, surrounded by dusty compounds. There were no signs of plant or animal life—none of the dogs or chickens that abound in other parts of Africa. The people were joyless and the overall impression was one of wretched desperation.

By contrast, the newish hotel in the centre of the city where I was to meet the Australian businessmen appeared surreal in its comfort as we left behind the noise and dirt to enter air-conditioned luxury. We were immediately whisked away to meet senior government ministers. The meetings continued throughout that day and the next. On the second evening I was at dinner at the Belgian ambassador's residence. He and I had been third secretaries together in Nairobi in the late 1970s. We had children of similar ages and had stayed in touch over the years. I was benefiting from his insights about the Democratic Republic of the Congo over coffee on his terrace at the end of the meal when shots rang out nearby. This incident marked the beginning of tensions that escalated throughout the week. Behind it all were the DRC government's efforts to evict the Rwandan military advisers who had been invited to remain in Kinshasa after they had assisted the government to gain power. The situation rapidly degenerated into a racist bloodbath that eventually led to civil war. The Rwandans in Kinshasa were physically different from the Congolese, being tall and slim. They were easily distinguished and throughout the week a vendetta was carried out against Rwandan residents. Twice my hotel foyer was invaded by armed military, pushing aside guests, ordering us to lie on the floor while they searched for Rwandans. There were bodies in the street.

Overnight, my job changed from promoting the business interests of an Australian company to protecting Australians in the Democratic Republic of the Congo—including the Australian group I was accompanying. The small number of other Australians in the country were either missionaries, residents married to Congolese, or officials working with the United Nations. I wanted to contact all of them to establish their whereabouts and to advise them to consider leaving. Again I was able to call for assistance from my Commonwealth colleagues, this time the Canadians. Australia had an agreement with Canada that its diplomatic mission in Kinshasa would assist with Australian consular interests. The Canadian office in Kinshasa, therefore, maintained the Australian consular resident list. At a time of rapidly deteriorating security, I found the Canadian officers extremely professional, managing in the trying conditions to help me contact Australians while at the same time working to protect their own nationals.

The situation was not without its bizarre moments. On the one hand, it was sobering to ring the contact number of one Australian in the far east of the country, to find he was talking to me on his mobile phone as he cowered behind the wall of a UN compound under attack. (He was later evacuated by the United Nations.) On the other hand, most of the Australians I contacted had been long-term residents and were not at all interested in leaving. The most difficult group to deal with were, in fact, my business travelling companions. They had invested heavily in the Democratic Republic of the Congo and were in a state of shock and denial for some days. By the time they accepted they had to evacuate their Australian workers from their mine in the north, a state of civil war existed in some areas. They then had to pay an extortionate amount to charter an aircraft from neighbouring Uganda to evacuate their employees.

Throughout this eventful week, as the law and order problems intensified, it was clear there were cases of blatant human rights abuse. I made an appointment to see the DRC's Minister for Human Rights. Intrigued that such a minister existed, and having been briefed by the Belgian ambassador that he had been trained as a jurist in Switzerland, I thought it important to express formally the Australian government's concern that human rights be

naturally the rights of families to be informed first, and privately, regarding developments affecting their loved ones, are paramount. Many Australian journalists understand this and the media's generally responsible handling of this sad case underlined for me that Australians care deeply about what happens to other Australians.

In the end, UN access to the site was obtained and confirmed our worst fears. I attended a briefing by the UN representative setting out in graphic terms what had happened to the plane. As I listened with my male colleagues, I realised I was the only national representative with uncontrollable tears flowing freely. The plane had indeed crashed fatally and there had been no survivors. At least, for the Australian family so far away, the uncertainty had been removed.

In my other countries of accreditation—Mozambique, Zambia and Malawi—my job was similarly to help Australians in trouble; to maintain and build on our existing good contacts with the country's leadership; to deliver small but highly valued development assistance through AusAID's excellent programs; and to facilitate commercial relations between these countries and Australia. Australia maintains constructive relationships with each of these countries, but over the past decade we have developed particularly close connections with Mozambique.

Mozambique then was a model of African development. Until the early 1990s, it too had been plagued by civil war. By the time I arrived in 1998,

Visiting the women at an AusAID project in Masuingo Province in Zimbabwe, March 1999.

however, the warring factions had made peace and set up a democratic, two-party government. For an Africa hand like me, who had worked in countries as varied as Kenya, Seychelles, Rwanda and Burundi, it was a pleasure to see how the two factions, who had so recently faced off against each other in the bush and fought a particularly gruesome and lengthy guerrilla war, now worked together in a parliamentary system. Mozambique, a former Portuguese colony, is a somewhat incongruous member of the Commonwealth. Australia supported its application to join the Commonwealth, in part because of the geopolitical logic of its membership—it is an African country surrounded by other Commonwealth countries—but also in recognition of its democratic efforts.

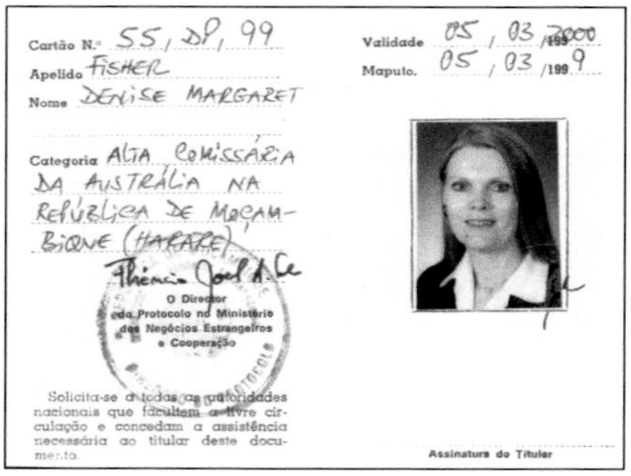
Cartão N.º 55/DP/99
Validade 05/03/2000
Apelido FISHER
Maputo, 05/03/1999
Nome DENISE MARGARET
Categoria ALTA COMISSÁRIA DA AUSTRÁLIA NA REPÚBLICA DE MOÇAMBIQUE (HARARE)
O Director do Protocolo no Ministério dos Negócios Estrangeiros e Cooperação
Solicita-se a todas as autoridades nacionais que facultem a livre circulação e concedam a assistência necessária ao titular deste documento.
Assinatura do Titular

Alta Comissária da Austrália na República de Moçambique—my identification card for travel in Mozambique.

The striking feature of Mozambique for me was its sense of history and the emerging political sophistication of this fledgling democracy. The capital is Maputo, formerly Laurenço Marques, a strategically located trading centre. The original Portuguese capital—with its grand old buildings decaying with neglect—is in the far north on the now virtually inaccessible Ilha de Moçambique, an island off the coast. So, although the Portuguese were in Mozambique for as long as they were in Angola, the capital Maputo does not bear the marks of colonial history in the way that Luanda does. But it is clearly a Portuguese town with some interesting architectural features—even its more modern structures have a decidedly Mediterranean flavour. Of special interest are a wrought iron prefabricated two-storey house in the botanical gardens designed by Gustav Eiffel and the 1930s-built cathedral, which is a monument to art deco taste. As you drive around the town you can see, glimmering through the neglect of years of war, what life in the old town must have been like at the height of Maputo's role as a bustling trade centre, with its gleaming coffee shops and department stores.

There is in Mozambique a recognition of the value of recapturing some of the beauty of the past, not only for a developing tourist trade, but also for the people themselves. Restoration projects are costly and time-consuming, but already Maputo has two fine examples. The railway station, one of the older buildings, has been faithfully restored, including the recent refitting of hand-painted wall tiles in the same design ordered from the same Portuguese firm that had supplied the originals over a hundred years before. The architectural gem of the capital, however, is the Polana Hotel. This is a classic colonial hotel on the water, built in the old Singapore Raffles tradition. It was ransacked by the departing Portuguese owners after the communists were elected in the mid-1970s but has been beautifully and lovingly restored to its former glory with the encouragement of the Mozambican Government as a matter of national pride. It is now one of the best hotels in Africa.

Far more impressive as visible evidence of maturing nationhood is the functioning of the Mozambique political system under its former guerrilla leader, Alberto Chissano. An excellent example of the country's political sophistication is the way in which the two main political parties work out their differences. I arrived in the country just after an election, where the opposition had bitterly denounced some aspects of the electoral system. Within twelve months, the Chissano government had initiated a parliamentary debate about these concerns and secured unanimous passage of legislation amending the electoral system to take account of some of them. This to me was an extraordinary achievement for a young country whose principal political parties had been at war only seven years before.

The Australian government has promoted development in Mozambique through a modest but effective aid program, largely focused on education. Our supportive, quiet approach has had effect. Additionally, contributions to Mozambique's development have been made by Australian states and individuals. These include the enormous Mozal aluminium smelter, for which Western Australia has supplied the necessary alumina. This export was worth over $200 million annually to Australia by the time I finished my posting. I was particularly proud to witness the work of one Australian manager involved in the South Africans' construction of the Mozal smelter. The undertaking imported 21st-century technology into one of the poorest countries of Africa, and through excellent management concluded the construction well ahead of schedule—a source of significant pride to Mozambique.

Other legacies of the past, however, still affect the daily life of ordinary Mozambicans. After decades of war, the country is riddled with landmines, some say numbering in the millions. Australia is supporting Mozambique's efforts to remove them from critical population and agricultural centres. In particular, we funded a demining unit headed by a former local soldier, Jackie d'Almeida, who was single-minded in his determination to enable Mozambicans to return to their former homes. This unit depended on mine-detectors, which they described as the best available, supplied by an Adelaide-based company called Minelab.

The dangers associated with demining activities were impressed on me during a visit to a site where mine clearance was under way. I had been briefed

With a team of deminers at a demining project funded by the Australian government in Mozambique. Demining Program Director, Jackie d'Almeida, at right.

by the organisers of my visit that a terrible accident had occurred that very morning, seriously injuring one of the workers. I did not realise that my visit in fact occurred only an hour or two after the accident. As I carefully walked between two lines of tape marking the 'safe' area, accompanied by officials, I came upon a break in the tape, and a large hole in the ground, with a mine-detector and other equipment lying haphazardly across the path. I later visited the severely burned worker in the local hospital, taking a long detour since the road to the hospital had been seriously damaged by recent floods. As we jostled along the trench-ridden path, I was struck by how the state of the roads would have aggravated the suffering of the injured man taking the same route only hours before.

But it is the spirit of Mozambique that gives hope to us all. Who will ever forget the television image of the young Mozambican woman who had just given birth to a baby perched in a tree above teeming flooding waters, during the disastrous floods of early 2000? Australia was one of the first governments to deliver assistance to Mozambique at that terrible time and I visited Mozambique shortly after the worst of the floods were over, to monitor how our assistance was being used. To observe the complex but effective coordination among donors, the United Nations and local authorities at various points along the Mozambican coast was inspiring.

For many of the countries in southern Africa, Australia, although a relatively young nation by international standards, is seen as an inspiration. For Mozambique this was particularly true and its government was interested in the skills and expertise to be found in its neighbour across the vast Indian Ocean. To demonstrate the strength of the relationship that Mozambique wished to see develop with us, they were among the first to agree to participate, modestly, in the Australian-led international force in East Timor in 1999. The regard and sincerity pervading Mozambique–Australia relations at this time made me proud to be representing Australia. An example was when one of Mozambique's ministers telephoned me after watching the televised opening night of our Olympics to congratulate Australia on our national achievement.

To witness Zimbabwe in decline over the three years of my posting was heartbreaking. In some ways, Zimbabwe is a microcosm of the challenges and successes of the African continent. One of the youngest African democracies, having secured independence in 1980 with strong support from the international community led by the Commonwealth, Zimbabwe had unending potential—particularly in its 13 million people, who were well-educated and skilled. Its climate, rich fauna and flora and attraction for tourists are incomparable. Within its compact borders the tourist can visit the breathtaking Victoria Falls to the west, the great Zambesi River and Lake Kariba, the dry low-veldt plains with their game parks and teeming animal and bird life, and the eastern highlands with their guest houses and Leopard Rock golf course perched on the side of a mountain that looks into Mozambique. It has resources of gold and platinum, besides its agricultural productivity in the north. By early 1998 when I arrived, Zimbabwe was enjoying the fruits of all of these resources. Its economy had grown by 8 per cent in each of the preceding three years.

At the same time, Zimbabwe had been plagued by the ravages of AIDS, the 'slimming disease' as the locals euphemistically called it. Situated squarely on the truck route from South Africa up to central and northern Africa, Zimbabwe succumbed relatively early to the disease. Natural modesty, time-honoured taboos and local tribal practices did not lend themselves to ready debate or publicity about it. In 1998, 25 per cent of the population were HIV positive. John Caldwell, Professor of Demography at the Australian National University, told me at the time that previous projections had put life expectancy in Zimbabwe at 58 by the year 2000, but the impact of AIDS had reduced it to just 37. Each week 1,500 people were dying from the disease. Throughout my tenure, it was normal to see people you met often, including officials and acquaintances, physically shrink into their clothes and die. Everyone lived with death on a daily basis. One day I was comforting our housekeeper, Edith, over the death of her grandchild, and asked if there was someone we could send for

Speaking to a group of eager school children in Zimbabwe.

from her family who could be with her as she grieved. She wept inconsolably, and sobbed that there was 'no one, all, all is dead'.

I will never forget the reaction of local dignitaries when I spoke to high-schoolers about freedom of choice and simple practices in the battle against AIDS. I was visiting a high school to present some assistance under our aid program. When I saw the sea of expectant young faces I felt compelled to address this subject that was so much on their minds. The provincial governor asked me to come back again and speak to their students about the disease. It seemed culturally impossible for them to do so. The programs that governments like Australia's are funding do have an impact and are often the only in-country programs to help Africans understand the disease and do what they can to prevent it.

Zimbabwe in my time there also demonstrated the fundamental weaknesses of a totalitarian state in our globalised world. No matter how outstanding the natural attractions and physical and human resources of a country, tourists and investors in mining and other industries will come only if there is peace and stability based on fundamental political freedoms and human rights. I was sickened by the change in my responsibilities relating to Zimbabwe itself over my time there. When I arrived in 1998, I was primarily involved in supporting greater Australian involvement in business, cultural activities and aid, all of which were thriving. Within two years, the economy was collapsing and physical intimidation of political opponents was rife. Productive farms and the livelihoods of thousands who worked on them were being decimated by officially endorsed takeovers by thugs. By the time I left, we were participating with other Western donors in contingency planning for anticipated widespread famine in one of the most agriculturally productive countries of Africa.

During that period, my main job was to keep Canberra informed about changes in local conditions, in order to ensure the safety of Australians, and to make appropriate policy recommendations as the situation deteriorated. We had a special role to play deriving from our status as a longstanding friend of Zimbabwe and a government that had supported its independence and subsequent development within the Commonwealth fraternity. Our Minister for Foreign Affairs was a member of a special Commonwealth Ministers' Action Group to ensure implementation in all Commonwealth countries of democratic principles as defined by the Commonwealth Declaration signed, somewhat ironically, in Harare in 1991.

My first meeting with President Mugabe took place when I presented my credentials to him soon after my arrival. At that time Mugabe personally took great care in ensuring regular contact with diplomats in Harare, particularly those representing Commonwealth countries. He received ambassadors and high commissioners early in their postings, and regularly hosted functions during which he made sure he mixed with us and provided opportunities for dialogue and conversation.

Having done some homework on Mugabe's background, I knew that he had surprised many when, following his election at independence, he had

Visiting a home for street children supported by Australian government funding in Bulawayo, Zimbabwe, October 1999.

With Dr Stan Mudenge, the Zimbabwean Foreign Minister, and a local constituent on a visit to a dam site in his electorate.

included white ministers and parliamentarians in his government and party. I was also aware that he personally had led governmental processes in his first decade in power that had ensured Zimbabwe had one of the most literate and skilled populations in Africa, enjoying high levels of health care. At the same time, Mugabe had been a hard and ruthless member of the freedom-fighting opponents of the Smith regime before independence, and since his election had orchestrated a massacre of the Ndebele people in the south in the 1980s.

When I first met him, in 1998, Mugabe impressed as a man of broad and reflective intellect, with a courtly, polished personal style. He showed great respect for the Commonwealth and all it represented, and for Australia. He expounded, in an extensive monologue, on the nature of change in Africa at the time, and welcomed warmly engagement by Australia in these changes.

In only a few months it became clear that he was under increasing political pressure both from a strengthening and articulate opposition and, more acutely, from within his own party. Mugabe focused anew on one of his earliest pre-independence promises—that of returning land to the blacks. He hosted an international land conference through which he hoped to attract political and financial support for redistributing land to small landholders. Mindful of a similar exercise soon after independence, when Mugabe had simply allocated land to favoured individuals, foreign governments, including ours, were sceptical. Indeed, Mugabe quickly tired of this process and his tactics became increasingly heavy-handed. He sent teams of 'supporters' to take over existing productive farms and to intimidate his political opponents with violence.

As Australia's high commissioner, I regularly expressed Australia's unambiguous opposition to these measures. I did this in my contacts with Mugabe himself, and with his senior ministers and officials, particularly in social settings, both on the golf course and tennis court, as official contact became increasingly strained.

Mugabe's foreign minister at the time, Dr Stan Mudenge, was a noted African scholar who made himself readily accessible to diplomats. Mudenge was low-key and unaffected. On one occasion he invited me and my husband to his home village (where I was impressed by work in progress on a hospital he was building), and then refused to allow us to thank him with a lunch invitation by taking us himself to his favourite restaurant in the vicinity, a humble cafe attached to the local petrol station. A historian, Mudenge had written extensively on the history of the Shona people, the original inhabitants of Zimbabwe, and was a mine of information about their culture and traditions. When he spoke of the Great Zimbabwe ruins, an immense and beautiful structure of intricate stone inlay in the south east of Zimbabwe, he brought to life the sophistication and order of the warrior peoples who created it. I felt he was seeking to explain the pride and dignity of the early Zimbabwean people underpinning Mugabe's goal of restoring true ownership of the land. At the same time this pride in history did not sit comfortably with the violence nor with the politics of fear and intimidation that his administration was instigating.

I attended regular lunches with Commonwealth high commissioners, where we exchanged information and discussed options for the Commonwealth to pressure Mugabe to change. I also pursued personal contacts individually with these Commonwealth colleagues, particularly the British, Canadian, South African and others who had become friends. I also followed closely what the EU ambassadors were doing, and associated Australia in some of their official démarches to the government at critical times.

National elections were held in June 2000 amid concern at Mugabe's tactics of intimidating his opponents. Together with other Commonwealth and EU governments, Australia sent a team of observers led by Senator Alan Ferguson and including Senator Andrew Murray, Senator Sandy Macdonald, and Kim Wilkie MP. Australian parliamentary participation in the election process was an opportunity to demonstrate, at the highest level, the interest of Australians in democracy in Africa, to influence a more democratic election outcome,

With the members of Australia's Parliamentary Observer Group to Zimbabwe's national elections, 20 June 2000: (L–R) Senator Sandy Macdonald, Senator Andrew Murray, Denise Fisher, Senator Alan Ferguson (leader of the group), and Mr Kim Wilkie MP.

and to increase the pool of Australian government representatives who were knowledgeable about southern African developments and their relevance to Australia. I felt some pride in our parliamentarians, who visited remote places and travelled long distances in difficult conditions uncomplainingly—in marked contrast to some of the other foreign observers. I was also impressed by their balanced approach to the racial and political complexities of Zimbabwe.

Meanwhile, I was attending to other serious consequences of the Mugabe government's policies. The impact of his totalitarian policies on Australians and fledgling Australian businesses in Zimbabwe was serious. Many young Australians were working in volunteer aid programs throughout Zimbabwe, often in remote areas, and our mission was in constant contact with them to monitor their safety as farm invasions and violence continued. Sadly the plans I had made to foster Australian business transformed into plans for assisting our businesses to wind down and many to move out—not without some difficulty. We had to contend with one major mining company's decision to close its large mine, which happened to be located within Mugabe's electorate. Another closure ran into union problems that resulted in the company's workers camping in front of the high commission in protest. Understanding their distress at losing their livelihood, I personally met them to listen to their concerns and liaised with the company concerned to resolve the issue.

A second area of consequence for us at the high commission was the dramatic influx of white Zimbabweans seeking visas so that they could leave. We had hundreds of applicants descend upon our small mission, many of them naturally in a state of high emotion, seeking special entry conditions into Australia. I had very early contacted the Department of Immigration and Multicultural Affairs in Canberra, which responded promptly, sending extra officers to assist. The mission's staff did their jobs with great professionalism.

An influential lobby of Australians interested in human rights and democracy in Zimbabwe was active throughout this period. These included former Prime Minister, the Rt Hon Malcolm Fraser AC CH at Care Australia; Justice Michael Kirby; Meredith Burgmann, President of the NSW Legislative Council; and former foreign minister Gareth Evans, head of the International Crisis Group, as well as a broad spectrum of non-government organisations. I was in contact with these individuals and groups when they visited Zimbabwe and when I was in Australia on consultations.

By the time of my departure, our government's message of concern was sinking in, but Mugabe's government did not want to listen.

Serving as head of one of Australia's missions in Africa was a varied, challenging and exciting opportunity, one where it was truly possible for Australia to make a difference in the lives of very large numbers of people through improving governance and economic development over the long term. Zimbabwe continues to be a nation that demands the consistent and patient application of diplomatic skills. And we need to reward and encourage fledgling democracies such as that in Mozambique.

At the time of my posting, I was one of just twelve female heads of Australian missions around the world. This put the proportion of women in charge of Australia's diplomatic posts in 1998 at approximately 15 per cent of the total of such positions. It is important that women continue to be appointed as heads of mission in numbers that better reflect the demographics of Australian society. Although there is an encouraging increase in the numbers of female officers being recruited into the Department of Foreign Affairs and Trade, the representation of women at senior levels, especially as heads of mission, also depends on the personal commitment of key people at the highest levels of government. In this regard, I would like to note with warm appreciation that Australia's foreign minister, Alexander Downer, has nominated more women as heads of mission than at any time in Australia's political history. I am also indebted to the department's secretaries Philip Flood AO and Dr Ashton Calvert AC, who nominated me for such positions and who attached importance to appointing senior female representatives abroad.

Afterword

Michael L'Estrange AO
Secretary, Department of Foreign Affairs and Trade

Since the political appointment of Dame Annabelle Rankin as Australia's high commissioner to New Zealand in 1971, 57 women have been heads of Australian diplomatic missions. There are currently 20 women serving as Australia's ambassadors, high commissioners and consul-generals out of a total of 88 such positions around the world. This constitutes a 6 per cent increase over the past three years in the number of women appointed as Australia's official representatives overseas and is a positive indication of the improved level of participation of women at senior levels of Australian diplomacy. While there is an ongoing need to promote this participation further, a natural change is taking place as increased numbers of women are now entering and assuming leadership roles in our diplomatic service. Fifty per cent of the department's staff are women, including 25 per cent of the senior executive service—working in senior management at home and abroad. Setting Australia's recent record against historical context and the experiences of other foreign services as outlined in the introductory chapter to this book, the new trends are very encouraging.

The improving profile of women in the work of today's Department of Foreign Affairs and Trade is the culmination of more than six decades of advances for women in Australian diplomacy specifically and Australian society more broadly. From the late 1940s through to the 1980s, when debate on gender issues resounded in international forums, Australia played a significant role in promoting equality. The efforts of Australian women, including Jessie Street and Elizabeth Evatt among others, in UN organisations such as the Commission on the Status of Women and the Commission on the Elimination of All Forms of Discrimination Against Women, enhanced Australia's reputation as an egalitarian, progressive society. Our international activism reflected a genuine mood in Australian society. Commitments in the international arena were readily translated into national programs and legislation. Improved conditions of service for female officers in the department occurred hand in hand with advances across the Australian Public Service and the Australian workforce generally.

The journey has been long and it has not always been easy. But as I read the recollections in this book, touching on the particular issues of the different decades, and as I reflect on today's departmental conditions of service, I believe it has been a road that women and the department have travelled together.

For the first forty years of the graduate diplomatic cadet program, the numbers of female trainees fell well below the numbers of males. The turning point came in 1984, when for the first time an equal number of women and men were inducted as graduate recruits—an outcome that overall has been maintained. The effects of this gender-balanced recruitment are now filtering into the senior management structure of the department, providing a larger pool of women from which heads of mission appointments can be drawn. A generation after the 1984 milestone, the policies underpinning the shift are bearing fruit. In an interview to the *Sydney Morning Herald* in early 2006, a former departmental deputy secretary (now Secretary of the Department of Agriculture, Fisheries and Forestry), Joanna Hewitt, noted the importance of reaching the end of this generational gap. She estimated that there was a 35-year horizon between gender-equal entry level recruitment and the equal representation of women and men in the most senior ranks of an institution's hierarchy. Staffing trends in the Department of Foreign Affairs and Trade reflect this outlook as more women from equal intakes begin to move into the Senior Executive Service.

In 2005, on the thirtieth anniversary of the United Nation's International Year of Women, I assisted in the launch of a departmental exhibition celebrating the history of women's participation in Australia's diplomatic life. The exhibition reproduced a letter written in 1945 to her parents by Julia Drake-Brockman, one of the three female diplomats in our first graduate intake in 1943. Julia related a conversation she had had with one of my predecessors, the acting secretary of the then Department of External Affairs, Mr John Hood. Expressing an attitude symptomatic of his time, Mr Hood had asked Julia, who was due to be posted overseas, 'Are you going to get married or go abroad?' Julia, who was in fact considering marriage, reflected to her parents, 'It's rather sad that I can't have my cake and eat it too'.

The handful of women who survived a sometimes hostile selection process to join the department in its early days entered a workplace that curtailed opportunities for advancement and postings on the basis of gender. For the first thirty years, they were mostly relegated to areas of 'soft' diplomacy (issues peripheral to Australia's core interests). They were required, until 1966, to resign on marriage and did not receive equal pay until 1969. Nevertheless, in that group of early female officers, there were those whose capabilities were incontestable. Cynthia Nelson, who in 1959 became the department's first female chargé d'affaires, heading our mission in Saigon for several months before the appointment of a permanent ambassador, is a case in point. Serving some years earlier as second secretary in Paris, her ambassador, Alfred Stirling, noted in his diary that she was 'worth three men: the answer to all the arguments against women diplomats'.

On some issues, attitudes changed particularly slowly. Almost thirty years after Julia Drake-Brockman was confronted with the choice of marriage or a diplomatic career, Penny Wensley, one of our highest-ranking female diplomats, also faced scepticism about her capacity to combine professional and family life. But as her chapter in this book illustrates, Ms Wensley has successfully done just that.

The department that Ms Drake-Brockman described in the mid 1940s is as unfamiliar to me as the one I administer would be unrecognisable to her were she to walk through its doors today. It is this gulf between past and present that makes this volume of reflections so important as a record of departmental and social history, as a celebration of the evolution in both, and as a signpost for future directions.

The introductory chapter to this book and the personal stories of nine of Australia's female heads of mission attest to the dramatic shifts in attitude and opportunity that have occurred since Dame Annabelle's milestone appointment. But what does the changing demographic of the upper echelons of Australia's diplomatic service mean for the conduct of our diplomacy and the character of the department, both in Australia and its overseas representation?

Perhaps most importantly, the equal representation of women at all levels of the department makes it possible for us to truly represent modern Australia in international affairs. The Department of Foreign Affairs and Trade, of all government and private sector agencies, plays a unique role as the institutional projection of our nation to the world at large. It is therefore important that we genuinely reflect the diversity of Australian society.

Victoria Owen and Sue Tanner in this book offer anecdotal support for the view that, at least while women heads of mission are in the minority (as they were in the Middle East and Latin America), there is a certain quality attaching to their appointment that can be employed to advantage. Ms Owen also identified access to informal but influential women's networks in some cultures as being of great assistance to her work. Conversely, Penny Wensley's experience is that the rarity of her appointment as a woman in the position of Australia's ambassador to the United Nations in New York, in 1997, was occasionally a hindrance. Her gender, for the media at least, was a distraction from the core issues that she was managing, for example as Chair of the United Nations' Fifth Committee, which handles administrative and budgetary matters.

The role of female ambassadors can generate its own special focus, particularly in cultures where there is more firmly entrenched gender stereotyping. But as Sue Tanner points out in her chapter, this focus brings with it particular responsibilities; namely, to ensure that the reputation of a senior female diplomat is derived primarily from respect for her competence and professionalism, rather than issues of gender. As female head of mission appointments become more commonplace, these artificial distinctions will disappear and it will be easier to look objectively at what role, if any, gender does play in diplomacy.

There is often debate about the impact of gender-specific attributes on the practice of diplomacy. Having observed Australia's highest-ranking diplomats—women and men—at work, my view is that any gender-specific attributes which may exist do so in the margins of the conduct of diplomacy. The core skills required of a diplomat are evidenced equally in the performance of both genders.

Progress towards a gender-balanced Australian diplomatic service is far from complete, but the goal is within reach and there is a strong commitment to it. The department's recruitment and promotion practices over the past two decades position it well to realise a balanced representation by women and men at all ranks—both in Australia and overseas. We have created an environment where women can be confident that recruitment and career advancement are equitable, transparent and merit-based. All officers are encouraged to aim for senior positions. It is critical, however, that the department avoid complacency. It must remain responsive to the emerging needs and concerns of officers and monitor closely a tendency that has been observed in other workplaces, and at times its own, for women to self-select out of top-level promotions or high-profile positions due to the difficulties of balancing work and personal life.

Climbing a professional ladder in any workplace entails new responsibilities and obligations and erodes leisure time. This is especially true for diplomats whose everyday work, at home and abroad, frequently involves crisis management, extensive travel and after-hours official engagements. Overseas postings bring particular complications and disruptions to family life, including to spouses' careers and children's education. To assist in alleviating these undue stresses, the department has assiduously and creatively structured itself so that staff can pursue rewarding career paths together with fulfilling personal lives. Examples of this approach are evident in the in-house childcare facilities provided by the department (one of the first of federal government agencies to do so) and the availability of flexible work arrangements (permanent part-time and job-sharing positions) that are being utilised by officers through to the first level of the senior executive service. Wherever possible, we have negotiated agreements with host countries overseas to enable accompanying spouse employment while government officers are on postings. The department is also actively encouraging a culture where non-standard working patterns do not prejudice the long-term career prospects of its staff.

Many of the measures implemented to remove barriers to women's professional advancement have, of course, entailed improved opportunities for male staff too. As gender roles and social conventions continue to evolve, conditions of service originally instituted in response to the needs of our female officers are also enhancing prospects for their male counterparts. Both women and men are now better able to combine and enjoy more satisfying professional and personal lives.

Of the twenty women currently serving in a head of mission capacity overseas or as our Canberra-based ambassadors on particular issues, several have had a particularly high profile in recent times. Lyndall Sachs, as ambassador to Lebanon, managed the largest evacuation of Australian citizens in our diplomatic history during the 2006 crisis in Lebanon. Margaret Twomey, our ambassador to East Timor, has skilfully represented Australia's interests through periods of major political upheaval and civil unrest. Caroline Millar is our ambassador to the United Nations and the Conference on Disarmament in Geneva at a time when the security environment presents new demands and international non-proliferation arrangements face serious challenges. Environmental issues, too, are integral to global security and Australia is fortunate to have Jan Adams representing its voice as our Canberra-based ambassador for the Environment.

This book demonstrates that generations of women diplomats have laid the groundwork for gender equality by working effectively around institutional obstacles, fighting discrimination in the international context and in the workplace, striving for professional excellence and seeking, sometimes against the odds, to fulfil their career potential and to be role models for future generations. The contributions of these nine heads of mission provide an important insight into the achievements of the department's female staff. There are many more stories that could and should be told. But the ones that *are* told in this book provide insight and inspiration as the career opportunities for women in Australia's diplomatic service continue to broaden.

Appendixes

Appendix I

Extract, National Library of Australia Oral History Transcript—Maris King

Maris King, MBE (1922–1997)

High Commissioner to Nauru, the Gilbert Islands (later Kiribati) and the American Trust Territories of the Pacific, 1977–1979

High Commissioner to Tonga, 1980–1984

[Editors' note: Additional material in parenthesis not attributed to editors is derived from responses given to questions put by interviewer.]

I was born in Wynnum, the youngest of four children, in the early twenties which meant that I really grew up during the Depression years. I had four years at the Brisbane Girl's Grammar School on a government scholarship, at the end of which I matriculated into the University of Queensland with a good senior pass, but not quite good enough for one of the very few government scholarships which were available in those days. My father was away for a lot of my childhood working out in the bush. My mother had the problem of looking after the children more or less on her own, including two of us who had become victims of poliomyelitis when we were very small and needing treatment and hospital visiting for many years.

I had decided that since I couldn't go to the university—the fees were quite out of our reach at that stage—I would like to become a teacher. So I applied for an gained a scholarship to the Teachers Training College in Brisbane. But when I went for my interview I was told that they couldn't accept me into the training college because I was lame.

Very reluctantly, I went to a business college to do shorthand, typing, book keeping. In three months I managed to get to a standard which took most people a year. Then I sat for the Commonwealth stenographer's entry examination. I came about eighth of the four hundred and in due course I was offered an appointment in Canberra at the then Department of External Affairs. Early in January 1942 I took off on the train for Canberra and found myself in a place very, very different from Brisbane.

In those days we had only a few overseas posts, but we still had a very busy Communications Section and that was headed by a man called Ted Tilley. The Communications Section was staffed by men—male clerks—but of course they were drifting off to war in 1942 and eventually some of us girls from the typing side of the department were offered acting clerical positions in the Communications Section. Fortunately for me, I was one of them.

Maris King, Brisbane, c. 1959. [Photo courtesy Michael Wilson]

This suited me much better than typing—I'd never been enamoured with the idea of pounding a typewriter for a living. I did that for about eight months. Then the opportunity arose for an overseas posting. It was not the department's habit in those days to post clerical or typing staff overseas. The few missions we had always employed somebody locally—an Australian if they could get one or, if not, a British subject - to do this sort of work. But in 1941 the department had set up a mission in Chungking, and there was no way in Chungking that they could find anyone to do this work.

The diplomatic staff, Keith Waller and Charles Lee, had tried to cope with the typing and communications but neither of them were very good at it, and the Minister [eds: head of legation], Frederick Eggleston, eventually sent a despairing cry to the department asking for help in this area. This telegram came in quite late one night. I took it in to [Mr Tilley] and said, 'Here's a great opportunity for someone. I wish it was me'. He just laughed and I didn't give it any more thought.

However, a couple of days later I was summoned to the holy of holies, the Secretary's office, and asked if I would really like to go to Chungking. In a state of considerable excitement and nervousness, I said, 'Yes'. So, the Secretary said, 'Well, I'll put it up to the Minister'—who in those days was the Prime Minister responsible for external affairs—'and if he agrees, you'll be going'. I went back in quite a daze. Three days later it was confirmed and I was on my way.

My work was secretarial for everybody; communications; I was also able to study Chinese. Before terribly long I had learnt enough of it to be able to more-or-less read the local newspapers and write very simple letters. [I was in Chungking for] about 15 months all told. Then I was in Canberra until

1947, working in the typing pool again. I was offered a job in Shanghai [that year], again as a secretary-typist. I was there for almost two years; then the communists really began to take over from the Chiang Kai-shek government in China and we were offered evacuation to Japan. I wasn't all that worried about the need for evacuation, but I'd never been to Japan so I thought it was a good opportunity to see a little bit of that country.

The embassy in Japan really had no jobs for most of us but they found things for us to do. I was occupied in revising the whole filing system and setting it up into a decent order. This occupied me quite happily for a couple of months. By this time, Nanking was in communist hands [eds: legation relocated May 1946] but the communists had not got down to the south of China. Two of our people from the embassy were able to get out and came to set up an office in Canton. I was asked to go across from Japan and locate myself in the Australian Trade Office that was in Hong Kong and work basically with these two men in Canton. This involved travelling up and down to Canton—the two men occasionally came down to Hong Kong on a weekend—and this went on for the best part of twelve months.

It was difficult. We had no security in the Trade Office which meant that we couldn't house our cipher books and things there and these were all kept in the naval dockyard which was about a mile and a half away. I had to traipse backwards and forwards to the dockyard, and usually I had to walk because I was not supposed to use a taxi when I was carrying classified messages. I don't see why I was any safer walking than in a taxi, but that seemed to be the thing.

[I was in Hong Kong] about twelve months, and then I came back to Australia. [Early in 1949] the Labor government opened the third division [eds: diplomatic/consular/administrative officers] to women for the first time. So, I came home and I wanted to transfer to the third division. Unfortunately I was just a little bit too old, by about two months, so I had to wait and do a wretched exam—a clerical exam—which didn't give me any trouble. I passed that all right and then became a clerical officer. That was early 1950.Then I applied for and got a part-time free place at the Canberra University College and started to work on a degree. I did the three years part time there with very good results. Then the Public Service Board, for the very first time, started to grant full-time free places, only a few, but they gave me one of these because my results had been so good. I came out with an arts degree, but with two majors in economics and a sub-major in economic history.

There was no scope for economists in those days in Foreign Affairs. I went to the Prime Minister's Department and was there for about twelve months. I didn't like it. I found the work uninteresting. Then the Department of

Foreign Affairs decided to set up one economic position, they called it an Economic Liaison Officer. I think they were beginning to realise by this time that economics and foreign affairs do go together a bit. I applied for that and got it, so back I came to Foreign Affairs. I did this work for the next ten years. I had a few promotions and ended up with an economic section with several people in it, which later on became a branch. I suppose you could say that I pioneered that part of the department.

I have vivid memories of Sir Arthur Tange as Secretary telling me one day that, while he was there, no woman was ever going to be head of a diplomatic mission for Australia. I didn't feel he had anything against me personally; in fact, I used to have quite a bit to do with him. He'd come to me for all sorts of information and advice from time to time. I think that he was just old fashioned about women and didn't really think they could do the same job as a man. Over the years, though, apart from a few incidents like that, I never felt that the department had a discriminatory attitude towards women. On the whole I thought they were very fair and very good. Once the actual barriers went, which they did in the fifties [eds: and sixties] mainly—the third division barrier, the marriage bar and equal pay and all that sort of thing—I always felt that the department treated me very well with few exceptions.

I was appointed as Deputy High Commissioner in Fiji in 1973. We were accredited also in those days to the Kingdom of Tonga and to Western Samoa, so there was a fair amount of travel to these places. [After three years] I came home for a very short time and then went to Nauru as High Commissioner. I was accredited to the then Gilbert Islands, now Kiribati, as Australian High Commissioner and I was also accredited to the American Trust Territories of the Pacific.

My departure for Nauru coincided with the opening of Nauru House in Melbourne, to which of course I was invited. This was at a time when Hammer DeRoburt, who'd been President of Nauru since independence, was temporarily out of power and the present Prime Minister, Bernard Dowiyogo, was in the chair.

The next morning we all took off in an Air Nauru aircraft for Nauru. I spent a lot of time talking to Bernard Dowiyogo on that trip. He was only twenty-eight, one of the youngest heads of state in the Pacific at the time—a very nice fellow. So we got there and I duly went into the High Commissioner's house, which is a big old wooden bungalow up on one of the very small hills on the Nauruan foreshore.

A couple of days later I presented my credentials, and since this was my first effort at doing anything like that—and it was the first time the Nauruans had ever had a woman diplomat—I decided to go to some lengths to make it as significant as possible. I'd organised myself into a Buck Palace garden party type of dress and a big hat and went off in a government car, being followed by our own car. The only problem with that was that the government car broke down half way there; I had to scramble out and get into our own car to finish the journey.

Then we arrived at the government offices and here I found the Nauruan peace-force all drawn up ready to be inspected by the High Commissioner designate. The ground, I might tell you, was very rough on this parade ground; it wasn't bitumen sealed and I was rather scared because I've always been apt to fall over fairly easily. I was a bit scared I was going to make a fool of myself. I knew the chief of police, I'd met him at many conferences in the Pacific. So I said to Danny—his name was Daniels and he was always known as 'Danny'—'Danny, I'm scared silly I'm going to fall over', and he said, 'Don't worry, I won't let you fall over. I'll grab you'. He was an enormous Nauruan; I'm quite sure he could have held me up.

We duly made our inspection and then I went into the office and presented my credentials. We did all the right things formally and made the proper speeches and so on; then we all sat down and had a very nice time over afternoon tea. I found being in Nauru as Australian High commissioner with Bernard Dowiyogo a very interesting experience because Bernard was not terribly experienced as Prime Minister at this stage. He rather used me (a) as a sounding board, and (b) as a primary adviser—looking back I wonder sometimes whether maybe I was too much of an adviser, but perhaps not. I saw a great deal of him and talked to him a lot. It was customary in Nauru too for the head of mission always to go to the airport when the President was going off somewhere and coming back. I saw him at the airport about once a month.

Once I had a really interesting experience. I had a friend staying with me from Australia and Bernard was going to a South Pacific Forum meeting in Papua New Guinea. I went down to the airport and took my friend Nancy with me to say goodbye to Bernard. While we were there, in the VIP room at the airport, Bernard said to me. 'Why don't you come over for the ride?'. He'd chartered one of his own aircraft. I sat back on my haunches and thought, 'I don't think I can do this', and then I thought, 'Well maybe I can'. So I rang my second-in-command and said, 'Look, I'm going to leave the country for a little while. Just look after things for me'. I had nothing with me: no passport, no money, no nothing.

Anyway, we went and we had a lovely trip over; it was about five or six hours I suppose on the small jet and it was set up for the President's travel which meant a rather different configuration of seats and tables and so on and of course the champagne was being poured liberally all the way. We got there and were taken into the VIP lounge at Moresby airport and the Papua New Guinean prime minister, whom of course I also knew very well—this was one of the big advantages in the Pacific, I knew everybody—took one look at me and said, 'I didn't know you were coming to this forum, Maris', and I said, 'No sir, I'm not', and explained what had happened.

In the meantime, our plane was being refuelled and in due course it was ready to take off. The only thing I'd really been worried about was that our prime minister might appear while I was there. However, we got back into our plane and taxied out to the edge of the runway just in time to see the RAAF VIP plane come in with Fraser aboard.

I think if I had had to stay in Nauru all the time I'd have gone bonkers, but because I was accredited to all these other places I was off Nauru quite a lot. I went to the Gilberts at least once every three months and I went to the trust territories about once every six months. I was away a fair bit. We had a big aid program going in the Gilberts, and the Gilberts too were very interesting because they were coming up to independence. The Chief Minister, who later became the President of Kiribati [Ieremia Tabai] was always very, very happy to see me. I'd walk into his office and he'd give me a big greeting and say, 'Come and sit down, Maris', and he'd curl himself up on a couch and there we'd sit and he'd talk to me about all his problems and he'd ask my advice on all sorts of things. One of the things that was worrying him an awful lot was that they'd been doing some negotiations with the Americans in Hawaii over fisheries and he couldn't make them out. I remember him saying one day, 'Outside the meetings they're so friendly and so nice and you feel they couldn't do enough for you. You get into the meetings and they're impossible. They won't listen, they won't agree to anything. What is it? Why do they behave like that?' I was trying to point out to him the hazards of international negotiations and things that people really cared about. That was fascinating for me. I felt that I'd been able to help him quite a bit with progress towards independence.

Once we presented [the Gilbertese people] with 26 blue Ford tractors. When I did the presentation some of the people said to me, 'But there's nothing on them to identify them as coming from Australia'. I said, 'Oh well, they don't have to be identified as coming from Australia'. When I went back the next time I was driving in from the airport and I saw one of these Ford tractors coming along the road and I could see that there was something written across the top of the cabin. When I got close enough I could see what it was—*Fraser*. Fraser was our prime minister at the time. They'd named this tractor after him. I thought that was great.

Another thing we did was we built four outer island airstrips. We'd had a bit of a fight over this and all sorts of things went wrong and they were delayed and delayed and delayed. A lot of the delay was on the part of the Gilbertese because, in the meantime, they'd been hit with a cholera epidemic and hurricanes. You name it, they'd had everything. The Australian Development Aid Bureau had almost given up but I put up quite a battle to get these airstrips and the Gilbertese knew about this. In the end the one on Nikunau Island now bears my name, which I'm rather proud of. It's the Maris King airport on Nikunau Island; I think that's nice.

The cholera epidemic was another interesting experience. The phone link between Kiribati and Nauru was very poor. They didn't have a satellite dish. We were supplying them with all sorts of medicines, cleansing agents and so on. Air Nauru was flying these up to Kiribati for nothing. The Governor used to ring me up every morning and give me a list of things they needed. My great fear was that I'd get some of those terrible technical names wrong because of the wretched phone contact.

I was [in Nauru] for two years. Then I came back to Australia. I had three months leave and after that I was sent off to Tonga [eds: as first resident High Commissioner]. Tonga was a British protectorate, it was never a colony and the biggest insult you can offer a Tongan is to say that they were a colony. They rejoined the comity of nations in about 1970 which meant the British protectorate came to an end. Since then it's been a monarchy with a king who can trace his ancestry back a thousand years or more.

Tonga was in my day a very traditional Polynesian society. When people had a grudge about something, when they were upset about something, they could go to the palace and talk to the King about it. He's one of the best educated men I've ever struck. I never found any subject I could raise with him that he didn't know more about than I did. He used to get some ideas which sounded a bit weird, mainly because they sounded very grandiose in the context of a small country like Tonga. It used to be feared at one stage that he was going to let the Russians in and let them set up all sorts of bases and things in Tonga. That, I think, he never intended to do. I think he was playing them for all he could get out of them and he never intended to give them anything. The same sort of thing happened with the Libyans. In fact I think he was a much shrewder man than he's ever been given credit for, by countries like ours.

[Australia's] aid program for Tonga was not all that different from aid programs in the rest of the Pacific. We did a lot of work in health and in education. We helped with their water supply. When the hurricanes knocked down houses we put up hopefully hurricane-proof homes. We helped them as much as we possibly could in agriculture. We rebuilt the Queen Salote wharf. We helped them quite a bit with fishing. We helped them a bit with their military people too, partly by training in Australia. We also had military advisors with in Tonga with them.

Quite a few projects—women's projects—we were able to set up in Tonga with some assistance from ADAB but done through the Soroptimists: a course for girls from all islands of the South Pacific in what I suppose you broadly call home economics, but it was much more than we understand as home economics because they were taught to build tanks—concrete tanks; they were taught to build stoves, toilets, all sorts of things like this, as well as doing the more usual things in home economics. I have a very interesting video that was taken on that course called 'Women can do'.

We helped with the radio station; we helped with telecommunications. I remember being asked to make the first phone call on their new ISD system which we'd helped put in.

It was a very formal place in lots of ways. One had to make one's presence felt, show the flag. On such formal occasions as, for instance, the opening and closing of Parliament, the diplomatic corps was very carefully drilled in the way it should behave. After two years I became dean of the corps because the British High Commissioner, who'd been *in situ* for about ten years, retired and I was next in line. This meant when there was something on, the diplomatic people were told when they should arrive—it was usual to be organised to arrive at two minute intervals and the dean of course, was always last [eds: and first to leave]. This happened at King's birthday parades and all this sort of thing.

I remember once being a little bit angry because there'd been some big event—it might have been Heilala week, their tourism week—and there were quite a few reporters over from Australia. Sometime after I was sent from home a small cutting out of, I think, the Sydney Mirror which said in effect, 'One of the most important people in Tonga is the Australian High Commissioner, Miss Maris King. She is always the last to arrive at any function and the first to leave'. I wondered what Australians thought of that one. It was quite correct of course, but a little explanation would have been a good thing.

[I had] four years in Tonga. I really didn't want to leave but I felt that I'd probably been there long enough. You're doing everything for the second time at the end of four years. I went back to the department. I took my leave and then formally retired in August of [1985]. [The place had been transformed between the time I joined it forty years before.] It's a much more professional body than it was, but it's also much more impersonal. When I was first there everybody knew everybody. It was like being one of a happy family. For instance, when I went off to Chungking, the department as a whole, small as it was, gave me a farewell party in the Secretary's office and I was presented with things like a lovely leather handbag. As time went on, maybe your little section would have a farewell cake for you but that would be about all. That's one of the inevitable things that happens with growth.

One of the things I did notice particularly when I came back from the last couple of postings, was the change in attitude towards women—and it wasn't all for the best. It's understandable, but a few years before if I'd started walking out of the department with a couple of bags and my arms full of books, somebody would have rushed up and said, 'Let me help you with that', but by the time I went back from Nauru, say, nobody would do that; they'd just say 'Hi' and walk on. It's a small thing maybe, but I think it shows a distinct change in attitudes between colleagues. A lot of people, for instance, would certainly not hold a door open for a woman any more, and maybe there's no reason why they should. I always felt that doing that kind of thing at least made life a little bit easier, not just for the woman either. You knew where you were. So, all of this has changed.

As time went on, the department as a whole came to expect a pretty high standard of professionalism from its officers, and on the whole I think it got it. At times the officers were not treated as well as they might have been, although I'm not sure whether that was the fault of the department or of our political masters.

If I had my life over again, I don't think I'd want it to be any different. I think I'd like to do the things I did, with perhaps a few minor changes here and there, but on the whole I've been fortunate and had a life that's been satisfying and that I feel—even if no one else does—I feel I've been able to do something for my own country, and that is something I'm quite proud of.

Interview conducted with Michael Wilson
11 March 1994
National Library of Australia, Oral History Section
TRC 2981/11

Appendix II

Women heads of diplomatic and consular posts: Appointments by year

1971	Hon. Dame Annabelle Rankin, DBE, High Commissioner to New Zealand *Political appointment*
1974	Ruth L. Dobson, Ambassador to Denmark
1977	Maris E. King, MBE, High Commissioner to Nauru Accredited to the Gilbert Islands
1978	Ruth L. Dobson, Ambassador to Ireland
1980	Maris E. King, MBE, High Commissioner to Tonga
1982	Mary McPherson, High Commissioner to Cyprus
1983	M. Rosaleen McGovern, Ambassador to Sweden Accredited to Finland and Norway E. Joan Norwood, High Commissioner to Vanuatu
1986	Diane K. Johnstone, Ambassador to Nepal Susan J.D. Boyd, High Commissioner to Bangladesh Penelope A. Wensley, Consul-General in Hong Kong
1988	Beris L. Gwynne, High Commissioner to Nauru M. Rosaleen McGovern, High Commissioner to Singapore Tonia L. Shand, High Commissioner to Sri Lanka Accredited to The Maldives Dr Helen R. Ware, High Commissioner to Zambia Accredited to Angola and Malawi
1989	Stephanie K. Daly, Consul-General in Bombay (Mumbai)
1990	Victoria M. Owen, Ambassador to Syria and Lebanon

1992	Ruth L. Pearce, High Commissioner to Solomon Islands
	Stephanie K. Daly, Consul in Bali
	Dr Jocelyn Chey, Consul-General in Hong Kong *Non-DFAT officer*
	Maurine Chong, Consul-General in Guangzhou *Austrade post*
1993	Penelope A. Wensley, Ambassador and Permanent Representative to the United Nations Geneva
	Jennifer E. Rawson, High Commissioner to Tonga
	Mary L. McCarter, High Commissioner to Mauritius Accredited to Comoros, Madagascar and the Seychelles
	Margaret A. Adamson, Consul-General in Berlin
1994	Annmaree O'Keeffe, Ambassador to Nepal
	Susan J.D. Boyd, Ambassador to Socialist Republic of Vietnam
1995	Merry S. Wickes, Ambassador to Jordan Accredited to Tunisia
1996	Judith P. Pead, Ambassador to Sweden Accredited to Denmark, Estonia, Finland, Iceland, Latvia, Lithuania and Norway
	Zena J. Armstrong, Consul-General in Guangzhou
1997	Lyndall A. McLean AM, Ambassador to Burma
	Susan E. Tanner, Ambassador to Chile Accredited to Bolivia and Peru
	Lisa K. Filipetto, Consul-General in Ho Chi Minh City
	Penelope A. Wensley, Ambassador to United Nations New York
	Karina H. Campbell, Ambassador to Laos

1998 Martine L. Letts, Ambassador to Argentina
Accredited to Paraguay and Uruguay

Victoria M. Owen, Ambassador to Arab Republic of Egypt
Accredited to Sudan and Tunisia

Denise M. Fisher, High Commissioner to Zimbabwe
Accredited to Angola, Malawi, Mozambique and Zambia

Susan J.D. Boyd, Consul-General in Hong Kong Special Administrative Region

Dr Janet M. Gardiner, Ambassador to Syria

Margaret A. Adamson, Ambassador to Poland
Accredited to Czech Republic

Sally L. Mansfield, Consul-General in Noumea

1999 Ruth L. Pearce, Ambassador to Russia
Accredited to Armenia, Azerbaijan, Belarus, Georgia, Kazakhstan, Kyrgyzstan, Moldova, Tajikistan, Turkmenistan, Ukraine and Uzbekistan

Susan J.D. Boyd, High Commissioner to Fiji
Accredited to Nauru and Tuvalu

2000 Dr Janet M. Gardiner, Ambassador to Portugal

Sharyn J. Minahan, Ambassador to Argentina
Accredited to Paraguay and Uruguay

Joanna M. Hewitt, Ambassador to Belgium
Accredited to European Communities and Luxembourg

Louise H. Hand, Ambassador to Kingdom of Cambodia

2001 Penelope A. Richards, Consul-General in Shanghai

Penelope A. Wensley AO, High Commissioner to India
Accredited to Bhutan

Denise M. Fisher, Consul-General in Noumea

2002 Elizabeth A. Schick, Ambassador to Chile
Accredited to Bolivia and Peru

Stephanie A. Shwabsky, Ambassador to Lebanon

Ruth L. Pearce, Ambassador to the Philippines

Lorraine M. Barker, High Commissioner to Bangladesh

2003	Pamela J. Fayle, Ambassador to Federal Republic of Germany Accredited to Liechtenstein and Switzerland
	Deborah A. Stokes, Ambassador to Austria Accredited to Bosnia Herzegovina, Slovakia and Slovenia
	Annabel M. Anderson, Ambassador to Kingdom of Cambodia
	Jennifer E. Rawson, High Commissioner to Fiji Accredited to Nauru and Tuvalu
	Susan E. Tanner, Ambassador to Spain Accredited to Andora
	Anna C. George, Ambassador to Croatia
2004	Lisa K. Filipetto, Ambassador to Kingdom of Cambodia
	Clare Birgin, Ambassador to Hungary
	Margaret E. Twomey, Ambassador to East Timor
	Jean M. Dunn, Ambassador to Turkey
	Zorica McCarthy, High Commissioner to Pakistan Accredited to Afghanistan until September 2006
	Corinne D. Tomkinson, Ambassador to Federated States of Micronesia Accredited to the Marshall Islands and Palau
	Jane Urquhart, Consul-General in Noumea
2005	Penelope A. Wensley AO, Ambassador to France Accredited to Algeria, Mauritania and Morocco
	Veronique A. Ingram, Permanent Representative to the Organization for Economic Co-operation and Development (OECD)
2006	Susan Dietz-Henderson, Consul-General in Shanghai
	Ruth P. Adler, High Commissioner to Brunei
	Anne M. Plunkett, Ambassador to Ireland and to Holy See
	Lyndall J. Sachs, Ambassador to Lebanon
	Anne M. Quinane, High Commissioner to Kiribati
	Caroline J. Millar, Ambassador & Permanent Representative to the United Nations Geneva
	Tracy F. Reid OAM, Ambassador to Croatia
	Sharyn J. Minahan, Ambassador to Denmark Accredited to Iceland and Norway

Appendix III

Women heads of diplomatic and consular posts: Appointments by country

Missions

ARGENTINA Accredited to Paraguay and Uruguay	Martine L. Letts, Ambassador (1998–2000) Sharyn J. Minahan, Ambassador (2000–2004)
AUSTRIA Accredited to Bosnia Herzegovina, Slovakia and Slovenia	Deborah A. Stokes, Ambassador (2003–2006)
BANGLADESH	Susan J.D. Boyd, High Commissioner (1986–1989) Lorraine M. Barker, High Commissioner (2002–2005)
BELGIUM Accredited to European Communities and Luxembourg	Joanna M. Hewitt, Ambassador (2000–2003)
BRUNEI	Ruth P. Adler, High Commissioner (2006–
BURMA	Lyndall A. McLean, AM, Ambassador (1997–2000)
CAMBODIA, KINGDOM OF	Louise H. Hand, Ambassador (2000–2003) Annabel. M. Anderson, Ambassador (2003–2004) Lisa K. Filipetto, Ambassador (2004–
CHILE Accredited to Bolivia and Peru	Susan E. Tanner, Ambassador (1997–1999) Elizabeth A. Schick, Ambassador (2002–2005)
CROATIA	Anna C. George, Ambassador (2003–2006) Tracy F. Reid, OAM, Ambassador (2006–
CYPRUS	Mary McPherson, High Commissioner (1982–1985)

DENMARK	Ruth L. Dobson, Ambassador (1974–1978)
DENMARK Accredited to Iceland and Norway	Sharyn J. Minahan, Ambassador (2006–
EAST TIMOR	Margaret E. Twomey, Ambassador (2004–
EGYPT, ARAB REPUBLIC OF Accredited to Sudan and Tunisia	Victoria M. Owen, Ambassador (1998–2002)
FEDERATED STATES OF MICRONESIA Accredited to the Marshall Islands and Palau	Corinne D. Tomkinson, Ambassador (2004–
FIJI Accredited to Nauru and Tuvalu	Susan J.D. Boyd, High Commissioner (1999–2003) Jennifer E. Rawson, High Commissioner (2003–
FRANCE Accredited to Algeria, Mauritania and Morocco	Penelope A. Wensley, AO, Ambassador (2005–
GERMANY, FEDERAL REPUBLIC OF Accredited to Liechtenstein and Switzerland	Pamela J. Fayle, Ambassador (2003–2006)
HOLY SEE	Anne M. Plunkett, Ambassador (2006–
HUNGARY	Clare Birgin, Ambassador (2004–
INDIA Accredited to Bhutan	Penelope A. Wensley, AO, High Commissioner (2001–2005)
IRELAND	Ruth L. Dobson, Ambassador (1978–1981) Anne M. Plunkett, Ambassador (2006–
JORDAN Accredited to Tunisia	Merry S. Wickes, Ambassador (1995–1998)

KIRIBATI	Anne M. Quinane, High Commissioner (2006–
LAOS	Karina H. Campbell, Ambassador (1997–2000)
LEBANON	Victoria M. Owen, Ambassador (1990–1992) Stephanie A. Shwabsky, Ambassador (2002–2006) Lyndall J. Sachs, Ambassador (2006–
MAURITIUS Accredited to Comoros, Madagascar and the Seychelles	Mary L. McCarter, High Commissioner (1993–1997)
NAURU Accredited to the Gilbert Islands and American Trust Territories of the Pacific	Maris E. King, MBE, High Commissioner (1977–1979)
NAURU	Beris L. Gwynne, High Commissioner (1988–1990)
NEPAL	Diane K. Johnstone, Ambassador (1986–1989) Annmaree O'Keeffe, Ambassador (1994–1996)
NEW ZEALAND *Political appointment*	Hon. Dame Annabelle Rankin, DBE, High Commissioner (1971–1974)
OECD Organisation for Economic Co-operation and Development	Veronique A. Ingram, Permanent Representative (2005–
PAKISTAN Accredited to Afghanistan until September 2006	Zorica McCarthy, High Commissioner (2004–
PHILIPPINES	Ruth L. Pearce, Ambassador (2002–2005)
POLAND Accredited to Czech Republic	Margaret A. Adamson, Ambassador (1998–2002)
PORTUGAL	Dr Janet M. Gardiner, Ambassador (2000–2003)

RUSSIA Accredited to Armenia, Azerbaijan, Belarus, Georgia, Kazakhstan, Kyrgyzstan, Moldova, Tajikistan, Turkmenistan, Ukraine and Uzbekistan	Ruth L. Pearce, Ambassador (1999–2002)
SINGAPORE	M. Rosaleen McGovern, High Commissioner (1988–1990)
SOLOMON ISLANDS	Ruth L. Pearce, High Commissioner (1992–1994)
SPAIN Accredited to Andora	Susan E. Tanner, Ambassador (2003–2006)
SRI LANKA Accredited to The Maldives	Tonia L. Shand, (AM 1990), High Commissioner (1988–1992)
SWEDEN Accredited to Finland and Norway	M. Rosaleen McGovern, Ambassador (1983–1987)
SWEDEN Accredited to Denmark, Estonia, Finland, Iceland, Latvia, Lithuania and Norway	Judith P. Pead, Ambassador (1996–1999)
SYRIA	Victoria M. Owen, Ambassador (1990–1992) Dr Janet M. Gardiner, Ambassador (1998–1999)
TONGA	Maris E. King, MBE, High Commissioner (1980–1984) Jennifer E. Rawson, High Commissioner (1993–1995)
TURKEY	Jean M. Dunn, Ambassador (2004–

UNITED NATIONS GENEVA	Penelope A. Wensley, Ambassador and Permanent Representative (1993–1996) Caroline J. Millar, Ambassador and Permanent Representative (2006–
UNITED NATIONS NEW YORK	Penelope A. Wensley, (AO 2001), Ambassador (1997–2001)
VANUATU	E. Joan Norwood, High Commissioner (1983–1985)
VIETNAM, SOCIALIST REPUBLIC OF	Susan J.D. Boyd, Ambassador (1994–1998)
ZAMBIA Accredited to Angola and Malawi	Dr Helen R. Ware, High Commissioner (1988–1991)*
ZIMBABWE Accredited to Angola, Malawi, Mozambique and Zambia	Denise M. Fisher, High Commissioner (1998–2001)

*Before this appointment Dr Ware had served with the Human Rights Commission, Department of the Prime Minister and Cabinet and the Australian International Development Assistance Bureau.

Posts

CHINA PEOPLE'S REPUBLIC OF	
Guangzhou	Maurine Chong, Consul-General/Senior Trade Commissioner (1992–1996)*
	Zena J. Armstrong, Consul-General (1996–1999)
Hong Kong Special Administrative Region	Susan J.D. Boyd, Consul-General (1998–1999)
Shanghai	Penelope A. Richards, Consul-General (2001–2002)
	Susan Dietz-Henderson, Consul-General (2006–
GERMANY, FEDERAL REPUBLIC OF	
Berlin	Margaret A. Adamson, Consul-General (1993–1999)
HONG KONG	Penelope A. Wensley, Consul-General (1986–1988)
	Dr Jocelyn V. Chey, Consul-General (1992–1995)*
INDIA	
Bombay (Mumbai)	Stephanie K. Daly, Consul-General (1989–1992)
INDONESIA	
Bali	Stephanie K. Daly, Consul. (1992–1994)
NEW CALEDONIA	
Nouméa	Sally L. Mansfield, Consul-General (1998–2001)
	Denise M. Fisher, Consul-General (2001–2004)
	Jane Urquhart, Consul-General (2004–
VIETNAM, SOCIALIST REPUBLIC OF	
Ho Chi Minh City	Lisa K. Filipetto, Consul-General (1997–2001)

*Non Department of Foreign Affairs and Trade officers

Appendix IV

Women heads of mission and post relative to total available appointments 1970–2006*

YEAR	WOMEN	TOTAL
1970	0	55
1971	1†	57
1972	1†	59
1973	1†	65
1974	2†	68
1975	1	70
1976	1	67
1977	2	68
1978	2	71
1979	1	74
1980	2	76
1981	2	76
1982	2	81
1983	3	82
1984	3	86
1985	2	86
1986	3	84
1987	4	81
1988	7	82
1989	6	82
1990	6	85
1991	4	82
1992	3	79
1993	7†	77
1994	8†	78
1995	8†	79
1996	7†	81
1997	8	79
1998	12	79
1999	14	80
2000	11	83
2001	14	84
2002	11	84
2003	14	84
2004	14	85
2005	17	86
2006	19	87

* Figures as at June of this span of years.

† Includes non-departmental appointees: 1970–1974 one appointee; 1993–1995 two appointees; 1996 one appointee.

Appendix V

Australian diplomatic missions and posts 2006

Country of location	City	Post type
Afghanistan	Kabul	Embassy
Argentina	Buenos Aires	Embassy
Austria	Vienna	Embassy/Permanent Mission to the UN
Bangladesh	Dhaka	High Commission
Belgium	Brussels	Embassy/Mission to the EU
Brazil	Brasilia	Embassy
Brunei Darussalam	Bandar Seri Begawan	High Commission
Burma	Rangoon	Embassy
Cambodia	Phnom Penh	Embassy
Canada	Ottawa	High Commission
Chile	Santiago	Embassy
China, People's Republic of	Beijing	Embassy
	Guangzhou	Consulate-General
	Hong Kong SAR*	Consulate-General
	Shanghai	Consulate-General
Croatia	Zagreb	Embassy
Cyprus	Nicosia	High Commission
Denmark	Copenhagen	Embassy
East Timor	Dili	Embassy
Egypt	Cairo	Embassy
Federated States of Micronesia	Pohnpei	Embassy
Fiji	Suva	High Commission
France	Paris	Embassy
		Delegation to the OECD
Germany	Berlin	Embassy
Ghana	Accra	High Commission
Greece	Athens	Embassy
Hungary	Budapest	Embassy
India	New Delhi	High Commission
Indonesia	Jakarta	Embassy
	Bali (Denpasar)	Consulate-General

*Special Administrative Region

Country of location	City	Post type
Iran	Tehran	Embassy
Iraq	Baghdad	Embassy
Ireland	Dublin	Embassy
Israel	Tel Aviv	Embassy
Italy	Rome	Embassy
Japan	Tokyo	Embassy
Jordan	Amman	Embassy
Kenya	Nairobi	High Commission
Kiribati	Tarawa	High Commission
Korea, Republic of	Seoul	Embassy
Kuwait	Kuwait	Embassy
Laos	Vientiane	Embassy
Lebanon	Beirut	Embassy
Malaysia	Kuala Lumpur	High Commission
Malta	Valletta	High Commission
Mauritius	Port Louis	High Commission
Mexico	Mexico City	Embassy
Nepal	Kathmandu	Embassy
Netherlands	The Hague	Embassy
New Caledonia	Noumea	Consulate-General
New Zealand	Wellington	High Commission
Nigeria	Abuja	High Commission
Pakistan	Islamabad	High Commission
Papua New Guinea	Port Moresby	High Commission
Philippines	Manila	Embassy
Poland	Warsaw	Embassy
Portugal	Lisbon	Embassy
Russia	Moscow	Embassy
Samoa	Apia	High Commission
Saudi Arabia	Riyadh	Embassy
Serbia	Belgrade	Embassy
Singapore	Singapore	High Commission
Solomon Islands	Honiara	High Commission
South Africa	Pretoria	High Commission
Spain	Madrid	Embassy
Sri Lanka	Colombo	High Commission
Sweden	Stockholm	Embassy
Switzerland	Geneva	Permanent Mission to the UN
		Permanent Mission to the WTO/Consulate-General

COUNTRY OF LOCATION	CITY	POST TYPE
Thailand	Bangkok	Embassy
Tonga	Nuku'alofa	High Commission
Trinidad and Tobago	Port of Spain	High Commission
Turkey	Ankara	Embassy
	Canakkale	Consulate
United Arab Emirates	Abu Dhabi	Embassy
United Kingdom	London	High Commission
United States of America	Washington DC	Embassy
	Chicago	Consulate-General
	Honolulu	Consulate-General
	Los Angeles	Consulate-General
	New York	Consulate-General
	New York	Permanent Mission to the UN
Vanuatu	Port Vila	High Commission
Vatican City (Holy See)	Vatican City	Embassy
Vietnam	Hanoi	Embassy
	Ho Chi Minh City	Consulate-General
Zimbabwe	Harare	Embassy

Appendix VI

Graduate trainee intakes 1943–2006

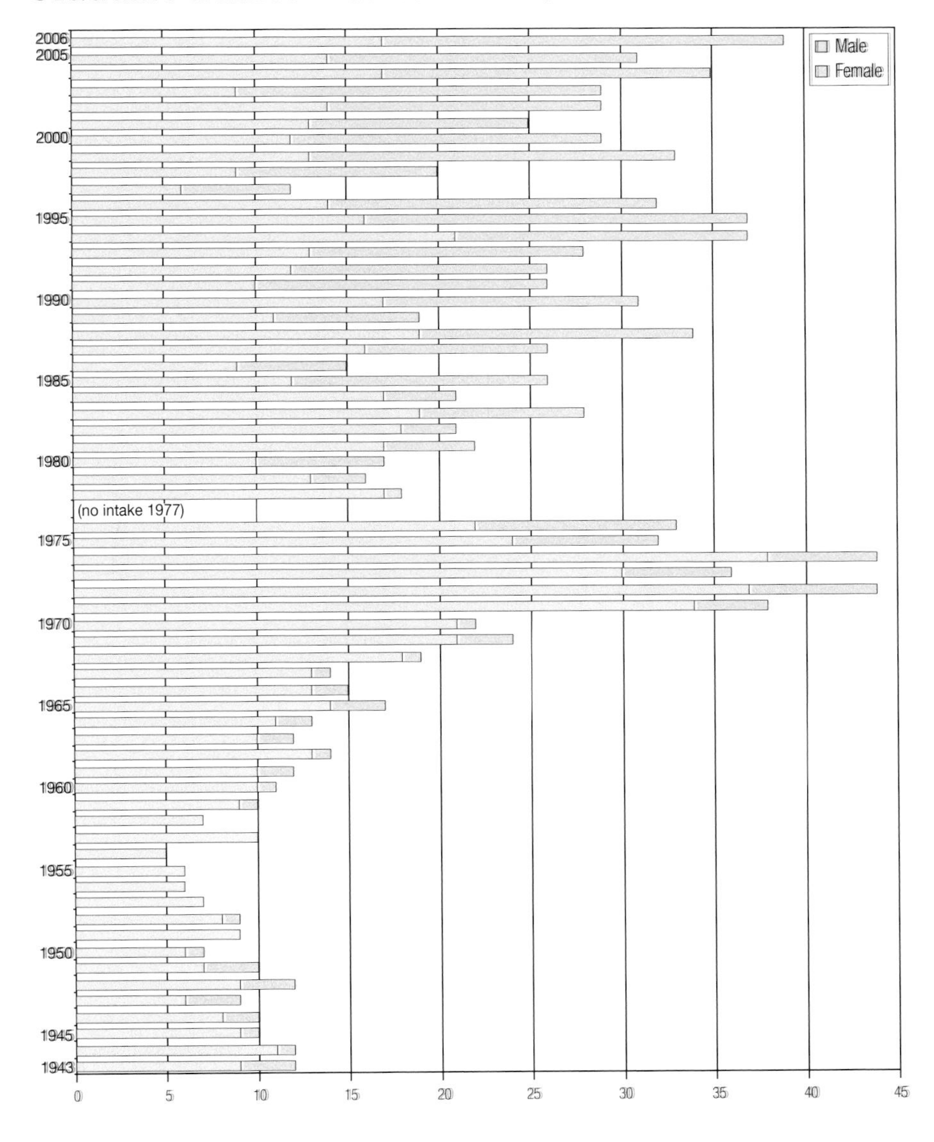

Index

Q

R

S